WHY DID IT HAPPEN ?

George Meeks

authorHOUSE®

AuthorHouse™ UK Ltd.
500 Avebury Boulevard
Central Milton Keynes, MK9 2BE
www.authorhouse.co.uk
Phone: 08001974150

First published by AuthorHouse 3/3/2010

ISBN: 978-1-4490-1337-0 (sc)

This book is printed on acid-free paper.

Quite a lot of the family information and incidents were given to me by my eldest sister, who´s name will remain anonymous, as well as the names of her family purely, for fact that the love and respect that I have for her four daughters who are still living will save them any embarrassment of their parents involvement in the telling of this factual story.

It all started one morning in a mining village in Co. Durham when my two sisters the twins Doris & Elsie were playing ball in the back yard, the youngest of the family Jane, was sat on the wall (so she didn´t interrupt their play) when a shout came from the house "you now have a new baby brother" the game was quickly abandoned, as was Jane, she was left sat on the wall which, she didn´t take too kindly to as, she had been the baby of the family until that moment and, now that I´d been born all that was to come to an end. She still, jokingly moans about it to this day.

Off scuttled the twins into the house to look in "awe" at this beautiful baby boy destined for a life of being spoilt rotten firstly, with love and affection, as there hadn´t been a boy in the family for 12yrs, and then, for more tragedies, and good fortune, than anyone could ever imagine.

My parents were from working class backgrounds. My father, (Jock as he was known) was born in Glasgow-Scotland in 1898. When he was 16yrs old he supposedly fell out with his parents as he wouldn´t go to sea as was expected by his father. He supposedly (once again) falsified his age and joined the army went into the 1st WW then after the war was over settled in the north-east of England. He was in lodgings at my mother´s parent´s home which was also in a small mining village called Blackhall and started working at the pit there, he was courting my mother´s elder sister Lizzie as well as my mother, and, eventually made my mother pregnant when she was 15yrs old, eventually they had to marry. They were described to me by my eldest sister Alice as total opposites Da as we called him, was a person who loved his drink and Ma was a kind and loving person, a good cook, never wore make up and, from what I was told she, never had any new clothes from being married, until the day she died, her family came first.

It wasn´t a good start in life for Ma, "Jinny", as she was called, to become pregnant at 15yrs old and have to wait until she was 16 to get married. It must have been one hell of a job hiding the pregnancy as her first born our John weighed 13lbs 14ounces when born. Now that is some size baby considering that my father was only 4ft 10ins tall but, my mother was approx 5ft 9ins tall. They had 9 children in all the first being,

John

Alice

Liz

James

Twins Doris & Elsie

Andrew   lived only 9 months

Jane   the brainy one

George   myself

There is very little that I know of my parents as I´ve already said and this will become apparent as the story unfolds.

Ma and Da lived with her parents Granddad Jack as he was known, and Grandma Jane, granddad Jack was described as, Spanish looking, tanned, with jet black loose curls and waving hair, Grandma Jane was described as a lovely kind lady who was an excellent cook. Ma and Da lived with them until at least our Alice their second child was born. Both my grandparents had died before I was born and had originated from South Shields in Co. Durham and the info I have to date is that they had 5 daughters;

Elizabeth

Alice

Jane   (Ma)

Mary

Rosanna   (Rose)

Granddad was some sort of night shift official at the pit, and it must have come as quite a shock as Da was supposedly courting two sister´s at the same time Ma and her sister Elizabeth Lizzie as she was called, and when Ma became pregnant, they had to get married. Ma and Da continued to live with them until at least my eldest sister was born.

My father told me he had been in a serious accident while working down mine, and showed me the results of the accident, on one of four meetings I had with him from the age of five, the whole of his back was peppered in blue mark´s which, was caused by a burst compressed air hose, which was used in those days to drive the coal-cutting machines, along with any other type of machinery used underground. I gather from what my eldest sister Alice told me, that Ma & Da left the village and the pit he worked at, soon after the accident, and went to live at Middleton, where, Da started to work at the steelworks or shipyards leaving the two children John and Alice with Ma´s parents, I suppose to help them get on their feet i.e. A new job and lodgings in a new area. Alice said our John was the apple of our grandparent's eyes. They were always well dressed and well fed while living with them.

It was some time later that Alice rejoined Ma and Da leaving John with grandma and granddad until he left school and eventually went to work and live on a farm. By then Lizzie, James, Doris and Elsie the twins and Andrew and Jane were born and then later moved on to Hart, a tiny seaside village between West Hartlepool and Blackhall. Their home there was a converted railway carriage so I´m told and, situated a field a little way back from the cliff edge. One story told to me by eldest sister was, Ma had left the twins alone and they had found Ma´s baking flour and it was all over the place when Ma returned, and that she was out of her mind as that was to last for the whole weeks bread baking. Being as hard up as she was, God only knows how she managed.

After a spell of living in the caravan Ma and Da moved to Horden where I was born it was once the largest coal mine in Europe, and now sadly it´s closed, and thanks to Margaret Thatcher and her government it´s a ghost town like the rest of the mining villages throughout the country, I can´t dwell on that subject now, as I won´t get this story told.

When Ma and Da had moved to Horden, he wasn´t working at the pit, where like every miner, he would have had an allowance of coal as part of his wage structure, so, in order to get coal for the fire, which was an easy task, all you had to do, was to go down to the beach an pick it off the shore, that was because all the coast pits tipped their waste into the sea, and coal, being lighter than stone it´s washed onto the shore. One day Da got his beach bike out, it had no tyres, no chain, and, no brakes it didn´t need any, as it was used "only" to carry bags of coal from the beach of which, there was an endless supply of, as well as drift wood, well one day, Ma must have been poorly and Da took the twins, Doris and Elsie on the crossbar and Da on the peddle down to the beach for coal, there was quite a steep slope down to the cliff top and could get a fair bit of speed up and, when they were almost at the beach cliff top Doris, manages to put her foot through the front spokes and of course they all went tumbling over the handle bars resulting in Doris, a broken leg, Elsie and Da with head injuries and if someone hadn´t been coming off the beach at that moment, who knows, how long they could have been laid there. However they ended up in hospital with Ma pacing the floor at home wondering, where "Jock" as he was called, is with her two bairns

Another story was when one day Ma wasn´t too well, Alice and Lizzie had kicked off again arguing and fighting, she asked Jane to pass her the sweeping brush and hit Alice on the head and knocked her out for a while but it did the trick they stopped fighting in the house for a long time after that but, I think by this time they realised that Ma was not a well woman, so much so that, she never ought to have had Jane or I after losing Andrew. I was told she had to lay him out herself when he died and was never the same health wise after that incident and who knows maybe her health would not have failed her at such a young age had that not happened to her. Another story, which is quite funny really is that Jane never liked the fact that when, Ma would bake, she make bread men (PASTRY ONLY) I got the biggest ones because, Ma would make mine (with a Willy on). We still laugh about it today and that happened 63yrs ago it must have been hard for her at the time, realising, she was no longer, the baby of the family.

Sometime before moving to Horden John my eldest brother had left our grandparents home to work and live on a farm was joined by Alice and were now both living, and working at the White farm which was in the next village to where Ma had lived. I can only imagine that they were living there as the results of having a job there. Soon after, James did the same, Alice worked in the farmhouse, and John and James worked on the land. I´ve never heard of them taking money home to Ma I just hope they did. It was John, the White family took a shine to, and treat him like a son, even in his later life right up until the day he died aged 47. John was called up for National Service and moved from the farm and during his army training he met and married Alice before he was shipped off to Burma, where he served until the end of that war.

At around the age of three to four Ma´s health must have been deteriorating rapidly. I can remember the girls taking me to school with them and, had to sit quiet at the back of their classroom, with a slate and chalk to keep me amused, while the girls had their lessons. I suppose it was the only way they could get any schooling in at all, as Ma would have kept them off school to help around the house, also, it would have given her a break from the constant bickering which all kids do but the twins have managed, it seems, to have carried it into adulthood, they are still at it night and day, every day, "BUT" have never ever fallen out with each other.

With having 5 sisters older than I, and of course girls, being what they are, all their friends wanted to kiss and cuddle me all the time, saying "poor bairn" and at that young age constantly being kissed by girls. "YUCK". Apparently I was a well behaved child, Jane has mentioned this many times over the years, and said that when no-one was about she would give me a crack and when I asked her why she replied for "being good" that's why, as all the attention had gone from her. We still laugh about that as well. On one occasion the twins had taken Jane and I down to the beach for the day. When I say beach the whole of the beach was filthy from the waste the pits would tip into the sea. It was like a war zone littered with huge stones and pebbles, coal from the mines and drift wood that had changed into all kinds of fascinating shapes and glass pebbles of different shapes and colours that would keep us all busy for hours and hours seeing what we could find among it all. We would have with us if we were lucky, dry bread and jam sandwiches and a bottle of water. I can remember that I always had to have my drink last as I always managed to put chewed bread in the bottle after I´d had a drink from it. We would if the season was right steal potatoes from the edge of the farmers field, take to the beach, light a fire, and have black roasted potatoes and of course on the way home we would take a few more out of the field and take them home with us and have chips or roast spuds again. It sure was a whole lot better than jam and bread. One outing we had to beach, on the way back, Jane was told to carry me, and when she refused Elsie hit her on the forehead with the glass pop bottle resulting in a large egg shaped bump. Jane said she blackmailed her for ages as she would have been in deep trouble if Ma found out about it. We all still have a laugh about that as well Elsie insists it was through that bash on the head that made her brainy.

I can´t ever remember John, Alice or Lizzie living at home before Ma died in 1946 but Alice told me when Lizzie was in her teens Da was having a go at Ma and Lizzie pulled him off her, pushing him into the corner of the room, resulting in him splitting his head open, on the airing cupboard door, taking a piece out of it, and Lizzie was frightened to death in case Da had a go at her but, it settled him down for a while, as regards to roughing Ma up, until, a few years later James had to sort him out by cracking him for doing the same thing to Ma. Good for them I say. . Our John´s wife Alice one day had made a visit to us from Chesterfield sometime before Ma died. We went down to the beach, goodness knows what she must have thought of it but I do remember that we had found a clear spot and they were all sitting on the sands close to the shore, Jane said I had gone in for a paddle and this large wave had come from nowhere and covered me and was drawing me back into the sea when they noticed what was happening they were screaming and shouting and pulling me out. Jane had to run home to get me some dry clothes. God only knows where they got a change of clothes for me as I didn´t have any. That was the first of three incidents in my life where I was almost drowned two of which were down at that particular beach

It would have been around about 1942-3 when John would have left the farm where he was living and working to do his army training when he met and married Alice, who was expecting their first child Christopher, where shortly after he was sent to Burma for the duration of the Far-east war, Lizzie and our Alice were in the A.T.S and James was living on the Collingwood farm until he was called up for National Service. James settled in Derby when he was demobbed and worked as a bus driver where he met and married Eileen and eventually had five children.

One of the most vivid memories I do have as a child and it's so vivid in fact it's as if it had just happened the other month when Ma had her accident. I happened around 1945. Jane must have been at school and Da at work or more likely down the beach picking coal. Ma had left me in the front room and closed the passage door to the stairs when she went upstairs to clean the bedrooms and stairs, when, all of a sudden there was this almighty BUMP BUMP and then an awful UUUUUGH as best I can describe it. Well when I shouted "MA" "MA" for what seemed ages and when I didn't get an answer I went to see why. Well, first of all the door was closed and, the round door handle was half way up the door, where I couldn't reach it, so, I got a high back chair and put in place so I could turn the handle with both hands, I got down off the chair moved it out of the way, only to find that the door was still closed. That took me ages to fathom out I had the chair too close to the door so, when I finally, got inside, my Ma was laying face down, I thought in my little mind that she was asleep I don't remember seeing any blood and, try as I may I couldn't wake her up and, eventually I fell asleep on top of her. With Ma being in poor health one of Ma's neighbours Hannah used to look in on her from time to time and as she hadn't been seen for a while came to see why, and found us like that. What had happened was, she was cleaning the stairs when she took an epileptic fit and tumbled down the stairs and hit her head on a baby gas cylinder which they used in case of gas attacks during the war, stood up, turned around and collapsed not surprising, as turned out she needed 35 stitches in her head and sadly that was the beginning of the end for her.

At 39yrs old she hadn´t even had a life, but, I do hope, the good lord has made it up to her for the short life she had here. My memory of Ma was, that she was always, dressed in black clothing, and I can´t ever remember her having me on her knee, which, I´m sure she must have. Had I not been shown one, of only two photo´s in existence of her I would, have gone through my life without knowing my own mother´s face. That´s what I have missing in my memories, as a child, the cuddles and hugs, you give to a child in everyday life. God only knows why that gas cylinder was still there after the war had ended; perhaps, Da was going to weigh it in for scrap at some stage. I can only go from what I was told that he liked his whisky and beer more than he liked giving Ma his wages (when he was in work) He was a Dab hand at getting drunk in the town on the way home from work on wages day, and what was left Ma only got a portion of what was left and had to feed the family. Just a thought, maybe the good Lord took her because like his son J.C. who could feed a multitude with five fishes and needed her up there with his lad, because each and every one of the family have said, she was a miracle worker making meals out of what small amount of food she had available. That is what Ma had to do with the pittance Da gave her as housekeeping money.

Money was so short Ma had a job at the local butchers, washing the place out when they closed, to make ends meet , her wages I´m told was only a pittance, and in order to get meat Ma would give the butcher our clothing coupons. When you think about it, what good were clothing coupons to her when she couldn´t afford to buy clothes anyway. An old joke about those days was sending one of the kids to the butchers for a sheep´s head and to ask the butcher to leave the eyes in to see us through next week. Seriously though what hard times those were and, thankfully, kid's today don´t have to endure that poverty.

It was on Ma´s first admission to hospital and Ma and Da must have had a blazing row because as she was being put into the ambulance Da´s parting words to her were " I hope they bring you back in a box and sadly that´s exactly what happened the second time she was sent to hospital. There she died of an epileptic fit. Is there any wonder that the family and neighbours hadn´t a good word for him. Another memory that I´ll never forget is, when she was in hospital before she died, I had been taken to see her, the lady in the bed across the ward a Mrs Rowntree, called me over, and of course I was thinking she was going to give me a sweet, went over and when she tried to pick me up to give me cuddle, I screamed the place down, it frightened the living daylights out of me, and Ma had to take me in her bed to console me. Not the kind lady´s fault I just didn´t like the look of her. On another occasion when I was taken to the hospital by Alice and her future husband Alf, Ma must have known she was on the way out and living on borrowed time, and it´s also just like it happened the other month, I can remember her saying to Alf will you look after my bairns, (Jane and I) I can´t remember the answer she got but, I do remember, her saying that, which I found a bit strange at the time, because, Da was at home.

One of the many stories Alice told me, was that, when she and Lizzie were at school, Ma used to inspect their hair for "nits" which was rife in those days. Ma took a fit while looking in Lizzie´s hair and by the time she got a neighbour in to help, Lizzie was almost bald, another time Ma had an epileptic fit and fell into the fire and badly burned both hands. Just imagine the pain and suffering she went through with those injuries and bringing up a house full of kids, the frustration also, Ma must have had, when she couldn´t give the two girls a crack for fighting like cat and dog, which, they did all day, and every day, all of that sounds funny now but, it must have been Hell for her. I think by this time they realised that Ma was not a well woman, so much so as I mentioned earlier, she never ought to have had Jane or I and maybe her health would not have failed her at such a young age.

Another memory of mine is of being down at the beach was when Da was bringing his bags of coal up from the beach and me dragging a bag of driftwood which was it seemed as big as me, and him telling me not to let it slip and can remember it hurting my hands and arms, but was so proud what I´d done, I never said anything about it, he probably didn't notice anyway.

Also as a small child, our James had made a sledge out of an old bed frame and, at the bottom of our street there was a steep incline, covered in thick ice and, a huge crowd watching us on this "SUPER" sledge well, when we got to the bottom on this bed frame it, had cut all the ice up so there wasn´t a sledge run after that. James picked me up and had to run home, being snowballed all the way.

At around the age of three to four Ma´s health must have been deteriorating rapidly. I can remember the girls taking me to school with them and, had to sit quiet at the back of their classroom, with a slate and chalk to keep me amused, while the girls had their lessons. I suppose it was the only way they could get any schooling in at all, as Ma would have kept them off school to help around the house, also, it would have given her a break from the constant bickering which all kids do but the twins have managed, it seems to have carried it into adulthood, they are still at it night and day every day "BUT" have never ever fallen out with each other.

On one occasion the twins had taken Jane and I down to the beach, and on the way back, Jane was told to carry me, and when she refused Elsie hit her on the forehead with a glass pop bottle resulting in a large egg shaped bump. Jane said she blackmailed her for ages about that in case she told Ma about it. We all still have a laugh about that as well. Another story is, Jane never liked the fact that, when, Ma would bake she would make bread men (PASTRY ONLY) I got the biggest ones because, Ma would make mine (with a Willy on). We still laugh about it today and that happened 63yrs ago it must have been hard for her at the time, realising, she was no longer, the baby of the family.

I can´t ever remember John, my eldest sister, or Lizzie living at home before Ma died in 1946 they must have all been in the services. John in Burma and the girls in the ATS, but she did tell me of an incident, when Lizzie and her were in their teens, Da was having a go at Ma and Lizzie pulled him off her, pushing him into the corner of the room, resulting in him splitting his head open, on the airing cupboard door, taking a piece out of it, and Lizzie was frightened to death in case Da had a go at her but, it settled him down for a while, as regards to roughing Ma up, until, a few years later James had to sort him out by cracking him for doing the same thing to Ma. Good for them I say. About 1943, John went to live in Chesterfield, and married, his wife Alice, who was expecting their first child Christopher, when he was sent to Burma during the war, Lizzie and our Alice were in the A.T.S and James was still living on Whites farm. By 1945, Doris and Elsie had gone to work in service, for some Jewish family in Bradford, and then later, went on to live in a hostel for mill workers in Halifax, and worked in the wool mills there until they both got married. Funnily enough they had one child each and each child had two mothers imagine that as a child and, in later years they both became widows at around the same time. It´s a good job they have each other and, when their time is up I hope the good lord chooses a day when he can take them both together.

One of the most vivid memories I do have as a child and can remember it just like it happened the other month, that´s how vivid it is, when Ma´s accident happened. Jane must have been at school, and Da at work or more likely down the beach picking coal. Ma had left me in the front room and closed the passage door to the stairs when she went upstairs to clean the bedrooms and stairs, when, all of a sudden there was this almighty BUMP, BUMP, and then an awful UUUUUGH as best I can describe it. When I shouted "MA" "MA" and didn´t get an answer I went to see why. Well, first of all the door was closed and, the round door handle was half way up the door, where I couldn´t reach it, so, I got a high back chair, and put in place so I could turn the handle with both hands, I got down off the chair moved it out of the way, only to find that the door was still closed. That took me ages to fathom out I had the chair too close to the door so, when I finally, got inside, Ma was face down, I thought in my little mind that she was asleep. I don´t remember seeing any blood and, try as I may I couldn´t wake her up and, eventually fell asleep on top of her. With Ma being in poor health one of Ma´s neighbours Hannah used to look in on her from time to time and as she hadn´t been seen for a while came to see why and found us like that. What had happened was she was cleaning the stairs when she took an epileptic fit and tumbled down the stairs and hit her head on a baby gasmask which they used in case of gas attacks during the war stood up, turned round and collapsed not surprising, as she needed 35 stitches in her head and that was the beginning of the end for her.

Another memory that I´ll never forget when she was in hospital and I had been taken to see her, the lady in the bed across the ward a Mrs Rowntree, called me over, and me, thinking she was going to give me a sweet, I went over and when she tried to pick me up to give me cuddle, I screamed the place down it frightened the living daylights out of me, and Ma had to take me in her bed to console me. Not the kind lady´s fault I just didn´t like the look of her. On another occasion when I was taken to the hospital by my eldest sister and her husband Alf Ma must have known she was on the way out and it´s just like it happened the other month, I can remember her saying to Alf will you look after my bairns, (Jane and I) I can´t remember the answer she got but, I do remember, her saying that, which I found a bit strange at the time, because, Da was at home. I can vaguely remember when Ma was laid in her coffin under the front room window and people were coming into the house to pay their respects and me saying Shhhh Ma's asleep. If Da at that time wasn't riddled with guilt then he should have been after that unforgivable statement he had shouted to Ma as she was being put in the ambulance.

After Ma died, Jane and I, couldn´t attend the funeral, apparently, we were told Da couldn´t afford any clothes for us at the time. And when the funeral service was over we were playing in a shop door way which, had a full mirror on the side wall of the entrance to the shop, where you could stand in front of it and stick an arm and a leg out to make it appear

15

that you were two people looking in the mirror, cheap fun for kids who had nothing to play with, and I remember Jane saying to me "that´s Ma´s" funeral going up the street and she is going to heaven now, and standing there in "awe" knowing she wasn´t coming back. Jane did take me to the cemetery at some stage, and I remember her grave was right up against a wall with no headstone or flowers like most of the others had but, too young then to understand why. I seem to remember that I hadn´t to tell anyone that we had been to the cemetery, maybe, those concerned didn´t want us kids to see, the offhand way, Ma had been buried in what seemed un marked grave.

It wasn´t too long or it didn´t seem too long after that, that my world fell apart, for a little 5yr old boy, whose, only fault, was to have been born.

Prior to Ma´s death as soon as anyone in the family was old enough to leave home, they did, as Da could start a row "in drink" before he went bed and carry on with it when he got out of bed the next day. So eventually there was only, Jane and I left at home. I can remember "once" and only once where he had me on his knee sitting in front of a small fire and he was rubbing his whiskers on my face, just a bit of fun but I remember that I didn´t like it. And try as I may I can never remember "ever" being sat on Ma´s lap although, I´m sure I was. After Ma´s death when we were sent to bed at night there was a bucket on the landing, in case we needed the toilet as the toilet was outside. At times Da left the house so quiet, to go out boozing that Jane wouldn´t know whether he was in or out, and even if I was asleep, I would be woken up to stand on the landing, and call down stairs "Da I want a drink of water" repeatedly, until she felt sure that he had definitely gone out, as Jane wanted to play down stairs, and knowing full well, I wouldn´t get shouted at, as much as her. On the odd occasion he would trick her, and he would still be in the house, and when we got down stairs, we would be chased back to bed.

I know I was very young but I can never remember there being sheets on the bed, only rough blankets, but, can always, remember, the army great coat, what would we have done without them in those days? There were never any curtains at the bedroom windows and on clear nights Jane would count the stars in each window pane or looking at the moon which looked much closer then than it does now, looking for faces on it, until we fell asleep. There was no wallpaper on any walls they were whitewashed with dye added to make it look posh. Being sent to bed cold and hungry are without doubt one of the most vivid of my childhood memories. I also remember things around the house like glass domes with flower arrangements in them and light bulbs and bottles with ships in them, apparently, they were made by prisoners of war. I often wonder where they went to, probably sold for beer money no doubt.

I didn´t know it at the time, but, every house around us had "BLACKLOCKS" the whole country was plagued by them so, once you got in bed and it became dark, you stayed there until daylight, or picked something up to hit the floor and they would scatter, or when you put the lights on. That kept kids in bed when it was dark that´s for sure. It wasn´t until detergent was used, on a large scale, that they disappeared, well, that´s my theory, and a lots of other people´s too. We wore the same clothes until someone took pity on us and gave us some cast off clothing. One thing for sure was that no one teased, or called you names about your dress because almost everyone was the same. I for one didn´t have socks I wore the sleeves from worn out jumpers or cardigans with my worn out wellington boots which always had holes in the soles of them which I wore winter and summer. The constant slipping down of those sleeves to the front of those wellingtons was a nightmare that you had to endure in order to keep your feet warm it´s a wonder my feet aren´t deformed. As best I can remember Jane always had sandals without socks and of course the inevitable holes in the soles. She often remarks on the fact that she never had underwear her pants, was her vest fastened with a safety pin between her legs. By anyone´s calculation that is poverty in the highest order. A short while after Ma died things started to happen and this is how the story was related to me by Alice my eldest sister. She and Alf had married and were living with his mother at Blackhall where, Alf worked at the pit. Alf was small in height but, I was told years later, he had the reputation, of being a street fighter. She couldn´t get along with Mary his mother. " Thomas" their first child, had been born there, and, according to her, he cried none stop, for the first nine months of his life, creating, even more tension, and so, they got themselves together and, got Da to sign the tenancy over to them and, we would all live there together with Alf paying the rent. Looking back, it was a "ploy" but Da must have thought it a good idea as it meant, more money for his boozing and, someone, to clean house and do the cooking. My sister and Alf must have taken the rent arrears on as he was always in arrears.

One of Da´s favourite stunts on rent days was to put the rent card and money on the front room window sill, take me up stairs and play a game of who could keep quietest the longest. More often than not I would fall asleep. When the rent man Joe ...... came to the back door and didn´t get an answer, he would go around to the front of the house to peer through the front room window to see if anyone was in then notice the rent card and money on the windowsill and write in his book Mr .... willing to pay "but not in". He also had a shilling coin with a hole drilled in it and a piece of wire attached to it for the electricity meter where he could drop the coin in the meter and it would register for a shillings worth of electricity and with careful manoeuvring he could retrieve the coin for use later. Of course he couldn´t use that trick too often as some money had to be in the meter when they came to empty it but, it would have got him three or four pints of beer in those days. Because Da, being like he was with drink, started to take coal from the coal house (which was Alf´s allowance for working down the pit) to sell for drinking money, instead of going down the beach for it, and like Da, Alf also liked his drink and when Alf found out they had a huge argument about it and Alf kicked him out, he then, went to live above a cafe in the village, but I can´t ever remember him coming to see us. Maybe his past was catching up with him and couldn´t take it ie. the resentment people had for him the way he had treat Ma over the years and that damning statement he had made in front of Ma´s best friend as she was being taken to the ambulance "I hope they bring you back in a box" I hope it haunted him for the rest of his days. Looking back I suppose Alice and Alf had finally got a good enough excuse to kick him out of his own home which I suspect was their plan all along. Sometime later Alf spoke to uncle Bill, (Ma´s sister´s husband) who also liked his drink, and one night when they were out drinking he said, that as "Jock" was not paying any money for our keep, Jane and I would have to be split up and the start of my nightmares began.

Jane was sent to live with aunt Rose and uncle Bill. They lived a short distance away from our home but can't remember ever going to their home. They had three children of their own at that time.(all girls) Uncle Bill was, as I remember him, and, will never forget him, for the rest of my days, was, a huge man, always with a menacing look on his face, and, I can´t remember him, other than, him shouting and bawling at the top of his voice. There was a huge conflict of personalities between Jane and their eldest daughter Doris, and after a short time Jane was sent back to live with us at our Alice´s and Alf´s and I was sent to aunt Rose and uncle Bill´s. And "that" is where my first "nightmare" began.

Uncle Bill would often come home in a drunken state and start by screaming and shouting, and, banging together a great big, pit coal shovel, and a massive steel poker at us kids, frightening, the living daylights out us, no one could imagine a grown man even in "drink" would do the things he did "having fun" as he put it. Aunt Rose didn´t make things any better at the time as she would be screaming at the top of her voice, telling him to stop. I was absolutely petrified with nowhere to go to, and no one to tell. There was on more than one occasion when I wouldn´t stop crying he´d pick me up and take me down the yard and lock me in the coalhouse, aunt Rose would be begging him not to, and, him saying to her "your next" if you don´t "shut" it, I felt safer in the pitch black dark of the coal house than being anywhere near him. That´s how petrified I was of him. He would eventually, go to bed and Aunt Rose would take me out of the coal house and things would return to normal, I can´t ever remember her once consoling me in anyway. I was absolutely petrified of that man and avoided him at every opportunity, the short stay I had there was the "first" of the most frightening events in my life as a child, something I can´t and have never forgotten to this day and, there was plenty more to come. There was another occasion when he was in another of his drunken states (looking back as an adult) he was trying to have it off with aunt Rose on the living room floor and she was screaming and begging him to stop, we all ran out to get away from him. On another occasion he was wrestling with her on the floor in a drunken state again laughing so loud it scared us all, he had a pair of pincers which he managed to get on her nose and when she started screaming we all ran out of the house and God knows what happened to her after we ran out. Jane was to tell me years later that she had, had to endure the same ordeal of being put in the coalhouse, she was on several occasions given a hiding by aunt Rose with a short piece of hose pipe aunt Rose would use to fill the boiler at the side of the fire when she would back answer and, as always, the threat of being sent into a home, whenever she and Doris were fighting. Doris was the apple of her dads eye, so, no matter what she had done wrong, Jane, would always get the blame. At ten years old her life was also one of hell.

During my short stay at my aunt Rose's I can remember there was one occasion when it was quite funny. It was the time Doris who, nearly always got her own way, saying, I want to go to the pictures and Aunt Rose would reply, there's pictures on the wall, but they don't move Doris would say and aunt Rose's reply was I'll make the buggers move. Strange, how incidents such as that, stick in your mind.

It was years later I was to find out the full effect it had on poor, Aunt Rose living with Uncle Bill, and the "insane" person that he was.

It was only a short time after being sent there that apparently Alf and uncle Bill, had got themselves together again, and made their minds up that they were not going to keep Jocks kids, after they found out that Da, had moved out of the village, where to, no one knew, but it was discovered later, that he had made his way to Chesterfield, where our John was living when he came out of the army, when the Japanese war was over.

Up to that point in my life I had only been out of the village twice or three times and that was when I was taken to Alf´s mothers. I can always remember that we were given something to eat other than jam and bread. She was a stout built woman and as I remember her she didn´t shout and bawl at me as was the norm since Ma had died, and she would always reward me with a homemade biscuit or small cake after running an errand for her as she never seemed to do anything but bake and cook meals all day, there was always the gorgeous smell of cooking in the house. She always had at least two or three Irish lads as lodgers staying there who worked on building sites. How they all fitted in, in not so big a house I don´t know. I remember being fascinated by their strong Irish accent and always complimenting Alf´s mother on the meal they had just eaten. At night she would play cards with them which was one of her weaknesses the other was backing horses, however I do have fond memories of my visits to their home. Alf´s dad Johnny was as I remember him, a very placid man who never raised his voice and absolutely adored Thomas it was no wonder as I was to find out years later that Thomas would want to spend as much time at his grandparents as he did.

One day and a day in my life I will never forget, uncle Bill and Alf after getting their heads together, without any prior warning to Jane or I, took us to the Education Authority´s of Durham, who were in charge of children´s homes etc. in those days. It was a massive house where they took us, then into a room where a Mr Sherwood, a big chap was standing at a fireplace, I couldn´t hear what they were saying but, Jane could, and the conversation went like this. The "only" way we can accept these children is, for both of you to walk out of here and "abandon" them.

Uncle Bill said something to Alf, then Alf came over to me, ruffled my hair, and said, "Be a good lad", then he, and, uncle Bill walked out. I never, ever, saw my Uncle Bill again after that day, and "that" wasn´t a day too early. I was absolutely "petrified" of that man and thought at least my nightmares would be over, how wrong I was.

I was told by our Alice years later, that she and aunt Rose were heartbroken that we had been left there, because to their knowledge, we had been taken there to get it sorted out as to regards money for Jane´s and my keep. They couldn´t have been that heartbroken as, neither of them visited me in the seven years I spent there. Alice did say she had suggested visiting me to Alf but, he wasn´t interested. When I asked why didn't you come? She said she couldn´t afford it. Aunt Rose, uncle Bill and her family moved to Nottingham along with my uncle Bill´s mate Dave sometime after 1947 to work in the pits there. It was in 1967 the next time I saw aunt Rose again, and hadn´t the heart to bring the subject up. uncle Bill had died by then and aunt Rose was either married to Dave or living with him as man and wife by then.

The next time I saw our Alice and Alf after being abandoned and put in the homes, was when our Jane would take us sometime later, on week-end visits back to our home village, where, we would stay at our Lizzie´s mother in-law, I can´t remember staying at our old house, which, our Alice and Alf now had, and was seven years later, when, they learned from our Lizzie, that they would be paid money, if, they became my guardian, and take me out of the children´s home, which, they did. Not "once", in those seven years had our Alice or Alf been to see us, not even aunt Rose or any other of my mother´s family. Chances are they knew nothing of mine and Jane´s plight. The only visitors I had in all those years were the twins and Lizzie and Eddie.

After they "abandoned" us, we were taken to "Medomsley Cottage Homes" near Consett in Co. Durham, and, as Jane puts it, put "in prison" We arrived there sometime about lunchtime, there were no children about, Jane was taken to another cottage (house) where only girls lived, and I was taken to another, where only boys lived.

There I was, seated at a kitchen table, scrubbed clean like everything else, (not a bit like home), they asked my name then, given a saucer with three or four biscuits and a glass of milk. I didn´t touch them, all I wanted was to be with our Jane. I was really scared, "alone", with all these strangers around me, until this lady, with a kind voice said, eat them up, and drink your milk, I´d never had that before, a glass of milk all to myself, or, biscuits on a saucer, there was only one saucer in our house, the one Da used to drink his tea with, there were times when there were no cups, we would drink out of jam jars. They also gave me a comic which, I was glad of, which I hid behind, and cried, cried and, cried without making a sound (too frightened) I wanted our Jane so badly but, I didn´t know where she was. There I was just turned five, dressed in rags, not knowing, what was going to happen to me next. "This" was the start of a seven year "nightmare" for me, which still haunts me to this day.

I was introduced to Mr and Mrs Peverly (a name I will "never ever" forget for the rest of my days) Mr Peverly was a big made man, that never said much to anyone, he had a false leg and used a walking stick, I found out later that he had lost his leg during the

24

war when he was in the navy, and was secretly called "PEG LEG" by all the kids. They were the husband and wife team that ran the house as were all the cottages run by a husband and wife team, as I seem to remember there were 10 in all 5 for girls and 5 for boys and each house was called a cottage, and named after trees and flowers. It was Primrose cottage, where I was to live for the next 7 years, and hated every second of it.

 Eventually they took me to the bathroom, put me in the bath and, I suppose they de-loused me, as I now smelled like a bar of carbolic soap, took all my rags away and kitted me out with clean clothes that fit. At that stage in my life you could count almost every bone in my body. The next scary thing was, when all the kids came from school and them staring at me and asking my name. After tea the next scary thing to happen was, after a cup of cocoa before being put to bed in a huge bedroom along with 11 more kids and given a night shirt to wear I´d never had that before either. At home I was always sent to bed in the clothes I was wearing to keep warm. I didn´t go to school the next day, but taken for a medical and kitted out with more clothes, boots and socks I´d never had socks before always cardigan or jumper sleeves. I´d never had so many clothes even handkerchiefs and still, I, haven´t seen anything of our Jane, I was getting very worried by now but daren´t ask anyone. (Too scared)

I was taken to the school the next day, and was dressed in the clothes I´d been issued with the day before, all the children from the home I seem to remember were better dressed than most of the local kids. I was taken to my classroom, told where to sit, and told what was expected of me, and I´m still scared to death but, when we were given a school dinner it made up for it, it was the most food that I´d ever been given that I could remember. At home it was "always" dry bread and jam mainly, sometimes a cup with an oxo in it, and break a couple of slices of bread into it and eat it like it was soup. That was the substitute of a hot meal Jane and I had. Is there any wonder why the most "vivid memories" of my early, early childhood is one of "always" being hungry and cold.

It still puzzles me to this day how a man, our father could "not" have noticed that his children are unkempt and "must" be hungry knowing what food you are giving them and yet do "nothing" to put the situation right.

That night after tea (more food) I was taken to one side by Mrs Peverly. She was a tall woman, with her hair pulled tight in a bun, with a "wart" on the right side of her nose and one on the right side of her chin. I don´t know if she noticed but I couldn´t help looking at them every time I looked at her She always wore a flowered wrap round apron with keys hanging from the waist, and really shiny shoes. The two other women wore a khaki wrap round apron and a white hat.

She told me, I had a job to do every morning, and it was then explained to me that "everyone" has a job to do and, it must, be completed before you have your breakfast (sounds simple enough) and then told "if" you don´t finish your job before breakfast is finished you go to school without it. Whenever she spoke it was an order, there was never any warmth or sympathy in her voice. The vibes that came from her, you knew immediately, you had "not" got to bother her. The same vibes came from Mr Peverly.

Well my job was polishing any of the brass taps, door handles and copper piping anywhere down stairs and needless to say for the first few days I never got any breakfast as it was too big a job for me to complete in the time allowed. After a couple of days that nice woman, who did the cleaning and washing and always spoke nicely to us kids, showed me what I was doing wrong, I was putting too much brasso on and it was taking me too long to take it off. I got the hang of it after that. What a lovely kind lady she was. She eventually fostered a boy out of our cottage I can´t remember his name now, but what a lucky kid he was at the time. Well, I quickly picked things up after that, and I suppose not knowing it I was becoming institutionalised.

Discipline was strict, there were so many rules to follow, that I was being shouted at constantly by Mr and Mrs Peverly, something that I wasn´t used to i.e. Going in and out of the house whenever I wanted to, was one of them. Having to do chores every day, being put in the bath every night, and having to whisper when you went to bed, these were the things you just had to get used to or, you wouldn´t fit in.

I remember the first Saturday I was there we all had to line up for a large spoonful of cod liver oil and then a spoonful of neat orange juice to stop, me especially, from being sick from the taste of that cod liver oil. I was then given 6pence pocket money. I had never in my life had 6 pence to spend and like most of the kids went straight to the local sweet shop and spent the lot. Not even that could make up for me being there, I just wanted Jane to come and wake me up from this nightmare, and take me home. In my little mind, I had no idea that I was better off there than at home with all the poverty that went with it. It was the mental effect that it was having on me. I hadn´t seen any of my family, or anyone I knew, for what seemed a life time and wondered why, always asking myself "why" a question I would always be asking myself throughout my life. Why, am I here, what have I done wrong, no one has told me and I´m too scared to ask, not even our Jane has told me that. After what seemed a life time Jane came on the scene, the first thing I asked her was, can we go home now, no she said we have to stay here, but I don't know for how long. That didn't make me feel any better but at least she was here. She showed me the cottage where she lived, and that she had to look after babies, which, I found strange as I hadn´t seen any babies. I never asked her anymore questions, as I was just so pleased to see her again and now knew she wasn´t too far away from me, although, she may as well have been in another village because, she couldn´t come into my cottage and I couldn´t go into hers.

Looking at it from an adult point of view, it wasn´t a bad place to be in ie. I had better footwear, better clothing, and good, regular food, although I wasn´t keen on the large spoonful of cod liver oil we were given every Saturday but, compared with what I had at home I was better off by far, except for the restrictions, and, bearing in mind at home everyone used to spoil me as best they could until Da left us. I suppose the best way to describe the feeling of being in that home was similar to that of having to do National Service in the forces "everything" is there for you except those damn rules and regulations that you´re not used to "but" have to conform to and, you want to go home but you can´t.

When Jane started to appear she would turn up every Saturday morning (pocket money day) to take me to the cinema matinee whether I wanted to or not, usually to see Johnnie McBrown, or Gabby Hayes and Hopalong Cassidy the cowboys of that era, and another episode of Sir Gallahad and if Jane didn´t get to me as soon as I got my 6pence, I´d be off, to the village sweet shop, and as I say would spend it all in one go. I hated it when Jane took me to the pictures, as she never sat with me, and besides all my pocket money was being spent on bus fares and pictures entrance. Looking back at it all, the local sweetshop must have had our sweet coupons allowance as things were still rationed at that time. The outing to the cinema cost, 1penny on the bus to Consett, where the cinema was, and 4pence to get in, but, if we walked home, and bought a penny worth of broken biscuits, we had to fore go our tea, (4-30) as it would be over by the time we got back to the homes at Medomsley, and you only had one chance at it. Jane would use me to the best advantage ie. send me into the shop to ask for the broken biscuits, usually the young girl would ask me if I was from the homes, (I couldn´t be mistaken for a local kid as I was too cleanly dressed) and that would mean some chocolate ones, and even some whole ones, "sometimes" we would get some bruised fruit as well out of Jane´s money, which we ate on the way home. We were all sent to bed around 6-30pm summer or winter, after having been bathed every night, something, that didn´t happen at home although we did have a bath in our house as it was a private house.. None of the colliery houses had a bathroom it was a case of using a galvanised bath in front of the fire. For most kids it was usually on washdays after the clothes had been washed and the "poss" tub was to be emptied the kids would be put in it for their bath. For anyone that is unfamiliar with, what a "poss" tub is, it was a galvanised tub that clothes were put in, and bashed with a three pronged wooden post, before they were put into the boiler. It was called various names throughout the country but it was the same thing. The other tool they had for washday was a wringer or mangle for squeezing water from clothes and no matter what anyone says, in most houses where I was born, the wringer was the most expensive thing in the house, and that is why we could leave our doors unlocked at night because there was "nothing" worth stealing. By today's standards most people were living in poverty and there was no taking the mickie out of you because you had patches on your clothes, or holes in the soles of your footwear and a piece of cardboard or lino in them to stop the grit getting into them, because, "everyone" around you was in the same predicament.

After being sent to bed it was, as I was told by the kids who had been there long term, it had to be total "total silence" or "PEGLEG" Mr Peverly, would come up and "thrash" you, well, that was enough to frighten a 5yr old little boy. We used to take it in turns to tell stories and that would put us, and sometimes even, the story teller to sleep. I remember the stories I told, were nearly always about cowboys and my hero´s were Johnny McBrown, Gabby Hayes and Hopalong Cassidy. We must have had super hearing because, once that bedroom door was closed every word was a whisper.

Every morning was another nightmare "until", I got used to it, there were two kids who wet their beds every night, and every morning they were bawled and shouted at unmercifully, one of them Tommy became my best friend, Tommy, had an older brother Billy, in the same cottage, they looked alike, they both had tight curly hair but, Tommy had black, and Billy had almost white hair. I found out many years later they had a sister in the same home.

Every Sunday morning after breakfast, we were dressed in our Sunday best clothes, and taken to the village church for the sermon, and sing hymns, brought back to the homes, did a quick change of clothes and then, outside, for a little play, brought back in after a while, given our dinner, and about an hour later, and sent off to the local Sunday school. On one occasion, one of the kids from one of the other cottages, and, not knowing at the time, had an epileptic fit, a woman from a house opposite the chapel put a blanket around him, and a clothes peg between his teeth to stop him biting his tongue during the fit, there was all this white froth coming out of his mouth, and him shaking like mad, it was really scary, I never saw that kid again maybe, he was put in another home.

On the way to and from the chapel, we had to pass a garage, and at side of it was a huge stack of used tyres. We kids in the homes were not allowed to have "BOOLERS" as they were called, every boy in the land must have had a wheel of some sort usually a bike wheel to run alongside of, well, when we saw all those tyres, and being Sunday, and no one there, the temptation was too great so, after we came out of Sunday school we all took a tyre and ran our little legs off, until it was time for tea. Well before we went in we had to hide them and they were all over the place, under bushes, covered with grass anything at all, just so we could find them later. It wasn´t long after that we were all paraded outside the Masters house a huge house in the middle of the grounds where the offices and the living quarters were for the head man who ran the place. So there we were on parade so to speak, and, told of the crime we had all committed, "stealing tyres", and that if everyone didn´t return them, we would be sent to prison, and that nothing would happen to us on this occasion, if, we did just that. So our little bit of pleasure was short lived. On another occasion we were paraded in front of the Masters house, and when we got there, there were baskets of unripe fruit from the orchard i.e. Apples, pears gooseberries and plums then, told that someone had been stealing fruit from the orchard, before it was ripe, so in order to get the right culprit, we all had to take an under ripe apple, pear and half a dozen gooseberries and a couple of plums each. Then everyone, had eat them there and then, and couldn´t leave until they had all been eaten. Needless to say we all had belly ache that night or the day after, "but" no one ever raided the orchard after that.

One morning I woke up and decided, that I wasn´t going to school that day so, I feigned illness by saying my throat hurt and that I felt poorly, so, I was told to stay in bed until, all the other kids had, had their breakfast and gone to school leaving me, I "thought" to play or sit around reading comics. Well, after the kids had gone to school I was told to get dressed and come down stairs and told because I had a sore throat it was best for me not to have any breakfast and to drink a cup of hot water which would do my throat good and would be taken to see the matron to be examined, by this time I was starving and it didn´t look like my plan was going to work. The matron took my temperature and said I should stay in bed "ALL" day and to be given a "very" small bowl of rice pudding at lunchtime with a cup of hot water and again at teatime and if I felt better the next I could go to school. Well by the time teatime came around my stomach thought my throat had been cut, I was absolutely ravenous and knew for sure I "wasn´t" going to try that again.

After a while and it did seem a long time, the twins came to see me and told me how well I looked and, how well dressed I was and, was I being a good lad and that they had come from Halifax were they were now working and living, and that it was a long way away, they both gave me some money as they left which I went straight to the sweet shop and spent it. They did come quite often, I suppose every month or so, at least they did visit me which, I shall "never

ever" forget them, when I needed support they were the first to visit me. But in my little mind I couldn´t understand why they couldn´t take me out of there. I remember them coming just before Xmas one year, I´d be about 7yr old at the time and, they had brought me a football a "proper" leather football and a tin of dubbing to keep it waterproof. We did get "one" present each at Xmas from the home but mainly colouring books, fruit and sweets which was very good but, this football was something else and I wouldn´t let anyone play with it so I hid it. Mrs Peverly found out, made me bring it out, and took it off me and gave it to everyone to play with then "called me a snake in the grass", we share "everything" here she snapped, which I knew didn´t happen, well, that hurt like hell, I didn´t cry, nobody cried in there or you were called a sissy, and no one liked sissy´s but, my most prized present "ever" had been taken off me, I must have sulked for weeks over that. When I told the Twins on their next visit they gave me a cuddle and said, never mind but that didn´t help either. I shall "never" ever forget the twins for their kindness shown to me when I needed it most.

The only other member of my family as I say, who came to see me was our Lizzie, along with her future husband Eddie, they came, I would think, about once a month or so but, they did come, and once again I will never ever forget that, no other family members did which, makes me think of the old saying "out of sight, out of mind" Did all the rest of the family have a conscience, apparently not I often think to myself what will Ma say to them? If and when they meet up providing there is such a place.

I remember one occasion, on one of the school holidays, I´d be about 7-8 years old, a man and woman taking me to their home for a week-end. It was a beautiful house, nice furniture spotlessly clean, but I remember it was mainly the woman who spoke to me more than the man, and on the first day there when I went into their sitting room, where the man was trimming his moustache in front of a wall mirror I was fascinated by it, I had only been stood there a couple of seconds when he looked down at me and screamed, "WHAT" are you doing in here, "WHO" told you, you could come in here, he really frightened the living daylights out of me, memories of uncle Bill came flooding back, and remember the woman telling him to stop shouting and giving me a cuddle, but he went on and on about it and the next thing I knew I was taken back to the homes and never saw them again. Apparently they had taken me out on a trial run with a view to fostering me. Thank God that didn't work out I'd just got away from that environment.

One day after that (and by this time Jane had been fostered out) I was about 8yr old I said to Tommy if, we run away we can stay with our Lizzie (as she had a two bedroom bungalow by this time) Tommy thought it was a great idea. So instead of going to school that day we set off as best I knew how to get to my home village, via Chester-le-street the way our Jane took me on the bus for week-end visits. Along the way we ate blackberry's and Tommy re- assuring me he wouldn't have anything to drink after his dinner so he wouldn't wet the bed at night (Bless him)

Well we got to Chester-le Street which is about 8 miles from Medomsly and asked a lorry driver who was parked up at some shops, if he could give us a lift to my village. When he asked us where we had come from, we said Consett and that we had lost our bus fare, he must have put two and two together looking at us, blackberry juice all round our mouths and had just walked 8 miles. So he asked us if we were hungry, "HUNGRY" we both thought our throats had been cut, we were that hungry, so, he gave us his sandwiches poured us a cup of tea from his flask and told to stay there, as he would have to phone his wife as he would be a bit late getting home after taking us to home.

We could see him in the phone box and had no idea that he was phoning the police, well, in a very short time the police arrived. They took us took us to the local police station where, we were too frightened "not" to tell them that we were from Medomsley cottage homes. Looking back as an adult, the lorry driver did the right thing phoning the police, I would have done the same thing, but, it wasn´t what we wanted that day. The police were good to us, gave us some sandwiches and talking friendly, and even, gave us a proper catapult and some rubber to make it work, although, we didn´t know "how" we were going to hide them when we got back to the homes as they were definitely "NOT" allowed.

Eventually, a man from the Education Authority came, and took us back to prison "oops I mean the homes. We were scared, and it must have shown, as he kept saying "nothing" is going to happen to you "don´t worry" but little did he know what was to happen to Tommy and I. On arrival at Primrose cottage we were taken into Mr and Mrs Peverly´s front room, which was really "scary" as that room was somewhere where "no one" ever went near at any time. We were asked why we had run away, and I said because I don´t like it here and that I wanted to go home, bearing in mind I´d been there almost three years, and couldn´t realise in my small mind that I no longer, had a home to go home to it had been taken away from me by sister and brother in-law. They asked us had we been beaten or interfered with in anyway, which we them told them no, and up to then we hadn't. Eventually we were taken for a bath, and taken back to their sitting room, to say goodbye to the man who brought us back, he seemed satisfied that everything was okay. Mr and Mrs Peverly and the man from the authorities were smiling and laughing as he left the room. Then "peg leg" took us out, and told us to go to bed and get undressed but, "don´t" put your nightshirts on he whispered. We had no idea why we weren´t to put our nightshirts on or, what was to happen next. All the kids were whispering asking where had we been what was happening etc.etc. We heard the man from the Education Authorities leave and then, we heard the "thump" "thump" "thump" of peg leg coming up the stairs, we still had no idea why we had to stand at our bed without our nightshirts on. And "never" in a million years guessed what was to happen next. A complete hush came over the bedroom as peg leg came in, with a leather strap about 2 foot long, with tassels on the end, he came to me first as I was the nearest. There I was a little boy of 8, naked, and frightened to death my eyes were popping out at the sight of the strap that peg leg was holding. He got hold of the back of my hair, pushed my face onto the bed, and started to thrash me with that strap. I don´t know how long he went on, but can remember as clear as day, that it stopped hurting after so long, and my screaming stopped. When he had finished with me, "GET YOUR NIGHTSHIRT ON" he snarled, and get into bed. It was Tommy´s turn next and, he had peed himself in fear, and peg leg was bawling at the top of his voice now, and it did seem as if he was thrashed for twice as long as I was. I remember being in bed "petrified" where was our Jane or anyone in my family who I could turn to. I had no feeling in my backside or my lower back, it was completely numb, it felt as if the skin was twice as thick as normal, and the only thought I had was the hatred of that man. As a child I didn´t know the word or had even heard of the word "BASTARD" but that best sums it up what

I thought of him, and the strange thing is, in all the time I spent there it was the "first" and only physical abuse I had, thank God, I also never had or heard of any sexual abuse at those homes and once again thank God.

Strangely, throughout my years I have never come across the name Peverly and knew as an adult no matter where I was "If" I had come across him I would have given him the hiding of his life, such was the impact that thrashing had on me.

A question I´ve always asked myself as an adult is, "how" could an adult do that to a child of 8 HOW? I had never experienced anything like that before or since in my life. After that night, whenever peg leg passed me, he always pushed me out of the way with his walking stick snarling, "get out of my way" and a look of hatred on his face whenever he looked at me. Tommy and I didn´t go to school for a few days, we were kept in our bedroom and let down for our meals and sent back after, it took ages before we even spoke to each other we were so scared. Tommy eventually stopped associating with me. But I can honestly say it took all thoughts about running away out of my head. We weren´t told not to say anything about the thrashing but, were so afraid we would get it again that we "never" told anyone. I can only think that the cleaners of the house must have thought we were poorly and that´s why we were off school. Looking back as an adult the Peverly´s must have been very worried about having enquiries made about children in their care running away, they must have felt their jobs were on the line "but" to thrash a naked 8yr old child I can only think their jobs must have been very precious to them.

 I can´t remember when Jane was fostered out but she must have been when that happened otherwise

I may have told her, I don´t know though, because, I was so petrified it would be given me again. She never came back to visit me once she left the homes, I was there on my own for about another 2-3 years. But at least I could now spend my pocket money how I wanted to. The first time I mentioned the thrashing to anyone was my sister Alice after I´d been taken out of the homes and I´d left school and knew I wouldn´t be sent back to the homes, as she had threatened me on numerous occasions up to then. That´s how huge an impact the thrashing had on me.

It was sometime after the time Tommy and I ran away, I can´t remember how old I was but, one evening when we were at the picture hut as we called it (in the grounds)after the film had finished the band master asked if anyone wanted to join his brass band so I joined. That man had the patience of "Job," he learned me to read music and play the "tenor horn" it was not the instrument of my choice, I always wanted to play the cornet, and whenever I got the chance to pick it up I would play it and when the band master saw me, he would then give me a lecture as to why the tenor horn was the best suited instrument for me. Looking back though I can´t remember his name and I should really because he was a very nice man, always spoke kindly to you, and of course the patience of Job. He was a train driver that much I can remember. All the instruments were owned by him, and it was a full brass band what a man. I wish I could remember his name though. Every year at Xmas he would give a small present and a card to each of us kids in his band and the same when it was our birthday, what a lovely man he was but, I do wish he would have let me play the cornet. Alas when I left the homes I didn´t get the chance to say goodbye to him which, looking back was so sad and, also I never continued playing in a band and to think of all the time and effort that nice guy had put in but, once I left the homes it was only my freedom that was my concern.

 Earlier, when our Lizzie and Eddie had got their own home, she and Eddie made enquires about taking me out of the homes. (Which was unbeknown to me?) The reason why they couldn't take me out of the homes, was because Lizzie was expecting her first child by then and, because they only had 2 bedrooms if the child was a boy then it would be okay if it was a girl then no, well, it was a girl so nothing became of it. It was a good job too that I didn't know of the enquiries because as they explained years later the disappointment would have been devastating for me. It was as I say years later Lizzie told me about it all. While they were waiting for the results of the pregnancy she was told that they would be paid a monthly sum for my upkeep and, pocket money per month for me and, a clothing allowance every 3 months by becoming my guardian which she mentioned to our Alice, so when it fell through going to live with Lizzie and Eddie, she and Alf pursued the matter and that's, why I went to live with them purely for the fact that they were going to be paid money for me. Their housing situation hadn't changed since Alf and uncle Bill had taken us to Durham and abandoned us 7yrs prior in fact they had, had two more children.

It came about when I was about to leave the junior school one day out of the blue, I was told that I was going to live with my eldest sister, not one word of it, had been mentioned prior, about me going to live with my sister and brother-in-law, just, get my things together and was taken in a car to my old home. I can't describe the feeling I had, but, as an adult now, and looking back at it all, it must have been on par with a guy having done his National Service and was being demobbed "God" how I hated every second that I was in those homes yet, still, had the fear of mentioning about the flogging I´d had, in case they took me back that´s how much fear it had instilled in me. What a "B....RD" peg leg was.

When I arrived at my sisters everything was "GREAT" I felt that the world had been taken off my shoulders. The lady who brought me to my sister´s told me I had a P.O. savings account, a savings account "ME" I couldn´t "believe" it. Well apparently, while I had been in the homes the 6pence pocket money I was getting weekly, there was also 3pence being saved each week as well, and by the time I was 11yrs I was getting 1shilling a week and savings of 3pence a week as well, and that my pocket money would continue to increase annually in the monthly allowance she would be paid for me until I left school, it didn´t take long for those savings to go, with her borrowing some of it, and never getting it back.

The pocket money allowance, died a death very shortly after going to stay there, as one day, I was sent to the shops with a pound note, and found that when I got there, I´d lost it, after tracing my foot steps for what seemed like hours, I went home and told our Alice expecting at least a good telling off but was told there´s no pocket money for you, until you've repaid it. I was given some more money for the errand. And looking back with the experience of her nature, which I didn´t have then, I probably hadn´t picked the £1 note up in the first instance as too little was made of the incident, bearing in mind that money was extremely tight in those days. Well I never got any pocket money again "ever" from that day, whenever anyone gave me money, as a treat i.e. Lizzie or the twins, who visited, now and again, it would be borrowed, and never repaid. I went working in the fields (potato picking) to earn some money for myself, in bitter cold weather, poor clothing. Why? I don´t know because she was being paid a quarterly clothing allowance for me. I´d have a pair of wellingtons with a holes in the soles and worked from 8am until 4pm with only 4 slices of dry bread and jam to eat and a bottle of water to drink, for 2shillings and 6 pence a day and 8am- 12noon on Saturday for the princely sum of, 15 shillings for the week, in today's money that would be 75pence and on the Saturday "pay day" when I got home my sister would say to me give that to me, it´s far too much money for you to have, and gave me 2shilling and 6pence (25 pence in today's money) and said I´ll buy some clothes with rest of it, well, it's a good job I never held my breath, as she never did buy me any clothes with that money. That without a doubt would have been, given to Alf, so he could go for a drink. As I say it seems ridiculous when they were being paid allowances for me, but that was the situation for me and, the threat of being sent back to the homes when I was cheeky, or saying the word "ORRRR" when asked to do a task, kept me in check.

There was one incident that I remember when I was about 12 yrs old. It was a couple of days before the first Xmas that I´d come to live with my sister and Alf she asked me what I would like for Xmas, I thought, this was something that had never happened before. I said I would like a large torch like one of my friends had, but if I can´t, can I have one of those lamps that they fit onto the front of a bike, they are only 5 shillings yes she said gave me the 5 shillings and said tell him to wrap it and bring it straight back here. Off I ran to the local bike shop bought it and took it home. At least I knew 1 present I was going to get for Xmas. On Christmas Eve tea time we all went to stay at Alf´s mother´s and on Christmas morning I was the first to get out of bed but when I got down stairs there were no presents laid out at all so I went back to bed until I heard voices down stairs. When I got down stairs there was my bike lamp still wrapped in the brown paper bag that I´d bought at the bike shop the day before, in the middle of the table and nothing else. Something else that was new to me, at least when I was in the homes we all got a present of some sort along with books an apple and orange and some sweets but there was nothing except the bike lamp. No one seemed to be taking any notice of me when I took it from the table and when I switched it on it didn´t work so, I quickly took the top of it to see why it didn´t work and found that there were no batteries in it. That made me cry and when I told my sister about it I was immediately given a slap at the back of my head and told that´s for being ungrateful. It was weeks later that I put batteries in it which cost 2/6pence by running errands for pennies and half pennies. That was my first Xmas at my new home, what else was in store for me? Little did I know then, but there were far, far worse things to happen in my life to come.

It was shortly after that time that my second near drowning experience happened. A lad who lived around the corner Jimmy Wood who was older than me and my mates was sort of leader of the four or five of people I hung around with. It was wintertime and we all decided we would go down to the beach, on the beach at the bottom of the cliff face probably about 100 yds from the sea shore was a fairly large fresh water pond I suppose about three to four feet deep which had frozen over. We were all sliding and skating on it and having great fun when Jimmy snatched the unusual shaped piece of drift wood I´d found on the beach from me and threw it into the middle of the frozen pond. Not realising at that age, the ice being thinner in the middle I went chasing after it, no sooner had I got hold of it when the ice gave way and I sank in it. What made me tread water

I don´t know I´d never had swimming lessons but I did and every time I put my arms onto the ice to pull myself out the ice broke and thinking when will the ice be strong enough to hold me while I pull myself out. No one dare come anywhere near me in case they ended up in the same predicament. I do know how long I was in the water, quite a while I suppose, keep lifting myself onto the ice only for it to break under my weight but at least every time I did it I was getting nearer and nearer to the edge of the pond. After what seemed an eternity somehow a rope had been thrown to me and was eventually pulled to the edge of the pond. It had been a beach lorry coming down to the beach for coals they left the beach by a different route when they were full. Had that lorry not come on the scene at that moment who knows what my fate might have been? I remember the lorry driver giving me his coat on and telling me to sit on the engine cover where it was hot. He took me home and explained what had happened down at the beach, my teeth and body chattering and shaking so much by this time Alice couldn´t make sense of what I was saying. She thanked him and the door was no sooner closed when I was given a good hiding for being down the beach in the first place never mind the inconvenience I´d caused the lorry driver. But after saying all that I´m sure the good hiding thawed me out quicker than the shivering did. Sadly Jimmy came to a tragic end only a few months after that incident. He had been walking along the cliffs of the same beach when for some reason he had fallen from the top of the cliff into a clay pit at the bottom on the beach. He had fallen head first into it. It was a treacherous area where it happened and we could only think that he had been bird nesting and lost his footing. I remember going to his house and seeing him in his coffin and he looked as if his nose, looked as if it was full of clay but not a mark on him which scared me. That incident kept me and most kids away from the cliff tops for quite awhile.

Looking back to those years in the homes I never once remember wishing that my Da would come for me, why I don´t know, after Jane was fostered out I do recall wondering when or why she hadn´t come back for me to take me with her "BUT" she never did. It must have been a year or two after when our Alice had taken me out of the homes, that she came to see me, and took me to see the family that she was living with. It was when she left school that she went to live with Lizzie and Eddie for a short while, then eventually with Doris in Halifax, where she got a job in a bank and worked there until she retired.

When I was about 12 to 13yr old, out of the blue our John the eldest of the family came to see my sister, I didn´t know him I had never seen him in my life, as he had been living on the farm or had gone to live at Chesterfield when I was born. I suppose he had been unaware that I´d been in a children´s home for 7 years. His marriage had broken down and his partner who had also been his secretary took me back to where they were living it turned out to be a huge caravan in a field near a farm house, my father was also there, in a converted railway carriage. I can´t remember anything about that visit, a hug or being asked any questions about my life, except that they left me in the caravan every night with some comics to read while they all went out on the booze. The day before I was taken back home it was the one and only time Da took me out on that visit, he took me into Chesterfield town, and bought me a kiddie´s pocket watch, with a cowboy riding a horse as the second hand and also his Clan tartan scarf. These were my pride and joy. They were the only presents he ever bought me in "his" entire life. I have often wondered if he was guilt ridden, when our John took me to his place and when he saw me for the first time in seven or eight years, after walking away from his two youngest children, and never making contact with either of them. No, perhaps not as, he "still" never came to visit or write, or send a birthday or a Xmas card to me even after that visit. I was 17yrs old, the next time I saw him. In the seven years I spent in those homes, my father, my two brothers or my eldest sister who I now lived with or any member of my mother's family ever paid me a visit or sent a letter, or a card only the twins, our Lizzie and Eddie ever came.

The longer I lived at my sisters the more my life was becoming unhappy, so unhappy because, I was being used as a dogs body, my sister, must, have held some sort of record for saying, pass me, fetch me, hand me, carry me, get me, give me, because, life for me was just, "that," every day it was my job to light the fire before anyone got out of bed, and a teapot full of tea made before she got out of bed, "But" it sure was better than being in those homes. There was only once that I can recall, where Alf told her to get off her backside and do it herself, as he was sick and tired of hearing her dishing orders out to me and it "was" only the once. He was at times just as bad as her, as I can remember him lying on the settee and telling me that the coals needed to be brought in from the street, when it was pouring down with rain, and think nothing of it, or, to take his greyhounds for a walk for a couple of hours, in the middle of winter, with holes in the bottom of my shoes while he would have a sleep on the settee.

After a while I realised that whenever the allowance cheque for me came, Alf, would have time off work, this is what she would be telling her neighbours, while I was making endless cups of tea for them. And I soon worked it out, that was the best time to ask her, if I could go out to play with my friends, because usually, it was only, when there were no more jobs to do around the house, i.e. wash pots, mend the fire, fill the coal buckets, sweep all the down stairs of the house, peel the spuds and prepare the vegetables ready for Alf´s and her next meal, run any errands and, if the youngest child was awake, take her with me in her pushchair. Can you imagine, a 13-14yr old lad, going out to play with his mates, and having a child in a push chair with him, I must have had good mates, as I can´t remember any of them saying, they didn´t want me around them.

By the time I left school I could cook, even bake pies, sew, iron clothes, and any other household chores, so, one good thing came out of it all, it put me in good stead for adult life, but, I missed out on a lot of playtime with my friends.

Another incident that I can´t forget, was, the time I was about 14yrs old, and was on an errand, when I realised that my pocket watch, which, Da had bought me wasn´t, in my pocket, so, I retraced my steps back home thinking it had dropped out of my pocket, or, maybe I had left it in the house, and when I told her of this, all I got was a telling off for being careless, and to hurry with the errand I´d been sent on, after completing the errand, I went out looking for my watch again, I must have spent a couple of hours, but, couldn´t find it, so I had to resign myself to the fact I´d lost it.

After maybe a few months, one day I was in the house on my own and wanting to know the time and as the house clock had stopped I went into Alf´s coat top pocket where his pit watch was, and low and behold there it was my watch with a rubber safety cover around it. I was gob smacked shaking like a leaf because God knows what I would have got by going in his pocket. After a while I took it out again after thinking "well" they wouldn´t have just made 1 of those watches so I took the rubber cover off got a knife and took the back off and there it was what I´d scratched inside it JG=GB my sweetheart Joyce G.... as a kid. I quickly put it back together again, and put it back in his pocket. I was mad, frightened and sick to my stomach to think my sister, had let me search the streets for hours knowing she had taken it "NO" stolen it and given it to Alf as a pit watch. And still I had the fear of being sent back to those homes so I daren't confront them about it. Looking back though, they wouldn´t have done that, they needed the money far too much. But as a child and the fear of it happening, I knew in my own mind to keep quiet about it. By now I knew that they couldn´t be trusted and would have to get away when the time was right, but when? It did come later though in a way, which would change my whole life and make me the person I am today. Shortly after the watch incident, when, I thought to myself, there can´t be anymore kicks in the teeth, well, low and behold, another comes along. It was summertime and Alice my sister was making what we in the north-east called, a clippie mat or Peggy rug as they are called in some area´s from old pieces of cloth, and there, in the "middle" of it as plain as day was my tartan scarf. Well I couldn´t hold it back I was crying and shouting at her HOW could you do that, that´s my scarf, that's what my Da bought me, the answer I got was "so what" you don´t wear it . I don´t in summer I replied, the next thing was, I was hit with the hearth brush on the neck and shoulders, and told "don´t" talk to me like that ever again. Taking, "NO" stealing my watch and then my scarf, meant nothing to her. I sulked for weeks after that. It was always the hearth brush or anything heavy every time I answered back or said the word, ORRRR.

One day our Elsie came to visit us, with her boyfriend Thornton, who, was to become her future husband. Thornton, was a nice guy, who asked how I was going on etc. and that he was in a cycling club, and asked, did I like cycling? I said I would but hadn´t got a bike, on their second visit a few weeks later, out of the blue, he brought me one of his spare racing bikes. "WOW" that was, even though it was second hand, the most expensive and best gift, I had ever been given, and later to become the worst. It was the "bee´s knee´s" no one had a bike like this, it had twin forks, a racing saddle with a pouch on the back of it with spanner´s for changing the wheel a puncture outfit and spare chain links, racing thin racing wheels and tyres "and" racing gears, it was as light as a feather and most impressive, it was a Claude Butler racing bike. "Yes" for the first time ever, I was the envy of all my friends. I never got to join a cycle club. I was kept too busy doing errands, at first I loved it, and then as time went on, I never seemed to get to ride it for pleasure, it was always for errands, in rain hail snow or blow, she took all the joy out of owning that bike, she had an awful habit of sending me on an errand and when I returned would send me straight back for something she had forgotten and when I would say why don't you write a list out it was always the same a hard slap around the head or the hearth brush across my shoulders. When I needed parts for the bike I would have to go and put loads of coal in for, a shilling a time, that was shovelling a ton of coal into a coal house for people, only, to be asked when I got home how much I´d earned and half taken off me which was turning me into a liar and cheat because I got to the stage where, I wouldn´t tell her all I´d earned, I hated it, but that´s what I had to do, so she wouldn´t take half the money off me.

It wasn´t long after I´d been given the bike, Elsie´s wedding came up, and Alice had to buy me a coat, to attend the wedding, there was a clothing shop in the next village, where she ticked on. You were given a card with the amount to spend at the top of it and, articles and price of them were deducted each time you bought anything leaving the figure you had left to spend. She had been to the shop herself and brought me a waterproof jerkin, the only one in the shop that looked as if it would fit me. It was twice the size I needed but, the only one she could get on pay weekly (tick) so; I had to have it, as the wedding was in two days time. She sent me down to the shop for other bits and pieces with the card, I was being served and there were three or four people waiting to be served when the young girl took the card off me to deduct the price of the articles and, said go back home and tell your mother to come to the shop, this card has been altered. It´s not my mother it´s my sister, my mother is dead I said, tell your sister then, to come down here immediately, she showed me the card, the figure six had been altered to an eight I was never so embarrassed in all my life. I don´t know how she got out of that one, probably blamed the bairns. That coat was still too big for me when I joined the army years later.

I was about 14yr old when Alf started to keep greyhounds, for a farmer, called George, a kind old man, who, was to be the first, of three people in my life, who took a shine to me, "maybe" because, he only had a daughter, and would have liked a son. I first met George at the dog track where Alf used to take me, solely for the reason, of walking the dog, or dog´s home, after the races, so he could stay on at the club drinking. After a while, I picked up on the race times that dog´s were doing, and knew what their capabilities were. George was impressed about it, and asked me if I would like to come to his farm, and walk his other dog´s and said, I´ll pay you he said. "Oh yes" I said, and of course Alf agreed, because of the deal he had with him on the other dog´s. Well, all went well and I was spending as much time at the farm as I could, here I was 14yr old and had a job "and" getting paid to do something I liked anyway, things started to look up as George would take me to various tracks so that his dogs weren´t in the kennels where they could be "got at" (nobbled) and George would say every so often when he was driving to the dog track, the dog is trying tonight George, and if it won, he would give me a fiver "WOW" a fiver for a 14yr old kid in 1956 it was fantastic. Even the ride in George´s car was a treat in its self as none of my mates were doing the things I was doing and, getting paid for it. Who knows what would have happened to my life had I taken up with his daughter who fancied me like hell but, being treat the way I was, I dare not take the chance of spoiling things by getting her into trouble. As young as I was then, I had a sane head on my shoulders, even though most of my brains were in my underpants, the same as any lad of that age.

 Eventually, I was doing farm work, as well as walking his dogs, and earning money which I would hide and not mention to my sister or Alf as it would, without doubt have been taken off me. I HATED it, as young as I was they were forcing me to be deceitful, when what I really wanted to do was show them how proud I was earning money for myself. And always no matter what time I returned home there would be household chores for me to do I could never get away from them.

   When it came to the time of leaving school, I asked George if he would set me on full time, but, he said he couldn´t as he already had two of his friends sons on his books, so that they could avoid national service, he was so sorry about it, that he got me a job on the next farm to his, and, so, not to throw kindness in his face, I took it but after about 6mths I left for three reasons, it was winter and I was inadequately dressed along with wrong footwear for the job. Which I'm sure had a great effect in contributing as to what was to happen to me in a few months time. Farm work pay was poor, and also because of the board our Alice wanted off me, and to have money in my pocket as well, it wouldn´t stretch to that so, I went to the pit for a job.

Well, I couldn´t believe that in late 1957, when I applied for a job at the pit, in the village where I was born, they told me, because my father didn´t work there, I couldn´t have a job there, but, could go to the next village, where that rule didn´t apply. I have often wondered if it was fate or destiny that I never got a job at the colliery in the village I was born in, was I to have an accident there, or what? Who knows, was someone looking out for me even then? I went to work at the colliery in the next village, not good at first because, as with most villages in those days, they were very clannish, especially young lads. Well everything went ok, and I made some good mates there.

After working in the timber yard for 6 months, it was 6 months on the "screens"; this is where the coal is tipped straight from the pit shaft and onto a steel conveyor to be handpicked of all the stone that is in it, before, it´s loaded into railway trucks. This job was staffed by people who were backward, but, were capable of doing a job and, miners who had been injured down the pit but were no longer capable of working down the pit again, and trainee´s like myself waiting until they were 16yr old, and, old enough to go and work down the pit. The noise on those screens was unbelievable, you would have to hear it for yourself to believe it, all talking was done by sign language, and by the time we were 16 we had picked quite a lot of it up. The underground shift times were awful to say the least and they were called

Fore shift which was   3-30am -11-30 am

Back shift   10-30am-5-00 pm

Night shift   10pm- 6-00am

I can remember the very first shift I worked underground, and was coming home, and travelling with a man of about 35ish and he said to me, are you tired kid?   Well, to be right, it had been the first time in my life that I had not been in bed all night, never mind flogging my guts out, and was so tired I felt ill, yes I said , one day he said, you won´t have to go to work, I hope its tonight I said, he said Automation will take over (I´d never heard the word automation before) what´s that I said, robots will do it for you and that was in 1958, and he´s not far out, when you think of all the people who have put out of work by computers alone? We were on the same shift so I travelled with that guy every day. We had to walk through a couple of fields to get to where we lived on a new estate one of these fields was used by the NCB for sick or injured pit ponies and the other used by the local milkman for his horse, well, one day as we were walking, this guy said to me, take a look at that youngen, you might never see that again, I looked, it was the milkman´s mare, with her rear end through the wire that separated the two fields, and, the pit pony servicing her. I often wonder what the milkman thought when his mare had a foal. "Immaculate conception" perhaps?

My take home pay was £2- 2 shillings a week and my board was £1-10shilling, the 12 shillings I had left had to take me to work, buy my clothes and my fags, when I started down the pit, my pay went up, to the princely sum of £2- 18 shillings, and then, had to pay £2 per week board, by this time I was getting bolder, and I asked, why couldn´t I have meat on my dinner?, as up then, the kid´s and I never, had meat on our dinner except, if it was mincemeat apart from that it was only gravy, and was told if you want meat on your dinner, you will have to pay another 10shillings, which I did, as I got another pay rise of 8 shillings, when I´d finished my underground training. As I was now working on shifts it was only at week-ends that I could go to George´s farm or meet up with him at the dog track and after a while I told him that it was getting too much for me and felt as if I was letting him down. He thanked me and said there was no need to apologise and that he understood. He said that he was pleased to have met me and wished me luck for the future and, put me onto two certain winners that night which was something he had never done before. I still think about his kindness towards me after all these years.

Things trundled on until the time Alice and Alf were going on holiday with the bairns for a week at the coast to Cayton Bay. My holidays started the following Friday. I was on night shift which meant by the time I got home in the morning they would have set off on their holiday. So I paid my board on the afternoon. After I´d set off for work that evening she showed Alf the groceries what she was leaving for me. Looking back why hadn't she done the decent thing and told me to keep myself that week instead of taking board off me. Well as I mentioned before about kicks in the teeth, when I came home from work I went to the pantry only to find a couple of slices of stale hard bread and a little jam in a jar nothing else, I was gob smacked, wondering why there was nothing in the house to eat and when I went into the front room I got to know why, there on the mantelpiece was a note saying that if I went up the street to one of her friends she would get what groceries I needed, and she would pay her when she got back. So there I was, starving and so shattered I had to go to bed. When I got up, I went straight to see the friend of hers, only to be told that she hadn´t been paid for the last lot of groceries she had bought her. Once again another kick in the teeth and I don´t know how to dodge them because I don´t see them coming. I´ve got about 12shillings to my name and it cost me about 7 to travel to and from work. So I went to our next door neighbour to tell her, and show her the predicament that I was in, and could she lend me some money until Friday, when I get my two weeks holiday pay, well, when she came around and saw for herself, and couldn´t believe it, as she was there when she showed Alf the pantry full of groceries. She couldn´t help me out with money which was understandable, as she had a house full of kids, but said, being as I was on the same shift as her husband, I could have my dinner with him. I was most grateful and that is, another person in my life who I will never forget. To this day I don´t know why I didn´t go to see my sister Lizzie, I can only think that I didn´t want to burden her with my troubles. Well, things went from bad to worse that week, on Tues or Wed I got a letter from her, saying, that she had lost her purse, and would I send £10 out of my holiday pay, and she would square up with me when she got home. Had I not been short changed and robbed prior to that there would have been no hesitation as to me forwarding her the money. So, to try and make it easier, for myself, I didn´t answer it, so when Saturday came I went to Halifax to stay at Doris´s for a fortnight which Alice already knew about.

Just as I think things can´t get any worse, another kick in the teeth comes along, and I certainly wasn´t expecting this, after she knowingly, left me without food, when she went on holiday. On the Tues or Wed while I´m at Halifax, I get another letter from her, saying, you, can keep your money, and don´t bother coming home. I kept those two letters and note, and, glad I did, as they would prove one day who was a liar and cheat, and who was totally innocent. Well, after telling Doris and Elsie, they are telling me not to worry and there is no need to go home they will get me a job at the mills where they worked but I didn´t want that so decided to write to my girl friend Carol at the time and explained the situation and would she ask her parent´s if they could put me up for a short while, until I can get some lodgings somewhere nearer to where I worked. I still to this day can´t understand why I didn´t ask our Lizzie to help me out.

I wrote to Carol and told her of my dilemma so she asked her parents if I could stay with them, and they were kind enough to put me up at their house but, it would only be temporary, as I would be sleeping on a settee. I was most grateful, and yet again they will always be remembered by me.

The unfortunate thing was that it was approximately 6 miles from where I worked there were no bus´s for me to use that would get me to the pit to start my shift at 3-30am and winter was approaching fast and the only shoe´s I had to my name were wearing out fast and couldn´t afford to have them mended so, when there was a good covering of snow, I decided to wear my pit boots. The first time I walked it in my pit boots was a disaster, I had set off too early, and by the time I got there, I could have cried with pain in my feet, and also the blisters, as I was wearing only ordinary socks. I had to go to the pit medical centre to get some plasters for my feet. It was a good job that the pit canteen stayed open 24hrs and I could get warm but couldn´t afford a warm drink because, of the extra travelling expense, I now had. I never told any of my work mates of the situation I was in because of the embarrassment of it being my own sister who had put me in it. I do feel sure I would have been given help if I had asked for it. Winter was approaching fast and furious now and the inadequate clothing I was travelling to work in was taking its toll I had to run a while and walk a while when I was on the fore shift just to keep warm. The coal seam where I worked was called the "LOW MAIN" and the district (as they were called) where I worked was aprox. 5 miles under the North Sea and it was "red hot", and when the coalface was exhausted all us young lads were transferred to another coal seam the 5-1/4 as it was called which, was further up in the pit shaft and as it was so close to the pit bottom it was freezing cold compared to the LOW MAIN, it was there I started working with pit ponies and, once again through inadequate clothing it must have had a bearing on what was to be the worst event in my life (health wise) that was to happen to me in the very near future.

I could sense somehow that, I had out stayed my welcome at the girlfriends house, they started to ask if I was having any luck in finding lodgings, after all, I had been there for a couple of months now, and they did say, it was to be "temporary". It was only a few days later, as I was travelling back to my lodgings on the bus, I met Jack, who had been the next door neighbour of our Alice and Alf; he asked me how I was doing these days, now that I´d left home. When, I told him the full and sorry story he said, you can come and lodge with us as long as you like George, it´s a three bedroom house where we have moved to so I could be nearer to the pit where

I worked and, there is plenty of room for you. (I had baby sat and ran errands for Jack and his wife Doreen when they had come to live next door to us. Well. I broke down in tears when he said that. I was very embarrassed about it, and apologised to him about it, and when he put his arm around me to comfort me, it only made me worse, as I can only remember myself crying like that when they took Jane and I into the homes and the thrashing I got for running away. I couldn´t thank him enough, and asked him If he would mind me coming to see them that night, to see if Doreen was in agreement with him, before I made any move. Which I did, she said she shocked at what our Alice had done and was pleased that she and Jack could help me out. I went out of their door with tears streaming down my face with happiness all the way to the bus stop. I was on "cloud nine" at last something good was happening for me. When I went back to my lodgings that evening and told them, they were so pleased for me. I thanked them for all their help, and had bought her mother a bunch of flowers; it was all I could afford. I said, I wished that there was something more I could give them, other than saying thank you, they said, they were pleased to have helped me under the circumstances, and, that I had been no trouble to them. My girl friend and I, with the few belongings I had, went to Shotton to my new lodgings the day after, and sadly, a short time after that, we parted company, on the "best" of terms though, and, I was glad looking back, we never had sex, (not for the want of me trying) but, that she could start a new relationship or even marriage as a virgin she really was a lovely, lovely girl. She and her parents will always be remembered as, kind and loving people who helped me when I desperately needed help and as I say, they will never be forgotten by me.

When I started lodging with Doreen and Jack they wanted £2- 10shilings board I was so grateful as I could now buy myself clothes and a pair of shoes for myself albeit they were on tick 5shillings a week until they were paid for. My travelling costs were less now, as I travelled on a contract bus to and from work, so I could now go to the pictures, and date girls. Everything was going great guns for me, when another kick in the teeth came, I was, as I mentioned earlier working with ponies down the pit by this time and, was supplying girders to a development team making new coal faces (a job I would do myself years later in life for 24yrs) the men on the development were on piecework and by keeping them well supplied with girders at the end of the week would treat me by giving me half a crown per man 3x 2shillings and 6pence which was great, yet more money to spend and I was also making a name for myself by being a good and regular worker at my new job (where I started as an outsider) The job itself was close to the Pit bottom and therefore very cold which I never felt as I was working so hard, it was when I´d taken the pony back to the stables and had to wait at the Pit bottom in sweat soaked clothes that you felt the cold when, one day, (I was on foreshift) I was ok when I got to work that morning, but as the shift progressed I was getting weaker, and weaker, I couldn´t throw the girders off the tram, as I normally did, with ease, it got to the stage where, I had to chain the pony to them and drag them off. I was getting so tired that I could easily have laid down and gone to sleep and this "wasn´t" me, I never said anything to anyone, (too proud) but when I got into the showers, I noticed that my knees were swollen to twice their size, no pain but, I was so desperately tired by now so, when I was on the bus going back to my lodgings I thought I would call and see the Dr. and ask why I was so tired thinking, I thought I might have some sort of flu, also, by now my wrists had become swollen. The

Dr. examined me and said go down to the pit medical centre which was in walking distance of his surgery and tell them I´ve sent you and to put you in a "HOT" salt bath straight away, and I´ll be down in a short while, by this time my head is in a whirl (Drs in those days were known for not telling the patient what was wrong with them, just take the medication) When the Dr. did arrive I was soaking in a hot salt bath and was feeling a little better when, he said you need to stay in it for a couple of hours and then told me that he was sure that I had Rheumatic fever and that you will need to take 4 aspirins every 4 hours until the fever subsides and that he would come to see me at home that´s, when I told him that I was in lodgings, who with, and that they would be worried that I´m so late coming from work. He knew Doreen and Jack very well as she had been a nurse before marrying Jack so; he called at their house to tell them. When I eventually got home she gave me my dinner and sent me to bed I was exhausted by this time. I just wanted to sleep more than I wanted to breathe. The next day I was in so much pain it was unbearable every joint in my body felt as if it was broken, any movement gave me such "excruciating pain" I couldn´t understand what had happened to me and how, in such a few short hours I could be in all this pain. To be honest every time I was falling off to sleep, I would wish I wouldn't wake up. It was such a struggle for me to go down the stairs to the toilet which was in the back yard that Doreen (bless her) decided it was best that my bed was moved into the front room, and there I stayed for 12 weeks in total, asleep, except to take medication and soup which was a monumental task as every bone and joint in my body was wracked with unbearable pain even my throat when I swallowed. At one stage because I hadn´t been to the toilet for so long Doreen, made me sit on a bucket of boiling hot water, to draw it out of me, which worked in the end but I was in excruciating pain. Towards the end of my stay in bed I now found that as my hands had been semi closed for so long, had locked and it felt like I´d had a nail driven through the palms, and the pain once again, was excruciating to try and open them. I was so weak that, had it not been for Doreen and her forceful help my hands would not have fully opened again I feel sure of that. During the time I was seriously ill, I don´t know where Doreen had got his address, but she wrote to my father telling him how ill I was and the reply was a pound note and the message that he could not afford the time off work to come and see me. Doreen and Jack were so shocked about it they seemed as if they never stopped talking about it. It was 12 weeks before I was well enough to get out of bed and the tiredness and the pain had eased a "lot" I had another 4weeks off work. 16weeks in all before I actually started back and another 4 weeks before I was back to something like normal once again. In that time I had not had a visit from my family Doreen couldn´t have told them "why" I don´t know and I never asked, but I wouldn´t have noticed them anyway as all I did was sleep, hoping not to wake up. It was never explained to me at the time why I contracted Rheumatic fever but of course inadequate clothing and footwear in adverse conditions must certainly have contributed to it.

I suffer with gout and anyone who has this complaint will know it´s "very", "very" painful, the pain I had then was same except, that it was in "EVERY" joint in my body that´s the only way I can describe the pain I was in.

When I eventually started back at work they gave me a light job, watching the transfer of coal from one conveyer belt to another until I got back on my feet as they put it. Jack suggested I apply to the Union about some convalescence at one of the Miners Convalescent Homes I applied, and was successful and went for two weeks to Ulverston Miners Home in Lancashire and was given money to spend as well. It was there that I met a girl called Joan a lovely girl who´s parent´s owned a grocery shop and also her father was the local bookmaker, we became good friends but because we lived so far away from each other we couldn´t court, we became pen pals.

Shortly after the convalescence and my life as it "seemed" was getting back to normal, yet another body blow came. I think that this was the "first" time in my life that I said to myself "what the hell have I done to deserve what was happening in my life. Life was so good for me now, I was loving it, staying with Doreen and Jack and wanted it to stay that way forever "when" Doreen´s mother died suddenly and Doreen´s daughter from a former relationship, had always lived with her, had to come home, and had to have the bedroom I had so, I had to find fresh lodgings, they didn´t rush me, and after a week or two I managed to get lodgings with John an old school friend, in the new village where I had lived with our Alice and Alf I still visited Doreen and Jack, for among many things, pay my debts for my clothing which they had paid while I was ill and to take her a bunch of flowers now and again. I will always be eternally grateful to Doreen and Jack for what they did for me and, sadly they are both dead now.

It seemed a life time had gone by and yet, it had only been about a year so many things had happened to me in such a short time when, one day while I standing around talking to my mates Alf my brother-law appeared, asked if he could talk to me on my own, I was fearing a bawling out and being shouted at but, to my surprise, he asked me how I´d been keeping and why I´d suddenly left home, "why" don´t you come home he said and, that he had "always" thought of me as his eldest son (that´s a good one I thought) When I told him the story he wouldn´t believe me so, I said to him, you go and ask the lady who wouldn´t get me any groceries then, ask Lilly the next door neighbour, who saw the next day, what in was in the pantry, read the letter my own sister, sent me, telling me she had lost her purse while you were on holiday, and, the letter she sent to me two or three days after I went to Halifax, telling me, "not to come home again". He looked at me and said I just can´t believe it she showed me a pantry full of groceries that she was leaving for you and she "never" lost her purse while we were on holiday, he asked me to bring the note and letters (which I had kept as, I just hoped and prayed that this day would come and here it was) and to meet him here the next night. When I met him the following night he took me into his local pub, I told him I wasn´t old enough and he said it didn´t matter, oh well I thought, and after reading the notes and the letters and probably had confirmation from Lilly about the pantry he actually cried I couldn´t believe it. He then went on to say come home "please". I did say I would and, went round the next day (to see how things were first, before I would go home for good.

 I can only imagine what went off in the house when Alf got home the night before, knowing him he would have questioned her, and given her enough rope to hang herself, I suppose denying everything and making me out to be a liar and, then giving her the notes and letters to prove that she was the liar. I did go home after a few days, the subject was never brought up again, the kids were pleased to see me though, but, you could cut the atmosphere with a spoon. Why I went back home goodness knows I can only put it down to fate and destiny as in a few short months another chapter started in my life which turned my whole life round. I was never asked to do any chores and my meals were as they should have been from the moment I started to pay board. I did mention on the first day back home, that I had been seriously ill with Rheumatic fever but, there was no interest shown, I might just well have told them I´d had a bad cold, thing´s were, it seemed, just as they were before, "no interest". Alf had only one quality in the time I knew him and that was, he never lied to my knowledge and never swore in the house not even the word "bloody". That quality must have rubbed off him, onto me as, I don´t swear in my home and I mortally hate liars and cheats, for obvious reasons, with what has gone off in my life.

I soon fell back in with my mates again, but couldn´t bring myself, (because of the embarrassment) to tell my mates, that my own sister had lied and cheated me, and told me not to come back home. I started to court a girl called Mary H... soon after I went back home but it was only short lived as her father had got a job in the oil fields somewhere in the middle-east and all the family were moving out there. We had a fantastic "last night" and she said she would write when she knew the address of the place where they going to be, I never received one letter from her, and the reason was, to be honest I had forgotten to give her my address in all the excitement of that last night. However it was "years" later this was confirmed, when I met up with her in the most unusual of places and circumstances.

It was a strained sort of atmosphere in the house as I say, and I was not really happy, after all that had happened to me. One day I came home from work from the back shift around 6-30pm and to my surprise who should be sitting there but my father, along with a woman older than him and, one of the ugliest women I have ever seen in all my life. I looked at him in shock, it had been 5 years since I´d last seen him. Before I could say a word he said to my sister and "who" is this lad? Are you kidding she said, he´s "your" youngest, our George. "Oh" he said looking at me, not saying another word but looking puzzled, then introduced me to this grotesque looking woman who was also called Alice. He never asked how I was keeping, or anything at all for that matter, it was Alice who did all the talking after the introduction, who turned out to be quite pleasant to talk to. By the time I had finished my dinner he said they were going to have a drink in the pub which used to be his local, before he left to travel back to Derby, where, he was now living with Alice. I said I would walk down to the pub with them, they never asked if I wanted to come in for a drink and, I don´t know why, but, I waited outside for them to come out after their drink, and walked them to the bus stop. All he said as he got on the bus was "be seeing you". I thought myself my God, this is only the second time, he has seen his youngest child since he walked away from Jane and I all those years ago, and that is all he can say. It must have been from that moment when the resentment for him, must have started. My whole opinion of him had changed forever. As a child I hadn´t had the resentment for him as I had for him now, a resentment that would never heal and turn to hatred on one particular night 26 years later. As I was growing up I had always told people, that both my parents were dead, I was so ashamed of him for allowing Jane and I to be put in a home. The twins were only made aware of the fact, long after we had been taken into the homes when, they made a visit back home, by that time Alf and our Alice had taken over the tenancy of the house. But "why" hadn´t our Lizzie who was living local at that time, come back home and looked after us? "WHY". That is something they have had to live with for the rest of their lives, and not once, was I given an explanation about it.

One day when I was almost 18, a lad who I travelled to work with, told me he was joining the army, and the regiment he was joining was in the armoured corps and that they were serving in Hong Kong, and why don´t I join up as well, it´s got be better than the pit he said. I thought about it all day at work and decided to ask him all the details about signing up. The thought of getting away from the environment where I now lived was uppermost in my thoughts. I never said anything at home about it until after I had signed up. There wasn´t any enthusiasm from either our Alice or Alf about it, except for fact that I would need to get my hair cut. That was understandable as I was dressing as a "teddy boy" then and, had a load of hair on, curly and combed into a DA style ("ducks arse" they called it)

As soon as I got my date for reporting to Catterick I went to tell Jack and Doreen and to say goodbye and that I would keep in touch as they were two people I would never forget. They both hugged me and wished me well for the future. I also went to see George and his family and said my goodbyes. George said you're a sensible lad and I´m sure you´ll do alright and gave me a hug as I left. I don´t mind admitting that when I walked away from Doreen and Jack´s house and George´s farm I was full up at the memories of their kindness towards me and was glad no one was seeing the state I was in as I walked home. I do remember the day I left, there wasn´t even a good bye said to me it was, as if I were going to work or going for a night out, and here I was, I was about to change the "whole" of my life forever. The kids had gone to school Alf had gone to work. I said to our Alice "well" I´m going now and the reply she gave me was "yeah ok" she never even got up out of her chair. I was expecting a hug or a kiss goodbye or some sort of comment but nothing, I picked up my few belongings and left. It was during the train journey that I reflected on what had happened to me so far in my life and thought to myself things can only get better surely. I must admit that I was feeling very apprehensive and wondered if I hadn´t rushed into something I would later regret but in reality I need not have worried. My life as a man was only beginning.

I arrived at Richmond railway station and was picked up by the driver of a 3ton truck from the 4/7TH Royal Dragoon Guards Regiment who I would be doing my training with and taken to Catterick Camp training barracks along with a lot of other lads some of whom were to do their National Service. The first job was to take us to our rooms it wasn´t a surprise for me as it reminded me of the homes, sleeping in a room with a lot of other kids just a few short years ago. Some of these lads had never even shared a room in their lives. The next job was to take us to the Quarter Masters stores to be kitted out with everything that that we needed for the rest of our army career and of course bedding and a mattress. I was the only recruit from the 17th/21st Lancers regiment in that intake and issued with a Motto not a cap badge. It had been awarded for bravery. It was one of two Regiments in the British army that don´t wear a cap badge, the other being the 11th Hussars. They didn´t wear a badge through disgrace. The "motto" and "never" to be called a badge was a skull and crossed bones (like the pirate flag you see in films) with a scroll, and on it the words "OR GLORY" it had been awarded for bravery to the 17th Lancers at the battle of Balaclava in the Crimean war in honour of their bravery, mentioned in Alfred Lord Tennyson´s poem "THE CHARGE OF THE LIGHT BRIGADE" ("Into the valley of death rode the "Gallant 600" i.e. The 17th LANCERS) it was all "very impressive" to me anyway. Winston Churchill had served in the 21ST Lancers during the 1st world war. The 11th Hussars had their badge take from them through disgrace by the fact the Regiment had been captured asleep in an orchard hence their nickname "The Cherry Pickers" and wore a brown beret with a red band around it to remind everyone of that disgrace. It was all "very" impressive to me.

We were taken back to our rooms and left to pick our own beds get them made and put our kit away and would be told and shown how to do this army style the next day. What came strange to me and to most everyone else was the different accents people spoke, but of course most of us had never been out of the villages we were born in up to then, which was to become a laugh throughout our training weeks trying to understand one another. The next morning at 6am we were woken up which was a nightmare for some. Once again it was no hardship for me as I was used to getting up early AND at first call (homes again) we were taken to the Cookhouse were we joined a queue that I thought would never end for our breakfast which was "best" described as some form of food, some of the lads couldn´t and wouldn´t eat it. I ate it, the memory of being without food as a child, made me eat it. After we had washed our knives, forks, spoon and tin mug it was back to our rooms where we were introduced to our troop leader and our drill instructor commonly called a "drill pig" but, only under our breath, whose name was corporal Durante we all had a laugh at that and that was the only laugh we had with him, we found out it was "Jimmy Durante" the name we were laughing at the "big nosed" film star. Then we were told to assemble outside in double file and were then taken to the regimental barbers and, what a con that was. I thought mine was ok as I had had mine nearly shaved off on the advice of our Alf only days before, we all had to have a haircut. The "con" was the haircut cost 2/6pence which was about twice the going rate at home and when you sat in the chair the civilian barber would ask you how you want it cutting and of course everyone would say don´t take it all off PLEASE and he wouldn´t and when we all had it cut and was back on parade that´s when the "con" was spotted. The drill pig would stand behind you and say "am I hurting you soldier? "NO" corporal was the reply given and he would say I should be I´m standing on your "f...ing hair" get yourself back in there and ask for an "army" haircut this time. The next part of this con was, if you didn´t have another 2/6pence it was strapped on, and because of that you had to report to the cookhouse after tea to wash pans, peel spuds by the cwt. sack full, and wash floors, it was one way, to get people to work in the cookhouse, as no one would ever, volunteer for that job.

Word soon got round you "never" complain about the meals because, during every meal, the "Orderly Officer" of the day, would walk round the mess, asking, are there any complaints about the food, and if the classic answer was "yes sir" these potatoes have eyes in them, the reply would be, they won´t have tomorrow because "you" will pick them out tonight, report to the cookhouse tonight for spud bashing, thus, getting men to work in the cookhouse, bearing in mind about 600 squaddies were using it at any one time. Good eh? This was my early introduction to army life. We all had to have medical and dental inspections and I remember when I went for my dental inspection, the dental officer was a gorgeous 20 something year old with a huge pair of breasts as she was examining my teeth she was, I thought she was pushing those huge breasts into the side of my head on purpose, I thought "WOW" should I ask her for a date but thought better of it as she was a officer, and I was only a raw recruit, and besides if I had ended up with egg on my chin I would probably have been sent to work in the cookhouse "every" night for the rest of my stay at Catterick. It was tempting, very tempting. There were rumours going round that there was a substance called Bromide in our tea to stop sexual feelings while we were doing our training if that was so it wasn't working on me that day I'll tell you. We all had an interview with the pay officer on how we wanted to be paid i.e. all of it or, some of it and, the rest kept in credit and to send a minimum allowance of 1 shilling a day to your home address I somehow signed up for it, I don´t know how I missed that, anyway what I thought I´d signed for was to be paid £6 a week and the rest left in credit and you never know what is in your credits until you specifically ask to see them and I never wanted any monies out of my credits until almost 3 years later when I found that I´d been sending 7shillings a week home to my sister, who I´d put down as my next of kin. I promptly stopped it. What a WALLY I must have been.

The guy who had the next bed to me was doing his National Service he was the son of a vicar and each night he would kneel at the side of his bed and say his prays and needless to say he had the mickie taken out of him something cruel every night but it never put him off but, I did noticed fairly quickly his prays were taking longer, and longer One night I woke up and he was actually sobbing and I thought to myself this guy is "NOT" going to make it, but he did as he was on National Service. There are times even now that I laugh about it but not the time it happened, when I think of some of those guys who couldn´t grasp the art of marching at first and when you´ve got the drill pigs face a couple of inches from yours and shouting and screaming things like, go and climb up the clock tower and jump off but before you jump SHOUT here comes f..k all because that´s what you are here f..k all and not being able to retaliate unless of course you want some time in the nick which was always threatened.

There was once a situation while we were still learning the basics of marching where we could not stop laughing, corporal Durante had stopped us marching, and told this one guy who couldn´t grasp anything, to repeat after him as loud as he could, "I am a f...ing idiot" which he duly did, shouting, "You" are a f...ing idiot, the drill pig stood with his face inches from his "screaming" at him, the veins on corporal Durante´s neck were standing out like varicose veins on an old ladies legs when he screamed at him and said, I told you to say "I" am a f...ing idiot and the guy said that´s what I´ve just said haven´t I? Needless to say we did a lot of marching that day, without smoke breaks. I still have a good laugh about that to this day.

It was 6 weeks when we finished our Basic training (square bashing), as it was called, and what a lot we had learned and achieved, i.e. how to polish boots to a standard of patent leather, make a bed pack and have every item of kit we were issued with, displayed on our bed, how to press trousers and iron shirts, we had all become firm friends and helped one another, the vicar´s son still, said his pray´s every night, but, the crying had stopped. At the end of our 6 week training, we were told it was the custom, to buy our drill instructor a present, as a way of saying "thank you" (for making or rather shouting at us into "soldiers") which, we duly did, we bought him a wrist watch. A small reward by any standard for turning a rag and tag set of civvies from boy´s into men. We could invite our parents, or anyone for that matter, to our "passing" out parade. By this time everyone had, had their uniforms tailored to fit, and we did look, and felt like soldiers now. I did ask my sister and Alf in one of my letters home if they would like to attend but, they never took me up on it. After the parade we were all given a rail pass, and a 72hr leave pass, it was I remember, much the same as getting out of those homes. I arrived home but, there wasn´t a welcome of any sort as I remember and it wasn´t many minutes before I was asked how long I was staying and asked for some board money. I went to see my mates to show my uniform off and my regimental cap "motto" not a badge like everyone else, and tell them all about my training. When I had signed on at Middlesbrough I had no idea what regiment I was signing on to only, that I wanted to be in the same one as my mate from work, at least I would know someone when I got there and, funnily enough I never met up with (George) until I joined the regiment in Hong Kong as he had Joined the week before me.

 It was Durham Miners Gala that week-end when I got home so, three of my mates and I went through to Durham City to it and that´s where I met Jan who was to become my wife. There were two girls to choose from, who I was chatting up, Jan and her mate who was good looking but, on the plump side, so I chose Jan. It was the first "catastrophic" mistake I made in my life, as the story unfolds.

 We swapped addresses at the end of the day and said we would write to each other which we did. The 72hr leave soon passed and I reported back to Catterick to start my trade training, ready for when I went to join my regiment. On the day I was interviewed, the training officer´s first word´s were "AH" just the man I want to see, I was very worried, and confused and wondered why, thinking all sorts things when, he said I want to apologize for reading your mail (prior to this all my mail had been opened) "but" he said, it had been delivered to me first, he went on to explain that the rank of 2nd Lieutenant (1 pip) and full Lieutenant (2 pips) they were called Mr until, they became a Captain and above, the calling then was the rank they were, and as his name was exactly the same as mine, he was sorry he had read them, and would I accept his apologies but it "was" a genuine mistake. "WOW" an officer apologising to me, that made me feel good. I went on to tell him it was the first time in my life that I had met anyone with the same name as my family let alone the exact same as mine, he went on to say, there are "millions" of us worldwide, which I was to find out later in life myself, when I began my family research. Most of the letters he had read were from Joan the girl I had met in Ulverston I suppose he got a laugh from them as they were a bit racy at times I suppose for those times.

After the interview, I was told I was to be trained as a tank gunner, most impressive I thought and, that it would take 6 weeks. It meant less marching around, while on trade training and, providing you weren´t on any duties i.e. Guard or fire picket duty you could go out of camp 4pm Friday until 6am Monday "if" you could afford it, the National Service men could never afford it on the pittance they were paid, some of the lads who had signed on as regular soldiers ie. 6yrs or 9yrs would pay them for bulling their boots or doing their ironing. I did genuinely feel sorry for them as a lot of them they were reduced to scrounging through no fault of their own. Some of them would hitchhike home and a few never made it back in time which would result in the dreaded cookhouse fatigues with mountains of pots and pans to wash and spud bashing. When Friday came round, off I went, as I only lived about 25mles away from Catterick to see Jan, it soon passed and couldn´t wait for the next Friday. I was in the pub the next time I came home, Alf introduced me to his mates son, who was a sergeant in the regiment that I was doing my training with and, that he came home every week-end if he was free and, if I was free, he would give me lift home with him, I took his offer and gave him 10 shillings every time he gave me a lift and he was delighted with that.

As part of the training we were taken up on the North Yorkshire moors to learn map reading, and while some of us were waiting to be tested we were laid back on the heather chatting, it was a warm day and I was looking up and ahead at a clear blue sky when, I noticed a black "dot" it was stationary about the size of your little finger nail, it was that high up in the clear blue sky, after looking at it for several minutes then closing my eyes looking at it again, even, looking away and looking at it again, I thought to myself what the hell is it, it can´t be a bird it the wrong shape and it´s too high up. After a short while I asked someone else if they could see it, and at first no one could, this, was causing quite a buzz by now and, after a few minutes, there were five or six of us, no more, could see it and giving explanation´s as what it could be when all of a sudden it went from "stationary" to our right in the blink of an eye and out of sight, confirmation of me seeing it and, "not" imagining it, was the comments from the lads who "could" see it, was, "f.....g hell" did you see "that". Looking back at it, it was like something out of "Star Trek" and that hadn´t been produced at that time and, besides "no" military aircraft to my knowledge "then" or "now" can fly that fast. That was the first of two unexplained sightings that I´ve seen in the sky. Of course, we, who had seen it, were cried down and ridiculed so much that in the end you stop mentioning for that reason. After all I was 18yr old, had 20- 20 vision and wasn´t trying to gain anything out of it then or now, but I know what I saw.

Two weeks before I was to be posted to my regiment I got home and Alice got straight on to me, accusing me of stealing the family allowance book worth 16 shilling a week, and that I had probably been cashing it in for the last two weeks. How could I do that I said, it´s an army camp. After awhile Lucy who was about 6 or 7 at the time asked me to get her raincoat down off the peg in the passageway, when she it put on she found in the pocket the rolled up family allowance book, she had not worn that coat since she last went to the P.O. two weeks prior .No apologies where given to me her only interested was in sending the bairn down to the P.O.to cash it in. Things hadn´t really changed at home if I could call it that. The fact that kids looked upon me as a elder brother kept me going back there then, they were really good kids and I loved them as such, it was also somewhere to get my head down and the knowledge of going abroad soon to join my regiment kept me going. And when I look back she was having 7 shillings a week sent to her from me and "never" once mentioned it and, to accuse me of stealing from her was an insult that I remember to this day. No one in the family is of the same nature as her as far as I´m aware thank God.

I went to Halifax to visit the twins and Jane who had married by this time, and had had a baby. It was the first time I´d seen her since 1958 when Alice had told me not to come home. I had gone to say my goodbyes and tell them where I was being posted to. Our Elsie´s husband Thornton who was a metal polisher took all my brasses and two motto´s to his works and had them polished to the standard which made them look years old, worn, as if I had spent hours and hours polishing them, which did me proud when I was to join my regiment. Years later my troop leader swapped his Stirling silver Motto for one of mine.

It soon came round when it was time to return to camp. I´d said my goodbyes to Jan, we weren´t courting as such, but that we would write to each other. I´d said my goodbyes to my mates and went home, the next morning I picked up the last of my belongings, I remember that I'd said goodbye to the kids before they left for school and told them I would write to them, and, when it was time to leave, only my sister was there and I remember to this day as I picked up my belongings and said well "I'm going now" and her words were once again "yeah ok" I was dumfounded I know a lot had gone off prior but, none of it was my fault, I don't know why but, I just thought she would have given me a kiss, a hug, a well wish or don't forget to write will you, not a "yeah ok" Here I was, her youngest brother who, had endured being wrenched away from his family at such an early age and, put in a home with my sister and when she was eventually fostered out I was left there alone, had joined the army and seeing that I had been transformed from a boy to a man, was now going to the other side of the world and didn't know when she is going to see him again. WHY was I being treated this way yet again the question "why"

I travelled back to Catterick camp with the feeling of utter loneliness and dejection, and wondered what was in store for me for the rest of my life, am I expecting too much of my family?. Thinking that way at 18 yrs old takes some believing I know but that's how I felt.

On arriving back at camp, our intake was billeted in a different part of the camp where you stay awaiting your travelling orders to your different regiments. A couple of days later a load of mates and I managed to get a night out on the town in Darlington for a drink and, while we were waiting for a taxi back to camp in the longest taxi queue I've ever been in, two girls came and asked if we were going to Catterick camp, we said yes so, one of them who was absolutely gorgeous whispered in my ear, if you give us a lift to the W.A.C's billets I will let you have me tomorrow night, I was shocked to say the least I couldn't believe what I was hearing, I agreed to let them share our taxi amid shouts and boo´s as, they had come from the back of the queue and would never have got a taxi in time to get them back to camp in time for lights out (midnight) We all laughed and giggled on the journey back to camp and when they were getting out I said are we "still" on for tomorrow night and never in a million years a girl as gorgeous as that saying yes, she leaned over and whispered to me, to meet her at her billet at 7 o clock where we dropped them off, gave me a kiss, thanked us and walked off. I told my mate what she said and, he said, I expect they pull that one every time they want a free taxi back to camp.

Well, the following night I went to meet her. "fully" expecting it to be a wild goose chase and to be stood up but, there she was, she looked even better than the night before, we talked for a short while, she said can you remember what I said to you last night I blushed and said yes I do, and then she took me to the back of her billet and down a short grass embankment where, it didn't take long to get down to the business. I soon wondered what was happening. I hadn't a lot of sexual experience then but, knew she shouldn't be reacting the way she was, I looked at her face and she was giggling, and then when I looked up, "oh my God" I couldn't believe it, "all" her mates and more besides we looking down at us. I´ve got to say though after the initial shock it didn´t put either of us off, we finished the business off, to shouts of "more, more" We pulled our selves together and she said, I hope you didn´t mind that but it was all "in fun" we went off to the local club for a drink. She said it was her last night in Catterick camp as she was being posted out to Germany the next morning. We had a few drinks and walked back to her billet, and parted company the way we had met earlier that night, down the embankment but without the audience. As Jan and I were only on letter writing terms then, I asked if she would like to exchange addresses but she declined.

Finally my orders came through I was to travel by train down to Stanstead where I was met at the station with a lot of other personnel and taken to R.A.F. Standstead boarded a plane and took off for Istanbul, then onto Bombay (refuelling) and up to then was the hottest place I'd ever been and then onto Hong Kong. The journey took 26hrs and by the time I landed at Kai-Tak airport (Kowloon) I was absolutely shattered. I was picked up at the airport by a 3ton truck which became known as the Regimental taxi and taken to my camp through Kowloon and up to the New territories to a place called Sek-Kong where the Regiment was stationed. It was on that initial journey the "smell" of China hit me. It was something I never got used to, for the whole of my stay in Hong Kong. It was the same smell as dead rotting animals all the time, there were street vendors cooking and selling all sorts of food which smelled and looked disgusting. Everything was hustle and bustle no semblance of order with the traffic. The drive up to the New Territories was scary, every bend in the road going up was a hair pin bend which the driver took at such a speed I seriously thought, that this day was going to be my last. We finally arrived at our camp it was laid out like a huge holiday camp, lawns and flowers everywhere a complete contrast to Catterick, I thought to myself, I could get used to this if it wasn't so damned hot which, by this time I was absolutely soaking with sweat. I was met at the guardroom by a sergeant who introduced himself as Sgt, R..., from 3rd troop "A" squadron which was the Squadron and troop I would serve in for the rest of my career. He was a Scotsman who, I didn't know at the time was to become my "tank commander" for a while and, who, I would be eternally grateful for his advice on many, many, things, regarding army life out there in the far-east.

I was taken to my billet which was similar to a large bungalow, Sgt R... asked me, was I hungry then took me to the cookhouse got me fixed up with a sarnie, and told me to get back here for an interview with the Squadron OC at 1pm. At the interview which seemed very informal, I was told that was how things were in the regiment, unlike the training regiment "But" break any rules or regulations and they would be on me like a ton of bricks. I was told I would I would be Sgt R...´s gunner and that it would be tomorrow before I was taken to the tank park, as we finished work here at 12noon everyday "WOW" I thought this is great. I was then taken back to my billet and by this time everyone had finished work and had come back to the billet where he introduced me to everyone and who to watch out for as regards lending money, playing cards with and, being led astray down at the brothels and who not to try and keep up with drinking beer. My God I thought, at last, somewhere, where it´s good and friendly and, it never changed the entire time I was in the army.

 The following morning Sgt R... who had been on guard duty woke the troop up with his ritual of getting us out of bed for work, this is how it went "every" time he was on guard duty there were four billets and he would enter each one in turn shouting incessantly "Morning morning morning morning" at the top of his voice, rise and shine get out of bed you've had your time, hands off cocks hands on socks get out of bed you idle lot, and then he would drop the troop bin lid in the middle of the floor as he left. Make no mistake you were fully awake when Sgt R... had left your room.

Later that day he took me to see film show and a lecture about V.D. which was compulsory to every new recruit to the far- east. I was both shocked and horrified at the film I'd heard about V.D. but never seen or given details about it, looking back I "wasn't" street wise far from it, he went on to how say, to avoid any of it was simply by "not" having sex, and I know that won't happen he said "BUT" when you do, wear a "rubber Johnnie" they are free from the quartermasters store and no limit to how many ok? Oh and other thing, always chose an ugly one he said. He could see the puzzled look on my face, and said she's less likely to have VD because everyone wants to bed the good looking one's does that make sense to you? And besides all women look and feel the same when the lights are out. He then went on to tell me where the brothel's were and that they were "ALL" out of bounds to any military personnel and, jail time if you were caught there. After seeing that film I never went without a condom. It was one of the best pieces of advice that was ever given to me as a young lad.

We also had room boy called Fan Mao I had to laugh at the time, this so called room boy he was old enough to be my father, he came in every morning and made your bed pack swept and "washed" the floor when needed gather your dirty clothing, take them to the Laundry which was free, clean your boots for work that day and if you were on guard duty that night he would have all your kit out ready when you finished work i.e. starched uniform, boot's bulled up, (spit and polished and all your brass's gleaming) All for $5 hk. aprox 6/3d old money. 31 pence per person, per week in today's money. I felt so ashamed of myself having this old guy doing all that for "ME" There was a couple of occasions early on when someone would start to snap his head off and I would step in and later told by the lads it's what he is used to leave it, but, I couldn´t stand it, I used to have to walk out when they shouted and bawled at him. We became friends in a sort of way I remember that I was the only guy in our troop maybe in the regiment who paid the room boy while out in field he had no other job so, he had no money coming in for whole time we were out in the field which, didn´t seem to bother anyone but me, "that", paid great dividends for me in the future i.e. when I was skint mid week, Fan Mao would cycle a 12 mile round trip to take my camera to a pawn shop and borrow any amount of money (within reason) on it, and on payday or, the week after, he would do the same again to get it out of pawn, he could also get credit at the NAAFI "no one" could get that, but he could. Whenever I was on guard duty, he would take particular attention to "all" my kit because, the officer of the guard, would award a soldier on guard who was exceptionally well turned out, "Stickman" and one of the perks when awarded this was, to miss your "next" guard duty. Well I had the pleasure of that award several times while Fan Mao was looking after me.

Life was really started to become good for me new mates new environment altogether. I became firm friends with Ray W... all through my service and also Nolly N....., who slept in the next bed to me, he slept with his eyes half open which I found very strange indeed at first. We spent a lot of our leisure time down in Kowloon boozing etc. Both of them could eat Chinese meals but I never could in fact I never had a Chinese meal in all the time I spent in the far-east, there were several stories about restaurant's being raided and finding skinned dogs hung up in their freezers but in later life I found out that the Chinese eat dogs anyway. One of the things that I couldn´t get used to and can´t even today was the repulsive smell of garlic, they must have used it by the shovel full whenever they had a meal. It was mega cheap to buy anything out there and, I mean "anything" it seemed that, if it was on this planet, you could buy it. There were no drugs being used by the lads, or if there was, I never heard of anyone being on them but, this was the sixties, too early perhaps and anyway we could get enough pleasure from beer drinking, and still can. I remember one week-end going to buy a measured suit, I was measured, and two hours later went for a fitting and two hours later picking it up ready to wear and that, also applied to shirts and shoe´s it seemed everyone and everyone was fighting for your custom every time you walked past a shop. I´d never known anything like that before and, the bartering for everything you bought was something you have to experience yourself to appreciate it.

I had only been there a few short weeks when I was sent to Hong Kong Island for 4 weeks to be a bus escort to the married family´s kids; this was the norm for any new arrival soldier to the posting. It was a simple enough job really, at 7-30am Mon-Fri we would get on a bus in the camp where we were billeted and a Chinese soldier from the R.A.S.C. he would drive us to our pickups at various married quarters and take the kids to school and pick them up again at 12noon and take them home, and all our time between and after the pickups was our own, No, guard or fire picket duties. What a skive that was, there were six of us from various regiments, that were stationed there, and one lad in particular who I got with like a house on fire was Alan T....... from the Northumberland Fusiliers who spoke "properly" as he was also from the north-east. He had been posted in Hong Kong for some time and this was his third time on bus escort duty, he was married but, after a while he and his wife couldn´t get along in any way at all she, wanted to go home but couldn´t afford it and the army wouldn´t pay for it. Well one night when he was in the town with his mates he decided to visit a brothel for the first time and asked if he could have a "white girl" and when they brought "two" out for him to choose from, one was his "wife". Well all Hell broke loose; he was in deep trouble now as, he was out of bounds, he´d given her, a prostitute (his wife), a good hiding, the police were sent for he was arrested, anyway, at the end of the day he was put back into barracks and she got her wish she, was sent home, and that´s why she was working in a brothel, to get enough money together to fly home. I never saw Alan again after we rejoined our Regiments and often think back to that incident and wonder how he fared in life, well I hope he has, as he was an all round good guy and wonder if he mentions the incident to his mates when he has been having a drink down at his local some time. It is certainly one classic story that´s absolutely true.

There was no regimental barber at the Hong Kong camp so we had to go to a civvie barber shop and I remember the barber asking me if I wanted a scalp massage and went on to say that if I massaged my scalp everyday it would slow the widow´s peak from receding and the onset of grey hair in later life. Well I´m not sure if it "did" or "didn´t" work but I have done it from that day to this and at 67 my widow´s peak has gone back "slightly" and I only started to get grey hair two years ago. Is it in my genes, my age, or did it work? Who knows? My father so I´m told was totally bald when he was 27yrs old so I´m not doing too bad, and I´m certainly not complaining.

The four weeks were soon over and it was back to camp where I got stuck into my job of being a gunner on a tank and "all" it entailed. There were a lot of Nottingham lads in the regiment as there had been a large recruitment drive a couple of years before I had signed on, and of course with me talking with a north-east accent I was always referred to as "Geordie" or "George" from then on. I didn´t mind as I knew these lads "couldn´t" talk "properly" like us from the northeast.

My life was so "good" now and, apart from the odd guard and fire picket duty at week-ends, it was like being on permanent holiday. Most of the weekends we spent in Kowloon we would pop in the Royal Navy club to play their bonus bingo to see if we could win anything, we had played in there, and we had won once or twice. On one particular afternoon, I was playing and out the corner of my eye saw this massive cockroach coming towards me and thought I´ll squash it when it gets closer, the next thing I knew it had gone up my trouser leg I daren´t scream because of them playing bingo, but dropped my trousers, and was stepping out of them when this guy came to me and said "WHAT " the bloody hell are you doing, and if he hadn´t seen the sheer size of that cockroach come out of my trousers I´m afraid I would have been in the nick for a long, long time. Of course everyone had a laugh and was the talking point over the week-end and when we got back to camp.

It was around this time that I had my third experience of nearly drowning. I´d been to the regimental swimming pool on several occasions but only in the shallow end and was just managing to swim from one side to the other in a fashion mostly lying on my back treading water to keep afloat. One day we decided to go down to one of the beaches down the coast where there were woman. We arrived there and sure enough there were loads of girls about but they were mostly diving off a couple of wooden rafts about 40yds out in the water. My first thought was how the hell I am going to get out there. I managed it in a fashion by swimming a little and then floating on my back a little I don´t think anyone noticed that I couldn´t swim. All went well until it was time to leave and I had to make the journey back and as it was my first time swimming in the sea I panicked and went under more than a few times and was pleased when my feet could touch the sea bed, that really frightened me and still no one seemed to noticed I couldn´t swim. The next time we went there I had bought myself a pair of frog flippers on the advice of one of the lads and eventually taught myself to swim and just as well as it came in handy being able to swim in another life threatening incident in the not too distant future. There were several times that day I thought I was going to drown, a day I will never forget, more frightening than the day I fell in the frozen pond as a kid.

There were some "real characters" I met in the Squadron and, one that I shall always remember was "Oscar" H....n, a cockney lad and the first name Sgt R... had warned me about lending money to. He was about 25 yr old a good 7 yr older than most of us, a guy who had done everything and seen everything, and, couldn´t talk without swearing, "Effing and blinding" all day and every day. He was ugly, and always looked menacing; he really took being ugly looking to the limit. And as he was that much older than me, at first, he gave me, the impression, of being a trouble maker but, once, you got to know him, he was an all round fun guy, making everyone laugh. One of his favourite stunts was to start at the end of the Naafi queue and ask everyone in to give him a 1 cent piece no more and as they were virtually worthless everyone gave them to him and most of the time he ended up with more money than anyone in the queue, neat con eh? His down fall was, he could drink, like he had hollow legs, never any money and, as we had been fore warned no one, would lend him any money either, so, one of his many party tricks, to get people to buy him a pint was, he would stub a cigarette out on his hands or arm for 1 pint and on his face for 2 pints and, as you can imagine this did not improve his looks.

He was the Squadron gunnery store man, and could strip "any" weapon down and put it back together again faster than any man in the Squadron. Every now and again someone would challenge him to a bet, including me, on several occasions but, "never" beating him, it was like shelling peas for him and he would laugh his head off as he took your money. These "games" of Oscar´s stripping down weapons were openly encouraged as it served 2 purposes, 1, to speed our stripping and assembling of our weapons and 2, the team spirit. Had Oscar not been so fond of his drink and daft antics I´m sure he would have gone far up the promotion ladder. But he was content to be a trooper and was never any other while I served. We were in the NAAFI one night cracking jokes, laughing, and telling stories, when, Oscar came out with a "classic" one of the few lads who were doing National service was looking miserable and Oscar said to him cheer up you miserable B.....d whoever told you, you can catch VD from laughing was only kidding. It´s a statement I use today after all those years, whenever, I see someone miserable and, more often than not, it sets them off laughing. What a "character" he was, the "life and sole" of any party.

There is one experience that happened while I was stationed there in the New Territories that I will "never" forget. It was the time that, one of the lads in our troop Chuck D....n was trying to work his ticket i.e. being awkward and not obeying orders, and by being put in Regimental prison often enough you would be discharged from the army as an undesirable soldier eventually. 28 days was the longest in Regimental prison and the shortest in H M M P was 56 days. The H M M P was on Hong Kong Island, and I, was given the task of taking him there for his sentence of 56 days. We arrived at Stanley Fort H M P both dressed in our best uniform, and him, with every piece of equipment he had been issued with. I rang the bell and after a few minutes a Sergeant came out looking like a German SS Officer, the peak of his hat tailored to fit flat to his brow, his uniform fitting him like a glove and his marching "pace stick" under his arm. The first word he "SCREAMED" at us was "ATTENTION" We both snapped to attention, "yes" he said, what can I do for you? Then it started, I´ve brought Trooper D....n for his sentence "Sarge" I said. He walked up to me and inches from my face "SARGE" he screamed at the top of his voice "SARGE" you don´t address me Sarge, you call me "STAFF" do you understand me? "STAFF" "Immediately" it brought back memories of the Catterick camp drill pig. The veins on his neck were standing out like really bad varicose veins you see on old lady´s legs. He marched us both inside at DOUBLE QUICK time and brought us to a halt at a drill square. The next thing he did was to tell me to run around the square at double quick time until he came back. He marched Chuck away at double time and after about 20 minutes came back to me. By this time I was wet through with sweat, he stopped me, and then marched me to the gates, stopped me and said "quietly" everyone in here is called "staff" except officers, now fall out, get back to your regiment and don´t "ever" let me see you again. I came out there feeling like I had been the prisoner. All the lads had a good laugh about it when I told them. When Chuck came out he was a "changed" man indeed, it took him a couple of months at least to slow down and get back to normal. He told us all about how he was treated from the second he got there to the second he got out. Utter humiliation 24 hours a day he said. It was an eye opener for anyone who wants to break the rules and regulations while in the army. Everywhere he went, he was screamed at and was marched everywhere at double time, you didn´t sleep on your bed because you wanted to keep your bed pack right and proper, any wrong doings put extra time on your sentence so you "do" conform. Chuck was never in any trouble after that and left the army, sadly, with a prison record. What never ceases to amaze me is, if it´s "humane" enough to run military prisons on those lines, then why, don´t they run civilian prisons the same way, because, I never heard of "anyone" having two helpings of Military Prison. Surely it would stop re offenders?

It was in was in Feb of 1961 that Jan and I got engaged by post. I sent her a beautiful ring of one diamond and two Safire's, she was well, well pleased with my choice of ring and then we started to buy things for the bottom draw so to speak, and looking forward now for my return home.

It was the year after that, that we were informed that "A" Squadron had been chosen to do some training exercises in Borneo. We were to drive down to Kowloon docks and load up on the S.S. Kittiwake. It was very exciting; here I was, seeing the world at no cost, a far, far, cry from all what had happened from the start of my life. We arrived at Jesselton port in North Borneo, which was a British Crown colony at that time. It is now called Kota Kinabaloo. It wasn´t a large town as I remembered it but, it must have been a bit scary for the locals, us driving down their main street in 45 ton tanks, something that the older generation would have remembered from the war when, it would have been the Japanese. After the short drive through the town we arrived at a jungle trail, then we drove for something like 2-3 days, and when we stopped that night, out of the jungle you could hear the sound of drums along with all the other sounds it was something like out of the Tarzan films and this was 1962.. At night there was a guard, as was norm when we leaguered up for the night, but there were no natives to be seen. We realised that there wasn´t any need for a guard as these people do not steal, unlike lots of the Chinese where we had just come from, unless it was nailed down they would steal it.

We arrived at our destination a place called Kota Belud, a small village where, the locals where dressed in sari´s and the women were bare breasted, and for young lads of 18-24yr old it was hard not to look. We drove about 2 or 3 miles the other side of the village and parked up uniformly as was norm, then made ourselves comfortable as we could i.e. Raking the ground level where we would sleep. It was then that Sgt. R... gave me another one of his "many" sound pieces of advice, as he was blowing up his beach airbed he said to me you know what "any fool can be "uncomfortable" and through the night while tossing and turning on the uneven ground, Sgt. R...´s message sank in. We got up next morning to find that the mozzies hadn´t missed anyone and as we were only issued with Palladrin tablets to stop us getting Malaria after being bit, we had to find a way of keeping the damn things away from us "and" to our dismay found there were mozzies during the day as well as night. I eventually realised later, that whenever we refuelled, the mozzies kept away from us and thought if, I wiped my skin with a rag with a drop of fuel on it perhaps they would keep away I tried it and it worked, and was mozzie free most of the time after that. How I never got dermatitis I´ll never know but I didn´t. At night we would make ourselves a campfire by digging a hole deep enough to pour a jerry can of petrol and oil in it and, when lit, it would keep the damn things away. We would drink our beers swap stories and jokes till the early hours. It was on one of those nights that the biggest Praying Mantis I´d ever seen, landed on my chest that sobered me up in a split second. I really don´t know how we would have managed with all those creepy crawlies at night without the help of a drink before going to bed. You name it and it seems it´s there in Borneo.

On parade the next morning we were told to be friendly with the locals at any cost i.e. not to chase them away when they stood around us, watching our every move with fascination and after a while realised, that we could leave things lying about and come back and everything was how we had left it. It was a long time before the natives who stood around us every day in their loin cloths and wooden spear came closer, we would try and communicate with them. Their language was Dyak and learned later from one of the lads (Tony) who, had been brought up Malaysia that he could make them understand him to a degree. A couple of days later, after we had done our jobs on the tanks, we were told anyone who wasn´t needed in camp, could go down to the local village Kota Belud. It must have seemed like an invasion to the locals everyone stared at us like we were "aliens" they were fascinated by our tattoo´s especially if they were on your chest, apparently, further in the jungle if a native had tattoos on his chest or neck they were a fierce warrior who they had much respect for, well most of had chest tattoo´s and that explained why the look of fascination of the natives who came to look at us every day The shops had fresh fruit, vegetables, fresh eggs and other things to buy. We had been paid a month´s wages before we left Hong Kong so, we all had plenty of money to spend. There was a couple of bars and we all ended up in them and, drank both of them out of draught beer and out of bottled beer in one of them so we all ended up in the one that had some beer left. There was plenty of loud singing and shouting but not any trouble. The bar owners must have thought all their birthdays had come at once. On one of our visits to the village a young lad came in the bar one night with a monkey, asking, if anyone wanted to buy it, after quite a few beers I bought it, what for I don´t know, I must have been mad, but everyone seemed to get a little bit of fun with it. We gave it the name of "bad man Pierre" as it was always pinching anything that wasn´t fastened down and trying to eat it or tear it up. We didn´t know it at the time, but, were later, going to come across some of his relatives, on a very, very large scale.

It wasn´t long before we got an invite from one of the natives who, through Tony could communicate with them. We asked permission to go and were told yes so that evening the native turned up and three of us were taken to his village and house. On the way there we could hear these jungle drums just like the Tarzan films it was fantastic but also a little worrying as we had no idea of the reception we were going to get when we got there (I´d seen a lot of Tarzan films) it was about a mile or so to his village and, when got there, the drumming what we could hear that sounded so "good" sounded nothing like it in the village there was no sort of tune as before, just the sound as if everyone bashing a hollow tree trunk willy nilly it sounded awful. Everyone in the village came to have a look at us. Women and kids which we hadn´t seen before and, once again looking at us like we were aliens, I thought surely these people have seen white people before. We were taken to his long house, up a wooden ladder, it was about 6ft-8ft from the floor and found it be very clean inside but no furniture. We were introduced to his young wife who looked to be about 14 or 15 and a child who looked to be about 3 or 4yrs old and his mother an old woman sitting further down the room the women were bare breasted. We were asked to sit with him and, then his wife brought a large leaf with fish on it, and then went back to sit with the child. I didn´t like the taste of it and told Tony, he said don´t offend them Geordie get it eaten. After the fish he gave us a half coconut shell each and brought a large bamboo pole from the corner of the room and poured us a drink from it. The smell of it was "awful" but, after the first drink surprisingly it was really good and tasted nice, apparently it was made from fermented coconut milk and called Toddy and, it seemed he had an endless supply of it in the bamboo poles stacked up in the corner of the room. After about half an hour of drinking Toddy we heard a loud scream from his wife looked over to see the little boy been thrown down the room head over heels, the old woman picked him and gave him her breast and he started to chew on her nipple which, we all laughed at, the little boy must have been doing that to his mother and was too painful for her. We carried on drinking for short while and Tony thanked him and his family and invited them to our camp and, told him we were going to make our way back to camp before it got too late. We weren't too bad drink wise when we set off but by the time we did get back we were all as drunk as lords it sure was powerful stuff. The next day we were on the move up country (into the jungle) so we don´t know if the local guy ever came to see us. A few days after we went further into the jungle Tony had an accident. He had climbed a coconut tree without his shirt or vest on and had slipped while chopping some coconuts down and trying to hold on had slipped down the whole tree with his arms wrapped around it. It took all the skin off his arms and chest and had to be transported to a hospital in the Philippines for skin grafts, and that was the last anyone saw of him.

We drove for a couple of days to a clearing the Gurkha engineer´s had made for us to camp up which was close to a river, at last we could get bathed, we got one of the lorry tow ropes and made a swing like when we were kids, swing out into the river and swim back. I had done this several times, and swimming back the cry went up George there´s a snake behind you, yeah, yeah I thought, but I would take a look anyway and a good job I did because this black and red snake was coming towards me, well, I swam for my life and just as I was being helped out of the water a Ghurkha soldier whisked the snake out of the water with a stick and chopped the head off it with his Cuckehrie (knife) he went on to tell me that it was poisonous and "would" without doubt would, have killed me had it bit me. We were all on the lookout after that incident. Also there were two incidents of women being eaten by crocodiles further up the river they had been attacked by them coming out of the bush while they were keeping a look out for croc´s in the water, while the other women washed clothes. It was on one of our frequent visits to the river to get bathed as well as have a play around on the swing, that, I saw the strangest sight. As I said earlier all the women were bare breasted and one particular day a group of women came walking by and one was feeding her baby which was tied to her back with one of her breasts slung over her shoulder the other hung down like a roll of wall paper it drooped down so much, everyone was laughing at her but she was oblivious as to why. We stayed there playing army games with the Ghurkha's for three months, the grass (called elephant grass) was as tall as the tanks, and we had to use disinfectant powder on our clothes every day, as the grass had insects on it, that when they bit, you got a decease called Scrub Typhus where your temperature would go sky high and kill you, only "one" person who got it and survived. While we were there was a Ghurkha soldier his name, and the temperature, he survived is in the Guinness Book of Records. While we were up country, a group of locals came to have a look at us as was usual whenever we stopped, our troop officer one day, managed to persuade one of them, to have a ride on the tank, we put tarpaulins on the engine decks and warned him several times about the engine exhaust being extremely hot, we drove round for a short while at a slow pace, and it seemed as if he liked it, but when we got back, to where we picked him up, he quickly turned round to jump off the tank and stood on the exhaust, and as he was barefoot it immediately burned the skin off his foot to the bone, that was the first of twice I saw human bone in the flesh it was whiter than white and you never forget it.

He "screamed" out in agony as anyone would, but after that he never made a sound. How he withstood all that pain without uttering a sound still amazes me to this day. What a brave man indeed! He was whisked away to hospital, how long it took to get him there goodness knows, but, it will be something "he" will never forget of that I´m sure! It wasn´t long after that incident, we were on our way back to Jessleton, and, instead of us driving back down through the jungle tracks, the Ghurkha engineers took us down river on pontoons (steel rafts) and what an experience that was "Oh my" we all had been paid for first time since we had arrived in Borneo and, after we had paid our debts i.e. Booze and fags we loaded the tanks on the pontoons and were on our way down river, we had only been going a few hours, when, we stopped and, one of the Ghurkha's threw a thunder flash into the water and immediately there were loads of stunned fish, floating about everywhere, I thought that´s a great idea as I hadn´t seen the likes of that before. After few more hours down river, there was this, "almighty" loud "blood curdling" screams, and when we looked where it was coming from, the "whole" of the river bank, for yards upon yards either side of us were these enormous Urang Utangs they were, "huge" swinging, and screaming, we hadn´t seen anything of them since we had been there and, if any squaddie said he wasn´t scared he would be lying. The Ghurkha officer said don´t worry about them; they are harmless, it´s because we are in their feeding ground, that´s why they are so noisy. I had "never" in my life seen a wild animal as big as they were and, so close. I for one wasn´t convinced, and was glad when we eventually got passed them. After a few more hours we came out of the river and onto a beautiful white sandy beach which was another first for me, a "brilliant" white sand beach as soft as talcum powder. We were told to get our kit off the tanks, as we would be sleeping there for the night. I remember it was a huge beach with the trees about 60 or 70 yards from the shore, there was good strong warm breeze blowing, so, a few of us and it was, "only" a few, buried our clothes, and marked it with a stick. In no time at all we were all in the crystal clear warm water and, after the trip down through the jungle where, it seemed you were in a permanent sauna with flies and mozzies it was sheer heaven. And then after a while, there was this "almighty shouting" I thought it was something in the water, but when we looked at the beach, it was almost black with monkey´s there was hundreds and hundreds of them, and when we ran onto the beach, I would say that "every" monkey, had some piece of clothing in their hands, and cleared the beach in seconds, and up into the trees. It was a good job bad man Pierre was tied up to the tank otherwise his relatives might have managed to get him free had he been on the beach. Looking back, at what was to be, his fate, I wished I´d never bought him in the first place and that that day had set him free to join his relatives.

Well you can imagine the language when the lads who hadn´t buried their clothes realised, that their wages in their trousers pockets were now up in those trees, and the closer you got to them, the further they went into the jungle. It was ages and ages before we dare laugh about it as you can imagine, being paid 3 months wages, hitting town the next day and, the monkeys had taken them into the jungle, Ouch! It was from that incident onwards the lads changed his name, from "bad man Pierre" to "you little B.....d" When we eventually arrived in Jessleton we had four, empty houses to live in, as the ship taking us back to Hong Kong, had developed engine trouble, and would be a couple of days before it arrived at Jessleton. Needless to say, those of the lads who hadn´t buried their clothes were now skint, and us, who had, still had our wages, became money lenders, so we could all go and hit the town, for a well earned booze up. The journey back to Hong Kong on the SS Kittywake was long and hot as we spent most of the time in the hold washing and cleaning the tanks luckily we were allowed a drink on the ship and spent the nights as usual telling jokes, swapping stories and singing.

Not long after arriving back in Hong Kong bad man Pierre or "you little B....d as he more commonly known now was becoming a nuisance in more ways than one i.e. he wrecked the tree outside our billet and on several occasions had crapped on the window sills and on the curtains.

One night when I´d been out on the beer, I couldn´t find him anywhere and after a search for him thought he had broken free. I went to bed, looked at the speed of the ceiling fan above my bed only to see him tied to the blade, how long he´d been there I don´t know. I said when I find out which one of you who has done this; they are going to get a fat lip at least. I stopped the fan and got him down, he was hanging onto me like grim death, when I did manage to get him free of me and put him on the floor he just rolled over, and over for a good five minutes to every one´s delight except mine. I was as mad as hell; it was days after before he became his normal self again. I was forever feeling guilty that I had bought him and brought him back to Hong Kong little knowing what a terrible end was to become of him.

We were told we were on standby to go up to the Persian Gulf as some trouble was looming in Iraq, it was then, we found out that, that had been the reason we had been sent to Borneo, as a show of strength against possible terrorists attacks, which, were occurring further inland. All the Chinese guys who were owed money were zooming round trying to get paid before we left for the Gulf. Oscar was one that was chased from one Squadron to another by all the char wahllers, ice cream men, and anyone else who gave credit they were like an invasion, Oscar owed one ice cream man $150 alone that´s besides others, he did have to pay up though, they all went to the Squadron Leader which Oscar never thought would happen and made him pay. It took poor old Oscar a while to get over that. Several times in the next few weeks we would be told we are flying out in a couple of days only to be told it had been cancelled but don´t leave camp. Our Squadron leader Major Joe K... had been christened "No go Joe".

In those few short weeks of being on standby I managed to get someone from "C" Squadron, who were not being sent up the Gulf, to take bad man Pierre or "you little B.....d as he was now known. We eventually, did fly out, our troop to Bahrain and B and HQ Squadron flew to Aden. We were informed we would be there for a year, and that our time would be spent alternatively 3 months on a ship, sailing up and down the Gulf with our tanks on board and, three months on land. It was our Squadron who had to wait for the ship to arrive in Bahrain. We were living under canvas in four man bivouacs at the side of Bahrain airport, and shared the cookhouse, a marquee with the 1ST Battalion the Parachute Regiment. It was by far the worst army food that I had in the six years I served in the army, in comparison it made Catterick training camp food like a 5 star restaurant.

It was shortly after arriving in Bahrain that I got another kick in the teeth. This time it was from Jan, she said that she had been seeing another guy and was breaking off our engagement saying that except for letters we hardly knew each other and thought it would be best for both us. It hit me like a ton of bricks but what could I do, I did ask her to reconsider but, she said she had given it a lot of thought and that was the end of it, she wished me well and said to come and pick the engagement ring up and the other things I´d sent her when I returned home. It was the first time in my life I´d been ditched by a girl and it hurt like hell. It was weeks later before I told anyone about my "Dear John" and found out that I was "one" of many including some married guys. We did a lot of cussing about it sitting around at night having a drink thinking of all those beautiful Chinese girls we could have had.

Bahrain was only a small Island and the main town was called Manama, and as it was Sultanate it was ruled under strict Islamic law i.e. "No" booze, we could only get that on camp. One day we were in Manama having a look around and went into a coffee and soft drinks shop when one of the lads said "hey" there´s a white girl working on the counter, I had a look and got a real shock I couldn´t believe my own eyes, and said I know that girl, I used to court her, of course everyone started to cry me down saying, in your dreams Geordie, when it was my turn to be served I said to her, you are English aren´t you? And you come from the north-east from P....... yes she said how do you know that? And your name is Mary H... she looked at me puzzled and when I told her my name and said I was courting you until you came to stay out here, she said sorry, I didn´t recognize you without your hair, which, like everyone, I´d had had it shaved off because of the heat. She went on to say she couldn´t write to me because, I hadn´t given her my address when we parted in P....... a couple of years ago. All the lads by this were sitting up and paying attention. You "jammy bleeder" George, they were shouting, who´s this George she said have you changed your name? (as she knew me by middle name) I explained to her that most of them came from Nottingham, and couldn´t talk properly like us from the north-east so, they call me Geordie I did my utmost to get a date but she was courting a Royal Marine, who was on a posting in Aden, you wouldn´t like being two timed would you she said, I already have I said, I´d been sent a "Dear John" 2 weeks earlier from Jan. Well I was the talk of the troop for ages after that, who would have thought all that way from home and meeting one of my ex girlfriends.

Bahrain was hot as Hell and, there were more flies than in the jungles of Borneo when you went for your meals you only ate with one hand, the other was used to swat flies away. It was inevitable that everyone would get dysentery and, of course no one would volunteer to empty the thunder buckets so it became a duty, and my name was on the first list, on my first duty, the Para corporal in charge said to save time, so that all the buckets wouldn´t, have to be taken away at the same time, on a 3 ton lorry to the beach and emptied in the sea, put your hands in and, if you can´t feel anything in the bucket put it back, if your hand touches anything bring it here and pour it into another bucket, and, when it´s full, take it out to the lorry. He then gave us a demonstration Can you believe it, but, that is true, and before we got started a French lad in the Para´s said I WILL NOT DO IT, and the next thing to happen was the corporal got the demonstration bucket which was full of diarrhoea and threw it over him, that was a good enough excuse for us to leave, and went back to my tent and await the outcome of it all. Well the corporal was stripped of his rank and would serve some time in their regimental prison when they got back to England. "And" more buckets were put out, so they didn´t have to be emptied one into another. The flies were unbearable there was no escape from them. You only had to sit for a minute or two and you were covered in the damn things. It was, without doubt the worst place in the world I´d been to for flies and that included Borneo.

We borrowed the troop land rover on one occasion, to have a look around the island and to see the Sultan´s palaces etc. you would have to see them yourself to believe it they were magnificent buildings and proper turf lawns around them, there where huge American cars left at the sides of roads and of course with it being a small island no one would touch them. One day as we were walking into Manama a motor cavalcade of motorcycles came riding by and all the locals walking stopped and faced into the road with their heads bowed and not many seconds later a couple of motorcycles came by and they bowed even further so we thought it best if we did the same and seconds later a huge cavalcade of big American cars came by with Arabs sat in them with falcon´s on their arms, apparently if you didn´t bow you would be picked up and taken away and given some lashes for not paying respect to the Sultan or his family, such, was the power of that one man.

It was while I was up in Bahrain that if, we weren´t playing hockey or volleyball which we did every afternoon (mad dog the Englishman goes out in the midday sun) I learned an invaluable lesson as regards gambling, it was one Saturday afternoon when a card game had been set up (three card brag) and after a while I managed to get a game, it was usually a group of four that played to eliminate cheating (however there was always someone keeping an eye on things) after a few games only two were left in the game myself and Paddy Mc..... (whose favourite saying was, Holy Mary mother of God send me down a couple of bob) I´d been dealt 3 aces and after what seemed ages and I´d bragged four weeks wages, and not being as heavy a gambler as some of them, I asked to see his hand, the only hand to beat mine was 3 "3s" and, he had them, I was "gutted" and have never played cards since that day. Looking back it was a small price to pay for an invaluable lesson. Don´t gamble it´s a fool's game, you are only chasing your own money, put another way, do you ever see a bookmaker waiting for a bus? And another strange thing about gamblers is they always tell you how much they´ve won, they never tell you how much they´ve lost.

Another incident I remember in Bahrain was going to see the M.O. I had a terrific pain in my backside. I stood in the queue which was about 20 deep and by the time I was three away from being seen by the M O, I passed out with pain. I had never experienced passing out before, even, when I had Rheumatic fever. I woke up in an air conditioned R.A.F. hospital bed which, was great in itself to be out of the heat and flies, and was later told, I had an ingrown hair on my Coccyx. After a few days of drawing the infection out, it had left a hole which had to be plugged with a string of gauze held in place by a dressing, best described as a woman´s sanitary towel, kept in place with Elastoplasts until it healed up. After about 10 days all was well and the orderly removed my dressings and the sticky stuff off the plaster from my stomach, he told me to turn over, to do the same to my back and when he started, the Ether he was using ran down the cheeks of my backside onto my testicles it was Freezing and I told him so. I was discharged that morning and walked back to camp (tents) which wasn't far away. Before I got back the pain in my Goolies was so great I had to stop for a rest. I got back to camp after a while, everyone was out, working somewhere, I didn't bother to report in as the pain by this time was so intense, that I couldn't wait to get in my tent to get my shorts off and see what was causing this intense pain. After dropping my shorts I examined my Goolies and found they were covered in huge blisters and the only relief I could get was to stand with one leg up on the bench and, in no time at all, the blisters had formed into one which, was the size of a cricket ball, so I nicked it with my finger nails to burst it which eased it a lot. By this time I was feeling so drained I took one look at my camp bed and thought the is no way will I be able to lie down and keep my Goolies clear of my legs so, I got a sheet and pillow and laid on the table covering myself completely with the sheet to keep the flies off me and, must have fallen asleep as, the next thing I heard was someone shouting Geordie B .... is dead, (the troop had returned from work by then) Gus D..... was the first in the tent and saw there was a body laid out on table, pulled the sheet back and seen me laid there asleep, and thought I was dead. All the shouting woke me up and I explained what had happened then, Ray and Bob carried me down to the M.O.s tent, he was sent for and, when I explained what had happened that morning he said he must have used neat Ether gave me some cream and said stop off work for a few days. We had many a laugh about that incident later around the camp fires when we were out in the field.

We could only buy crates of beer to drink in camp, and there was an unending supply of it, NO fires though as we were tented on the side of Bahrain airport. But it was always the same telling jokes, singing our version of songs; we always had a good time. Sometimes the

Officers would make some excuse or other and join us.

I had a letter from my sister one day saying that Alf had gone to Yorkshire to work at a pit in and could I help out and send her 50 pounds to pay for their furniture to be moved down there as Alf had managed to get a house and couldn´t afford the removal costs for a while yet. I was thinking of the bairns, being split up as a family and so, I foolishly, sent her the money by a P.O. money order, paid only to P....... P.O. only for it to be returned, in a reply letter it saying it, had to be cash, because If, she had cashed it at the local Post office/paper shop where I had made it out to, he would take the amount she owed there, so I cancelled the money order and sent ordinary P.O. orders. She said she would pay it back once they got on their feet, I was never given that money back and years later found out that N.C.B. paid for removals "and" a settling in grant. Yet another kick in the teeth and, me being half across the world, I can´t see them coming.

The ship, the HMS Anzio, arrived in Bahrain and fearing the worst having to spend 3months on a ship, what a surprise we all got, the daily menu was as good as any good restaurant, it was by far the best food I had had so far "and", no cookhouse fatigues, fire picket or guard duties. Whenever we had our food and were eating it on deck because, there was only a small mess which the ship´s crew used, the Chef would come round everyday to ask us if there were any complaints. He couldn´t understand why there were none. We told him that during your army training days, you don´t make complaints otherwise you end up on cookhouse fatigues, and besides, we were all more than satisfied with the food. After sailing around the gulf for a while we made a courtesy visit to Persia (now Iran) to a port called Bushehr where a football match had been arranged with the local team, we were paraded on deck, and were told, to let the local team win. The local team, young boys, were playing without boots so you can imagine what kind of game it was. After the match we went for a look around the town, everyone seemed to look at us with suspicion, it was inches deep in dust, and the last time the shops had, had paint on them must have been when Ben Hur had been around. To give you an idea of how poor these people were, the barbers shop had a little lad pulling on a rope which was tied to a carpet above the barber's chair was their equivalent of air conditioning. It was like taking a step back in time and to think of all that wealth the country had from oil you just shook your head in wonderment.

After sailing around the gulf for a couple of months and, getting quite used to no mozzies and only the odd fly we eventually sailed down to Aden, disembarked, and drove the tanks to the edge of the desert where we would be staying as it turned out for 6 months. On the way down we were told we would be getting updated from the MK 2 and 3 Centurion tanks we had to MK 4 and 5. Sure enough we did, at that time we were the only country in the world which had a tank that could fire on the move. So before, we picked up our new tanks from Aden docks, we had to take the equipment out of the old tanks which enabled the tank to do this, ready to fit in our new tanks, clean and paint the old ones, then drive them down to the docks, unload the new ones and load the old ones onto the ship, that would take them to Iraq who, the British government had made an arms deal with earlier. Yet the reason why we were there was in case they caused any problems up the gulf. We all shook our heads at that logic. We spent a lot of time in the desert and by now I could drive a tank, and because I could cook a decent meal, I was now the troop leader's driver. It was during the spell we had in Aden that one of the lads from HQ Squadron told me the fate of Bad man Pierre. He told me that the guy I gave him to had sold him one night in a bar to a Chinese guy and that he had heard he had been killed and his brains were eaten as a delicacy. I don´t how true the story was but I didn´t feel good about it.

One day, when we were out doing an exercise we stopped in a dry river bed, my driving seat was at the feet of the gunner Dick R...... he asked if he could get out for crap, when he came back and got sat down, there was this stench of crap he had actually stood in some one´s old crap as he walked back to the tank, What are the odds on that when as far as the eye could see in any direction was sand? There was another time we had unpacked all our rations to fit in the tank stowage bins and had inadvertently left the tin opener and here we were in the middle of the desert without a tin opener when, out of blue an Arab walked up to us, and I noticed he had a couple of army tin openers on his belt which after a lot of persuasion sold them to me. That saved the day; it would have meant using a chisel. One incident I remember, when we were out in the desert, we came across half a dozen camels and decided to catch one and have a ride on it (BAD IDEA) Ray and myself got a towrope and set off chasing them in the scout car it was a miracle that we lassoed one them, the smallest of them, I don´t know how old it was but it could run like the wind. We got it back to where we´d stopped and, after several people tried to get on it never mind riding it, I had a go at it and as I said BAD IDEA I managed to get on its back and hung on for a few seconds only, and how I was able to father children after that God only knows, was also a miracle, my goolies hurt like hell for days after but, it was good fun. On most of our trips into the desert we stayed out for days on end and at night there was always a guard no one liked it, but it had to be done, it was freezing cold during the night, I would always take my greatcoat to wear on guard and, wish at times I´d had another to wear. Another incident was when we´d had been out, we had been firing live ammo and on our return were unloading the machine guns and ammo from the tanks and Daz J.... , the radio operator on another tank was handing Pete L......... gunner, the machine gun out of the tank and the worst thing that could happen did, he hadn´t cleared the breach and as there was no handle to that one his hand touched the trigger, the round that had been left in the breach fired and went through his shoulder and threw him off the top of the tank, and ten or more yards down the tank park, it was a small hole about the size of a sixpence but when he was turned over, it was the second time that I saw human bone in flesh, there was a massive hole in his back, where you could see his shoulder blade, as white as white could be. There was hell on about it and sadly Pete died in hospital Daz was charged and spent time in jail. It was an accident I know, "BUT" the "emphasis" given on that part of your training it should "not" have happened. Sadly it did. It was around that time when we had an addition to our troop a great guy scouse C.....r I don´t think anyone got to know his first name. He had been on loan to the A.P.L. (Aden Protectorate Levy) their job was to patrol the Yemen border; he was an old soldier with some 15 plus years service in. He had been with them for a year and told lots of stories which we all thought were a bit farfetched at times but, who were we?, we couldn´t challenge them. One day the C.O. sent for him and he was awarded a medal for what he had been doing up in the Yemen and also, in writing an invite to the beheading of two school boys who they had captured, who had been attacking their patrols and Arab caravans with stones, for quite a while. He declined the offer of the beheading, and after that we never doubted whatever he said. He was another character I will always be pleased I met, and will never forget.

When we were, in camp, we would go to the cinema at night, in the open air with wooden seats and a huge board painted white to show the film on, take a case of beer and providing we were not too noisy on our return nothing was said about being drunk as long as we were right and properly turned out for parade the next day. One night we came back to our billet and there was a rat as big as Jack Russell terrier sat just inside the door of the billet. I picked a brush up and hit it square on the head and it jumped straight over my locker and out through a hole in the wall at the back of it. On another occasion we heard a blood curdling scream coming from the regimental cooks billet one night and when we got there Harry B....s was standing beside his bed white as a ghost, shaking like a leaf and sweat pouring down his face, he said he had made himself a cheese and onion sandwich and brought it back to his billet, eaten it, and fell asleep, when he felt something touching his lips and thinking it was one of the lads playing about opened his eyes to tell them to F..k off, and saw one of these huge rats sitting on his chest eating the crumbs off his lips. We all had a laugh about it but he was clearly shaken up about it and who wouldn´t be. I won´t be doing that again he said after he had calmed down.

It wasn´t long after that incident our troop, sailed back up the Gulf, we had a visit to Kuwait city, and in those days it was the same as Bushehr and Bahrain, deep in dust and poverty everywhere, a trip along the Iraq Kuwait border where it was hotter than anywhere I´d been, there was no way you could touch anything metal for more than a second or two. We had canvas water buckets as part of our tank equipment and if it was filled with water and hung up in the direct sun it would keep the water very cool which was a valuable asset to have in that heat. How it works I have never been given a proper explanation for it but, I suspect it´s to do with evaporation. It rained one day when we were in Bahrain and, they said it was the first time for 115yrs, I don´t know if that were true but, there were grown men looking up at it with fascination, the rain drops were the size golf balls and with so much dust around it stunk like hell. One day we were invited to go on a flight with the Para´s to watch them do a drop, we were put on an old Beverly plane that they used in those times "Flying Pig´s they were called because of their shape. We were told to get "well" wrapped up which, was sound advice as, once we were airborne there was more patches on it, you could see daylight through them, it was like a patchwork quilt and perishing cold unfortunately we didn´t get to see them do a drop as it was too windy and so because of casualty risk they cancelled the drop. However we did land in Sharzah and had a look at the Sultan´s private army and air force which was very impressive indeed.

We had been on standby, for about 11 months when we were told, we could go to Mombasa, in groups, for a two week break "if" we wanted to, so naturally, no one refused. The only woman any of us had spoken to in all that time was Mary H... in that store in Manama, and as most of us had plenty of money, and desperately needed some female company, off we went, flown there by the R.A.F and taken to an army camp but, not run as an army camp, there were No restrictions at all i.e You could eat and sleep there if you wanted to and no curfew at night. We were housed in billets like in Honk Kong and advised to, "ONLY" take enough money to last you for that day or night and as many rubber Jonnies as need be. There was a beach close by and it was my second sight of a pure white sandy beach. That evening we went down to the town, feeling like stallions let loose, and found it was much the same as Hong Kong i.e. the main street was made up of bars almost every other building was a bar, and girls sat about in every one of them like Hong Kong they were dark skinned obviously except for a few who were jet black. I found out later that these were from Tanganyika but who was looking at the skin colour. We hit the first decent looking bar we came to and, after a few drinks I was propositioned by a tall fantastic looking girl, who looked was as black as my army boots and a face nearly as shiny, she looked just a little older than me, spoke good English, and after I had bought her a drink she said, "If I buy your drinks today, will you buy mine tomorrow?" I´d never had an offer like that before and took her up on it. Well I "didn´t" pay for another drink that day, and have got to admit it looked a bit dodgy to me being brand new to Mombasa and having my drinks paid for by a woman. However, it was how it worked for "almost" the two weeks I was there. She took me home to bed that night and as the story unfolds it was a better night than my honeymoon turned out to be, the next morning she woke me, and had another session in bed then she cooked me a "huge" mixed grill for breakfast which I was in dire need of, I returned to camp but, not before she reminded me it was my turn to pay today. We arranged to meet at 2 o clock that afternoon in the bar, which we did, and then I paid all day and, found out she had hollow legs, and could drink better than "any" lad in the regiment and that´s for sure. She was easy to get on with asking me what it was like in the UK and where did I live etc. I was being well, well bedded, and fed when she took me home so, I decided to slip her some money for the food but she never once asked for any which, I found very strange. We were offered trips from the camp where we were staying at, there were safaris out on the Serengeti or, up Mount Kilimanjaro, and, "bitterly" regret to this day that I didn´t. I had a large sexual appetite as any young lad of that age has and, my brains were in my underpants to a degree and as we were only there for two weeks I didn´t go.

On one of our daily trips back to the camp to pick up more money and Johnnie´s, someone said they had heard of a strip club that had "White" girls performing so about 10 of us decided we would give it a try and go to it that night. I met a girl in there, really good looking and thought, as she was white and spoke perfect English, she would be English, and as it turned out she was Seychellese. Later that night she took me to her home, and that´s when, a disaster happened that has never happened before or since, in my life. We got to her place, I had no idea where I was and didn´t care I´d been none stop drinking since I got there over a week ago and had plenty that night as well. It was sort of half light when she opened the door to her house and straight away I noticed a spider on her wall, it was bigger than my hand and in my drunken state picked up a sweeping brush to kill it, I hit it square on, and it fell to the floor and ran under a chair, and that was the last I remember of that night. I woke up with a hangover big enough for two, she was sobbing then hugging me and I thought to myself "crikey" was I that good last night. It wasn´t until I sat up and looked around and saw that the room was totally wrecked, what´s happened I said, she told me, that I had got her sweeping brush, and started to wreck her place looking for a spider, and after a while collapsed on the bed, and that I´d been there till now, she wouldn´t send for the military police or local police or an ambulance, as "she" would get into trouble for having me there and, I would also get into trouble for being there. To make matters worse someone had used a pole through her window and taken the money from my trousers. I said I would bring her some money to pay for the damages, and arranged to meet her at 7 o clock that night in the bar where I usually went drinking. A "BIG MISTAKE" as the story unfolds. I got back to camp and all the lads were asking, where have you been George? I said with that Seychellese girl from that nightclub, they said, that was the night before George, and it wasn´t until they showed me a newspaper I realised that I had been unconscious for two days, as the girl had been trying to explain to me. One of the lads said, you must have taken the "HORRORS" through drink, and, you have now found out what your phobia is. Funnily enough I´m not afraid of spiders but am a bit apprehensive of ones that are as big as my hand. I did take her 60 East African shillings as she asked for, I´d only just bought us a drink when, a couple of minutes later in walked the Tanganyican girl, I´d been with since I´d arrived in Mombasa, she came in with a face like thunder, she came over to our table and produced a machete, raised it above the head of the Seychellese girl, she screamed, and ran out, with me behind her, she ran up the street, and I ran down it with this girl chasing me with a machete. I don´t think I´ve run as fast as that in my life. About 300yds down the street was a high class hotel, I ran in there and when the doorman saw the girl with the machete, he quickly locked the door. I don´t know what happened to her but after an hour or so I got a taxi back to camp. I can only think that she thought we were courting or something but that was the first of two occasions where I thought I was in mortal danger. We only had a few more days left in Mombasa and never went into to that bar again, I was not tempting fate.

When we flew back to Bahrain (exhausted) boarded ship, and the next day sailed down to Aden at the tail end of a typhoon, and what an experience that was. These ships we were on were called L.S.Ts they were flat bottomed ships they had used in WW2, so they could drop anchor out at sea and sail straight onto the beach open the bow doors unload the tanks and other vehicles and then winch themselves off the beach. So you can imagine in any rough weather they were thrown around like a bath tub. Surprisingly, I was never seasick but when we sailed down to Aden for the last time there were lots of the ship's crew that was. I remember once standing at the stern holding on to the rail for grim death and could actually touch the water over the stern that's how much these ships were thrown up and down and side to side in rough waters. It was on that occasion that I saw for the first time a RN sailor "grey" through sea sickness and, it's "not" a pretty sight I'll tell you. While we were on board ship we were entitled to the traditional tot of rum which all Royal Navy personnel were given every day. Ours was watered down to a measure of two to one, an interesting story is attached to that, it won't keep for more than a day or two it goes bad and stops the crew from hoarding it and maybe cause a mutiny by getting drunk.

On several occasions while sailing down to Aden and reflecting on my outing to Mombasa I thought of the advice Sgt. R... had given me when I first arrived in Hong Kong about always choosing the ugly girl (prostitute) and why I didn't heed his advice in Mombasa but, as it turned out everything was ok God bless the man who invented Jonnies.

When we arrived in Aden we handed our tanks over to our relief regiment and were put in barracks awaiting the troop ship to arrive to take us back to Blighty. The food in the cookhouse was absolutely crap so most of the time we ate cheese and onion sarnies or bread and margarine and tins of tuna fish bought from a char wallah. One day one of the lads said he had, had one of the Ghurkha meals it tasted like lamb curry and was quite good so we gave it a try and to my surprise it was good it was actually curried goat. After that it was curry and rice every day until we left Aden. It had been almost 3yrs since I left home and yet, it seemed a life time had gone by, the places I´d been, the things I´d seen and done, the confidence I now had and the friends I had made who, I will always have fond memories of, "yes", I had "definitely" been transformed from a boy, to a man in that short space of time. There had been a lot of trouble brewing in Iraq and that´s why we had been sent there, then just as we were about to leave, trouble was brewing in Aden, we all thought we would be kept back, however we weren´t. It was late September and our ship the S,S. Nevasa which was to take us back to the UK, had finally arrived in Aden, we were going home at last. We boarded the ship full of excitement and told it would be three weeks before we arrived in the UK. Although I didn´t have much of a home life to go home to, I was looking forward to being back in England, to visit the rest of my family and my mates. No sooner had we got on our way when reports were coming through that there was MEGA trouble in Aden and we all thought that because we were so near we might well be sent back, thankfully we weren´t. The first major place of interest on our journey home was the Suez canal, it was weird something I´d never seen before or since, a huge ship just fitting the canal and fields of vegetation either side of it was a weird sensation just like sailing up a road. And of course some of the local Arabs standing along the banks of the canal shaking their willies at us shouting "HEY McGregor" OR "JOHNNIE" do you want some? And what must have been to the many women, who were looking over the side of the ship, something of excitement to the usually boring days of life aboard ship, we were told, it was the norm for any cruise liner that sailed through Suez to have the Arab guys showing their "willies" off. . Our next port of call was Cyprus, (Famagusta) where we were allowed on shore and of course a visit to the bars and girls and bearing in mind we hadn´t been in any female company since we had been to Mombasa we made full use of the opportunity. The next port of call was Gibraltar, where it was strange to see the local police dressed as British Bobbies. We had plenty of time to go drinking, up the steep hill which ran through the main street which ran up the middle of the town called the "Gut" it seemed every other building on either side of the street was a bar. We set sail from there and, our next port of call would be dear old "Blighty" (Southampton) We all filled what spare room we had in our kitbags with booze and fags from the duty free shop on board ship and I remember having 1000 fags in mine and crapping myself going through customs hoping, I wouldn´t be stopped, and later the sheer relief of getting through. We were now on 8 weeks leave, armed with Rail travel warrants to our home towns, it was a bit sad for me, to see that lots of the lads had families come to meet them, and that no one had come to meet me, I did look round half heartedly hoping that "maybe" but knew in my own mind there wouldn´t be (stupid really) however. I made the journey to my sister´s home town, got off the train onto a bus to where she lived and someone told me where to get off the bus for my sister´s address, with a kit bag and a huge suit case, dressed in my uniform. I knocked at the door and one of the bairns opened it and shouted its Uncle George, I walked in, and was greeted with a hello, no hugs or a kiss (but should have known better than to expect anything different) the bairns where all around me looking at me and asking why I was so dark skinned and talked funny which, I went on to tell them as best I could so they would understand that the soldiers that I´d been with all this time couldn´t speak properly like us so, I had to talk like them, so they would understand me, but they were too young to see the funny side of it and also it had been that hot there was why I was so tanned. After something to eat, I undid my kitbag and gave the bairns their presents I´d bought them in Aden, it was fascinating for them, as they wanted to know all about the places I´d been and, also for me as, they were the only one´s interested in me, making a fuss of me, in their own way. I love those bairns and although, there are only a few years between our ages, they still address me as Uncle to this day, along with my other nieces and nephews, now that´s respect you don´t get often these days. My sister Alice, Alf and I went out for a drink that night, and the only civilian clothes I had, were what I´d bought out in the far-east and middle- east, far too thin for this climate. Needless to say I was perishing cold all night and couldn´t get warm. Alf and my sister were surprised at the amount of beer I was drinking and not getting drunk. I said I´ve just had three years of training and didn´t even pass the course with some of those lads. I went to bed that night with my army Greatcoat on the bed, remembering as a child having one on the bed, and never in a million years think I would have one on my bed all these years later. And I was still as cold that night as I was as a child all those years ago. The next day I went into town, to buy myself some warm clothing, although the weather was good I just couldn´t keep warm. Among other things I bought was an overcoat, which, I wore, everyday and, put it on my bed at night, as well as my Greatcoat. Living in a house again with family was a bit strange at first, having to watch my language, as there were children around, I managed it though, as I have never swore in front of kids or women in my life. In today´s "modern society" most kids can give me lessons in swearing and, I, have been blessed, that "none" of my family, are foul mouthed, at least not in front of me and, vice versa.

During my leave I went to visit my sister Lizzie and Eddie where I got a real welcome home, and sent a letter to Jan (BIG MISTAKE)   the following day asking for the things I´d sent her from Hong Kong i.e. engagement ring, hand painted tea and coffee services, along with various other things that would have been used in a home had we got that far. And as she was going out with another guy now, I didn´t see why he or she should have them. She agreed, and we met up one night where she lived, and went for a drink, she said she saw a vast change in me and was sorry the way things had turned out but, we had only known each other a few short weeks before I went abroad. She did make a comment about my weight saying that I hadn´t put much on since I´d been away. I explained that for the past year no one in the Regiment had eaten properly due to the heat. I had actually put 7pounds on in the 3 years I´d been away and now weighed 10 stone 2 ozs I was best described as being built like a Gypsies greyhound all p.... and ribs. She suggested as it was so late would I call at their house the following night and pick the things up. From that time my memory is a blur I can´t remember getting back with Jan, I certainly wasn´t on drugs. I guess I must have had my drinks spiked, coupled with the fact at that time my brains were in my underpants, and also we had said a lot in our letters to each other during my time abroad.

Getting back together would haunt me for the rest of my life as this story unfolds. During my stay at our Lizzie's she told me that she had, had a win on the football pools while I'd been away, and showed me a photo of her and her mate holding the cheque for £23,000 a small fortune in those days. She then went on to tell me the problems she'd had after winning it. She had been in a syndicate of 23 girls at work, and she would send the coupon off every week after collecting a shilling a week from each of them. She had been doing that for a couple of years when one of the girls said she was leaving and moving out of the area but would like to stay in the syndicate so, on the day she left she gave Lizzie 5 shillings and said she would send Lizzie a 5 shilling postal order every 5 weeks to cover her coupon money. That was the last time Lizzie or any of the girls saw her. After the 5 weeks were up Lizzie told the girls she would continue to pay the girls shilling until she sent her the money. After six months went by, they all said that because, you have been paying that girls share Lizzie "if" we do win you can have two shares. After a year or so and the girl still hadn't sent any money, they had a win of £23,087 and 87 and all the money was shared out between the 22 who were left in the syndicate. The local newspaper got hold of it and printed the story. Two weeks later when Lizzie was at home, she had a knock on her door, it was a young lad who she didn't know and he said I've come for my mum's winnings Lizzie was dumfounded she invited him in, and explained that his mother hadn't paid her any money after the 5 shillings had been used up and that she had paid her share for 6 months to keep the coupon money right so, then the syndicate said Lizzie could have that share if she was willing to pay for it. He went away and seemed satisfied with the explanation. A week later Lizzie received a letter from a solicitor saying that she should send an equal share of the winnings to his client, Lizzie by this time was in a right state and was going to send the girl the money but after talking to the girls about it all the girls thought she had a cheek asking for it so they wrote a letter together and sent it to her and nothing more was said about it.

I also went to visit the twins and Jane and got a "real" welcome there compared, to the one I got when I arrived our Alice´s a couple of weeks earlier. When I visited Jane she showed me the copy of a photo of my niece I had, had done in silk for her when I was in Hong Kong, I had forgotten about it, but so much had happened during those three years I´d been away. They were all fascinated by the stories I told them. Even the story of the bike Thornton had given me, from being the best present "ever" to the "worst". They were shocked at the behaviour of our Alice and Alf which, I could now tell them as an adult, and, wished I had told them at the time, and maybe things would have worked out differently for me.

My 8 weeks leave was soon over and I had to report to Manchester airport but, our flight was cancelled due to fog and were sent to the Buxton hotel in Buxton it was a huge building a 4 star hotel. I had never stayed in a hotel as grand as that, things were looking "good" "and" paid for by the army. A few of us decided to go out on the town, I remember that the local beer was "awful" so Frank C...... suggested we drink Barley wine instead (BIG MISTAKE) well, everything was ok until, it 10-30 and, was time to leave the pub, when I got outside my legs went and, couldn´t stand up, I had to be helped back to the hotel which thankfully was just around the corner. I can´t remember any of that and, the next morning was woken up by the chamber maid with, about 20mins to get ready and onto the bus to the airport. My head was pounding and, it felt like I´d been drinking ink the night before I never sobered up until, we got to our camp in Germany. In my short experience of dinking (about 3 yrs) that was, "the" worst hangover I´d ever had and that included the incident in Mombasa, every time I had a drink of anything it seemed to make me drunk again. It was a lesson well learned, (leave the Barley wines to the girls, they seem to handle it better) I have "never" had a drink of Barley Wine since that night.

I quickly got settled in to our new barracks, it was a far cry from what we had been in, in the last 12 months. Our new posting was for 3yrs and it was looking good.

By January we were out on our first NATO exorcise it was on the Baltic coast. I have never been as cold in all my life as I was there. Every night the temperature would drop to – 27c or more, and there must have been times during the day it dropped even further. There was no heating in the tanks and, if we were driving for any distance my eyelashes would freeze up, there was no way you could keep warm except, when we stopped we would lift the engine decks up and stand on the engine to keep warm. It was on that exercise that I saw ice crystals forming in a bottle of cheap brandy that´s how cold it was. We were told not to leave our boots out at night but, to put them under spare clothing, we used as a pillow otherwise they would freeze, which they did for some of the lads who didn´t heed that advice, with having leather laces in our boots you could snap them like twigs, the next morning if, they had been left out. We only had one blanket with us in those days, sleeping bags were not issued for another couple of years after that exercise so, we slept in all our clothes and our tank suits which were insulated but were not that warm. We had bought a Tilly lamp between our tank crew and, one night it was nearly the death of all four of us. We had the fly sheet up at the side of the tank and packed the surrounds with snow to keep the cold and wind out, and using the heat from the Tilly lamp to keep warm we, must have made too good a job of that because, after falling asleep the Tilly lamp was belting carbon monoxide out the lean-to was full of it, and if one of us hadn´t woken up we would have all been dead. It was on that same exercise that, Dick R..... had to go for a crap one night while we were out, he dropped his tank suit down, his other trousers and did the business, unbeknown to him he had done it in the hood of his tank suit hood, he came back to the tank, oblivious, of what he had done , he got into the tank and, the best part of it was, it was "him" that was complaining of the stench, and, with him having his tank suit hood drawn up tight "we" couldn´t see it. We were all saying have you done another "Aden" trick Dick, check your boots, it was hours later when we had stopped and, all got out of the tank and he, took his tank suit hood off, that we realised what he done, it was plastered all over his beret. What odds could you get on that happening?

When Jan and I decided to get married, there were two bombshells dropped the 1st being the only available leave that I could have was from the 20th April and married on the 27th, missing, a tax rebate which, you could get in those days by getting married before 6th April. I found out later that April 27th was my father´s birthday. The 2nd bombshell was, Jan told me that because her Da had been off work so long with industrial eczema she had been handing her wages over and receiving pocket money so, her mother would only let her pay board for a month before the wedding, as her wages were needed for the upkeep of the house. There was a houseful of them, there were 9 in all living at home and only 3 working, which meant that I would have to dig deep or, wait until a later date which we didn´t. It worked out that Jan, would hire her wedding dress and bridesmaids outfits, the church fee´s and church hall for the reception. I would buy her mother a frock, and also one of her sisters and an outfit for her two younger brothers, the cake, catering for 60 guests and a drink for the toast, the photographer and album, train fares to Scotland and our honeymoon. Jan didn´t need a wedding car as her eldest brother would take her to the church which was at the top of the street. It was tight going but, we managed. I stayed at my sister Lizzie´s the night before and, can remember Ted my best man, saying to me that day of the wedding "you "don´t" have to do this you know" while waiting for our taxi. Had I known what "was" in store for me, I would have taken that advice. Looking back at it, the marriage should have ended that day because although it sounds like the script for a play or film it´s all true. Here´s, how it went, on Day 1. We were married and, the only people from my family to attend were the twins, Lizzie and Eddie who was my best man. Invitations had been sent to everyone of the family including my father, my mates from the army couldn´t attend because they couldn´t get leave. We were married at the church at the top of the street where Jan lived and as the church hall was next door where the reception was being held, we walked there, the catering had been laid out by Jan´s friends, so, as the guests were arriving Jan and I were stood at the entrance greeting our guests, before anyone had been seated, Jan´s mother came to us and said "Jan" come and have a photo taken with all my family "we" haven´t been together for 25yrs so, obviously I went to go with her when her mother said "not" you George, "family only" to which her Dad said he "is" family now Winnie. I didn´t say anything as I didn´t want to spoil the day. Jan´s mother took charge of any photo shots, then and, after the reception, and I´m thinking, I hope she´s enough money to pay for them. We all ended back at Jan´s home when I noticed our Lizzie coming out of the kitchen where, any catering left from the reception had been taken. Her face was like thunder, I asked what was wrong, "nothing" she said, I don´t want to spoil your day, you will, if you don´t tell me I said. Well she said, you told me to get some sandwiches, cakes and a piece of wedding cake for old Mrs Nesbit and Mrs Stevenson (my ma´s friends who were too old to come to the wedding and, they had even sent us a small wedding gift) Jan´s mother told me I can´t, as it all going to the club later. I was shocked I went straight into the kitchen and asked Jan´s mother for a couple of carrier bags and half filled them and, the bottom layer, of wedding cake, gave them to our Lizzie and told her to share them out. Jan´s mothers face that day was like "thunder" (these kicks in the teeth "never" seem to stop I thought) but there was much, much more to come. Jan had gone up stairs to get changed, as her eldest brother, so we thought was taking us to the local train station, to go on our honeymoon, he couldn´t be found and, when he was eventually found in the front room, he had drank the last of the sherry and whisky from the reception and was too drunk to drive.

Time was getting on and our Elsie´s husband Thornton was kind enough to take us to the railway station. We got in the car and saying our goodbyes and usual stuff when Jan´s mother put her head through the window and said "and don´t forget Jan" you "haven´t" paid your board this week, but, it can wait until you get back. I ask you, "what woman" could say that to her first daughter to be married, and, on her way to her honeymoon? And just when you think it can´t get worse, we arrived at Newcastle railway station, to find the trains times, had been disrupted through, an accident down south somewhere and, that our earliest train to Edinburgh would be 3-30am in the morning. We phoned the hotel and told them what, had happened, they were very understanding about it, ring the front door bell and the night porter will let you in they said. So now we had to find a pub to go to until at least closing time (10-30pm in those days) and sit in the station waiting room until the train arrived, or so we thought. It was a cold night and, at first, we were the only two in the waiting room, and then the local drop outs started to drift in and then, the police came and started to move them out. After they had all gone they came to us and said you will have to go out as well, as we are locking the waiting rooms up for the night, I explained that we had just been married that day and through no fault of our own our train would not arrive for another 4hrs. Sorry he said, you can sit on the station platform but the waiting rooms had to locked and, that´s what we did for the next 4 hrs instead of been in bed on our honeymoon. It was now Day 2 when we finally got to Edinburgh and luckily the hotel was a short taxi ride away, rang the doorbell and couldn´t get an answer for 20mins or more and was deciding to look for a room somewhere else and come back later in the morning when, the night porter came and, apologized for the delay and, that he had been getting breakfast things ready at the back of the hotel (asleep more like) When we finally got to our room I got a bottle of good expensive champagne out of my case and a couple of champagne glasses which I had brought from Germany as a surprise for her, she said it just tasted like cider and after the 3rd glass conked out and fell asleep. What the "hell" have I done to deserve "all" this I thought to myself, what a way to start married life, and if it that wasn`t bad enough Jan came on her period on the Thursday and thought to myself if it wasn´t for all this bad luck I was having I´d have no luck at all.

We arrived back from our honeymoon to Jan´s home where there had been a change round with the sleeping arrangements we had a small bedroom to ourselves for the short time I had left of my leave. We were asked for board money for us both and also the week Jan hadn´t paid before we left. The atmosphere was strained and can only put it down to the incident with our Lizzie and Jan´s mother on our wedding day.

It soon came time for me to go back to Germany and now that I was a married man, I could put my name on the list for a married quarter and, any of those lads who had married before we came out to Germany. Shortly after, one of the lads in our troop, Pete K...... had found rooms in a village, not far from camp and said, there was another two rooms going in the same house. I went and had look at them and paid a deposit on them. Some good luck was coming our way at last. Jan was as excited as I was, she went on to tell me she was pregnant had, had it confirmed, which hit me like a ton of bricks I sure wasn´t expecting that so soon. After two or three weeks Jan came out and we stayed in those two rooms until shortly after our Christine was born. We became firm friends of Pete and his wife Jean, the landlady Frau Walter (never got to know her Christian name) and her husband Otto was kindness it´s self to Jan she would fuss around her the whole time she was pregnant like a mother hen. During the time Jan was pregnant soldiering had to go on and both Pete and I were out on exercises quite a lot which I felt sorry for her but, at least she had the company of Jean "but" neither of them could speak German or Pete and I at that time and, Frau Walter couldn´t speak English so it was difficult for them both. I was at work when Jan started in labour with our Christine and Jean got Frau Walter to phone for an ambulance for her and as there wasn´t a military hospital in the area she was taken to a German civilian hospital at Padderborn, when I got there she had been born and, she was "beautiful" 4lb 6oz with a touch of jaundice which gave her a beautiful colouring, the nurse past her to me and, on holding her saw what I thought was a "wart" on the side of her nose she´s beautiful and thought, she doesn´t want one of those so, I asked the nurse how long would it be before the hospital can remove it, she was confused at first what I was talking about and, then went on to tell me it was a blob of cream on her nose where she had scratched herself. "WHEW" then, as I am holding her she seemed really, really small, I mentioned this and then, the red cross nurse explained to me by showing me Babies born in Germany don´t have nappies between their legs as we do in England their legs are folded as they are in the womb and wrapped round them "WHEW again"

After about 10 days we brought her home. Jean and Frau Walter were buzzing round her like flies "but" there was a problem while Jan was in hospital they found Christine wouldn´t have the breast and, was put on Glucose and water and, as she was so small she needed to be on four hourly feeds, the problem was, she was such a lazy feeder it took four hours to get a feed into her. She was a good, good; baby rarely cried even later when teething we hardly ever lost any sleep with her.

We managed to scrape enough money together to buy a second hand car which was used mainly to do shopping trips to the NAAFI (supermarket) and when we decided to travel home in it to have our Christine christened the worst possible thing happened we broke down on the Autobahn 15 kilometres Ostende where we were catching the ferry to Dover. We were towed into a garage and waited for an inspection report on the breakdown and cost to repair. It was what I feared the "big ends" had gone, I told them I wouldn´t need it repairing as the cost was almost as much as the car was worth so, I paid the recovery fee and told him he could have it for the scrap value which he deducted from the recovery fee. Jan was in a foul mood all the way home and no amount of explaining made her feel better about the situation.

There was to be another bit of bother with Jan´s mother and our Lizzie, on the day of the christening, Lizzie was to be our Christine´s God mother. So Lizzie and Eddie came over to Jan´s mother´s house and Jan´s mother insisted that she was going to carry our Christine to the church until Lizzie made it quite plain that she wasn´t and left her again with a face like thunder.

We travelled back to Germany to our lodgings by train which took about 14hrs in all. It wasn´t long after that incident Pete and Jean got married quarters and shortly after that we did, we were in a brand new complex of two story flats, with two bedrooms, we chose an upstairs one. Everything we needed was issued free, from cutlery to a cot and in those days rent free also, things were looking up for us a brand new home of decent furniture and totally free.

It was about 6 months later that one day in camp Pete came to me and said that Jean, and he, had decided to quit the army, I was really shocked as I thought he liked it as much as me, and also Jean having a job in the NAFFI and having Jan for company when we were out in the field, everything was ok. He asked me if I wanted his Mercedes, he didn´t want any money for it, just to take the payments over, otherwise, they wouldn´t let him leave with debt owing in Germany. I agreed, and although money would be tight it was too good a bargain to miss. Pete and Lizzie left Germany and it would be 8 years before I met them again. It was soon after they left I was to have the best driving lesson of my life with that Mercedes. Jan had gone back home for a week and I took some mates to a cricket match at another camp I was driving on the autobahn and seeing what speed I could get out of it, I was doing over a 100mph when a huge lorry and trailer pulled straight out in front of me. I hit the brakes and was certain we were going under the trailer and be killed. It frightened the living daylights out me and have "never" drove as fast as that ever again. That was a lesson learned that day.

Jan had difficulty picking the language up, where as I, was thanks, with the help of my troop corporal Reg. C.... who was married to a German girl and could speak it fluent, I was coming on with it, in leaps and bounds. So when the occasion arose that she needed anything from the local shops it was hard for her and something she didn´t like doing, and as time went on it really got her down. My duties in camp, i.e. guard and fire picket which would at times be at weekends still had to be done and, also the amount of time the regiment spent away on exercises was quite a lot i.e., 4-6 weeks away and 2-4 weeks in camp so, I can understand Jan, as a newlywed with a baby it wasn´t too good and, after about 18 months she dropped the bombshell. She was fed up with it all, she had found it difficult to mix with the neighbours, You are not at home enough, I can´t, and don´t want to pick the language up, and as well as all that, being home sick, I just want to go home she was starting to say every time I returned from exercises. We talked it over for hours and hours but I couldn´t talk her into staying, she had made her mind up. So now, I would have about 12 months to serve before, I needed to sign on again but, instead would come out of the army. I was both shocked and unhappy with the situation as I loved the army life, I had no idea life had been so awful for her. Looking back at it all maybe I should have stayed in the army but it wasn´t right to have a wife and child in England and me in Germany, also I would never have met the good and wonderful people ("and" some truly "bad" people) and "true" friends that, was to be another chapter in my life.

When Jan went home and because I couldn´t stay in the married quarter without my wife I had to move back into barracks. It was another bad chapter in my life and, I moved back into camp. Things were not the same after that, being married, having a life together with our baby and, now, we were back to writing letters and phone calls, and at the back of my mind finding a job, "what job"? I didn´t have a trade and didn´t want to go back down the pit again.

Of the many times when we were out in the field, we went to many places and, one of them was the German concentration camp "Belson" (Celle) which is one of the most vivid of my memories of Germany and, "that" is one place that I shall never forget. It´s strange and eerie place, and everyone who was there that day felt the same, the quietness of it and, being totally saddened at the amount of graves that there are in the relatively small area it covers, and, the epitaph "Lest we forget" in dripping blood red letters. Anyone who has seen that, I can promise will never forget it. But all the places weren´t all as sombre as that (for want of a better word) another place was when, we were billeted in barracks, that had been used during the war to give German officers a break from front line duty and help build the supposedly Aryan race, so we were told. And strangely enough in all the places I drove, I only came across 1 German who had fought the British, and he said he was a prisoner in both wars and glad of it. I shook his hand and thanked him for being honest as everyone else told us; they were on the Russian front. One guy told us he was in the Hitler youth and invited us back to his house providing, we brought our own drinks, which, we did, and during the stories he told us he cried telling us of the hardship and brutality he suffered in the Hitler youth, and couldn´t get out of it, and for "what" at the end of the Day. They were not the stories we have been led to believe about those young kids. Another time was, when I and another 3 tanks were broken down with engine trouble and, as it was almost at the end of the exercise they wouldn´t repair us, we were to towed down to the local railway station a by the A.R.V (armoured recovery vehicle) loaded up on flat bottom railway trucks, and after the regiment were on their way, we would follow on. Nobody said anything about lowest priority travel, it took us three more days than the regiment to get back to camp (one of the reasons that really got to Jan) Once we had started our journey we had to pull into sidings and let "any" train have priority so, we didn´t seem to make much progress and on this occasion we stopped at place called Buchen and as we were all running out of fags and could see over the field, some shops, I could speak a little German then and, asked the guard, how long are we stopping here for his reply was 2 hours and made him understand we wanted to buy fags from the shops we could see. Ok was his reply so, I collected monies from the lads and set off. It was a pub we could see and, had to buy the fags out of a machine I never had a drink as we had more than enough on the tanks and as I approached the point where I´d set off from I couldn´t see the train it had gone. Here I was scruffy, not had a good wash for over a week, in my denims no, beret on and can´t see the train. Panic was already was setting in I looked up and down the track then decided to make my way to the station and have a word with the station master about a mile up the track. I explained what had happened and he said that the train had been ordered to go to Buchen Holst which was 35kilometers away but it wouldn´t leave until 0800 next day that was for sure. As I couldn´t understand all he was saying he gave me note which would be a pass for me to travel and to show it to any railway staff. It read Here is a soldier who has lost his way and needs to get to tank train that is at Buchen Holst sidings (I felt like a little boy) the thing he "stressed" was, that at the next station I was to change stations go, across the road for the train to Buchen Holst and only had 5mins to do it in. Well I got to the other station and was running down the platform (when for the second occasion in my life, I thought my life was in mortal danger) Someone was shouting "halt or I shoot" I could understand that much German and had a look over my shoulder as I was running, and realised a policeman had his gun out and was pointing it at me. I was crapping myself, I stopped dead in my tracks (and wonder to this day if I hadn´t had the note in my hand and, had put my hand in my pocket for it, what, would have been the outcome that day) I gave him the note and he let me go on my way and just managed to catch the connection. I arrived at Buchen Holst and, had look up and down the track and couldn´t see the train anywhere so, off I went to the station masters office note in hand, the directions he gave me, was to walk down the track for about 2 kilometres and you will see the train that it will be there until 0800hrs I finally found the train I was absolutely knackered and all the lads could say (winding me up) was, where the f..k have you been for those fags George, to which I said I couldn´t get any. (Winding them up) Those that wanted any change were told to B....cks. I didn´t need any rocking to sleep that night.

Sometime after that incident there was another funny incident, it was when we had a spell in camp. Oscar the likeable rogue, had a letter saying, he had to go home, a. s. a. p. as his father was dying, he rushed around and was gone in a flash and on his way. Two weeks later he was back saying everything went off ok, as regards to the funeral, when he got home, no one at home had any money for the funeral so I soon fixed that he said. He had bought a load of TV's and a multitude of other things on HP and sold them off to pay for the funeral. About 6 months later it all caught up with him. He had to go back to UK to court and If he got prison for fraud that would be the end of his army career that´s for sure. Don´t ask me how he done it, but he had to pay it all back, at a few quid a week which, would take him donkeys years. That´s Oscar the lovable rogue that he was, nothing, ever bothered him, great to know "BUT" do not get involved with, at any cost. I often wonder how he fared in life after the army, well I hope.

On another occasion, we were at a place called Hone that was used as the firing ranges for tanks. I had broken down and was awaiting a spare part to be fitted and as everyone had gone to the ranges decided to go back to my lean-to (a piece of tarpaulin tied to side of the tank as a makeshift tent) and have another sleep after a heavy night on the beer when, I was woken up with poking and grunting at my feet, I opened my eyes to see the biggest wild boar in my life, it was the size of a calf, I let out such a scream I don´t know who was frightened most (that sobered me up instantly) it ran out of the lean-to and when I got outside it was standing about 10yds away it had about 8 or 10 young ones with it. It was looking at me menacingly so I threw a piece of wood at it to chase it away ("BAD MOVE") I hit it and then, it came charging straight for me. I hadn´t any boots on and climbed up a tree and, for ages it stood there looking up at me and snorting grunting my feet were killing me and my hands were hurting holding on so tight, it finally left but kept looking back I gave them a lot of respect after that (an invaluable lesson learned ("don´t throw sticks at wild boar") There were thousands of them running around those ranges but were told they were more than likely to be Rabid otherwise, we would have picked them up to eat, those that were shot on the ranges, and there was a lot. While we were up at the ranges and Hamburg wasn´t too far away, we had a few trips down to the Reeperbahn and even though I had a really healthy sexual appetite I didn´t go off the rails so, had to make do with watching the strippers and porn movies which were in every bar. Also it was while we out there on the ranges that I learned to drive a land rover which in so doing got me my civvy driving licence which has been one of my best assets.

Life trundled on for me after Jan went home, and because I was soon to leave the army was offered a job in the Officers mess as silver man/barman/waiter (which ever you looked and fitted in best) which I took. I learned a lot in the short time I worked there and was "even" given a reference on leaving, from the Adjutant which, he said it would get me a job in any high class hotel or bar in London. Who knows what job I might end doing, I had a whole horizon to go at when I left the army. As well as the skills of making drinks, I became my troop officers Valet which earned me a few extra bob and was left alone to spend my time as I liked when, not on mess duties especially when the regiment was out in field. Although he was an officer we were friends outside of normal army life and spent hours talking about lives as children and it was surprising to me, he had a similar life as myself to a degree, he was sent to boarding school which he hated then on to university, like myself, he had no family life, he had to spend at least 6yrs in the army to be included in the family will which, he hated. I picked up a lot of tips and skills, on cooking while in the Officers mess and, would be there in the kitchen at every opportunity. I became firm friends with the Chef, Jeff who, liked a drink and, it had gotten him in trouble somewhere down the line and, promotion had passed him by but, make no mistake, If he hadn´t been as good and professional as he was, he would "never" have been working in the officers mess. He was given an awful lot of respect by the officers and, was easy to see why, the meals that he created and served up especially, on what they called "Mess night" (When all the Officers who were married and lived out of camp, would bring their wives to the mess once a month for dinner) were "out" of this world which, I could understand they had a 1st class chef working for them and didn´t want to let him go and, until then, I hadn´t seen that side of life. One of the best things about working in the Officers mess was that I got to eat the same meals as the officers it was fantastic although there were things I didn't like. One night as I was in the kitchen eating my meal and Jeff was having a drink Sgt C...... who ran the mess came in and asked what I was doing in kitchen "and" eating in there which, was, strictly out of bounds to any one, Jeff said, he is eating "my" meal, have you a problem with that? He turned and left, the next day Sgt C....... said to me you must be a relative of Jeff´s for you to be allowed in the kitchen, never mind having his meal, and the subject was never brought up again, that´s how much respect Jeff had in the Officers mess kitchen. He was one of three great people in my life who took a shine to me and was very grateful for it, we became friends maybe, because I would get him a drink when he wanted one but, can honestly say I "never" saw him drunk. He was I thought always, deep in thought and sharp with everyone around him but he was never like that with me, why? I don´t know. He would let me help him but, only in much as, passing or sometimes arranging things on plates or dishes, never preparing "BUT" he had let me to a degree into the world of a chef. The tips he gave me on cooking I still use today and, had I been given that job in the officers mess earlier and had met Jeff I would certainly have done the courses and, taken cooking up as a career. I love cooking, I always have, and always will, it is not a chore to me either shopping or preparing or cooking. Maybe I missed my vocation? One of his quote´s was, George "all" meat is tender until the cook gets hold of it. I "still" use that quote to this day and, have been given some nasty looks in my time, when I´ve used it when, people or friends are telling me about how tough some sort of meat has been. The short time I knew him and, the lust I have for cooking I will be forever grateful to him. I do hope he fared well in life after the army I really do.

I managed to sell my Mercedes to Mr G....... 2nd troop leader and got a good price for it which I sent on to Jan as it was needed at home what with the bairn an all. I saved quite a lot of my wages as I rarely left the mess I was eating good food and the drinks were mega cheap. It was the "first" time in my life that I couldn´t spend my weekly wages. One day Capt P......e from B Squadron came to me and asked if I would go and pick his car up from a hotel for him, he had arranged for a land rover to take me there and drive his back to the Officers mess "WOW" it was a "new 250 SL Mercedes sport" a dream of car to drive. I was like a dog with two tails and, couldn´t get over the fact that, he had chosen me to do him this favour; I "never" thought I was that "well" liked. This was the another side of life I hadn´t seen where, money was no object to them, a far cry from being born into poverty and spending half a lifetime getting to where you are comfortable through hard graft and, not just by being born and given everything on a plate. The time came for me to leave the army. I was thanked by most of the officers for my services in the mess. I managed to have a great night out with the lads before leaving. I was both sad and happy to leave, sad, because I was leaving all my friends behind and the life style and, happy because, I was going to be with my wife and daughter again. I had saved quite a bit of money by the time I was to be demobbed from the army which was to be used to set up a home, when that was to be I had no idea what I did know for sure was, that it took years to get a council house in those days.

It took a bit of getting used to once I got home, not being in the army and the routine you get into and also the fact I knew no one outside the home, home being at Jan´s mother´s which I certainly didn´t like and after a very short time it was beginning to show. There was no privacy and, the meals were hardly ever what I wanted and, especially after the meals I had been having in the Officers mess, yes, I had been spoilt forever in that department. I searched everyday for a job and, there was, plenty on offer but, the pay was mega poor, sometimes even less than the army, in the end I decided to go back to the pits, at least until I could get a better job. After all, I now had a wife and daughter to keep. I´d been home about six weeks when I decided that I would go to the pit I´d worked at before, joining the army which, seemed a life time had gone by and not just 6yrs, only to be told be told there wasn´t any vacancies, I was gutted I was told the reason why, while I was in the army they had closed the West Durham coal field and any miner who wanted to be transferred to the coast pits could do so, and that´s why there´s no vacancies. The training officer went on to say there are lots, of pits in Yorkshire wanting workers and, even gave assistance to miners who wanted to transfer there and, as you are unemployed the dole will give you the same assistance, sounds good I thought if, that´s what you want, I thought, I would "always" get a job at the pit however, that´s progress for you. Something came to mind just as I was about leave his office I asked him how long this assistance payment transferring to the Yorkshire pits has been in force, 3yrs or more he said. I thought back to the time in Bahrain when my sister had asked me for money to move them to Yorkshire. The subject hadn´t been brought up when I´d arrived back from the middle-east as I had forgotten about it. I went home, told Jan the prospect of moving to Yorkshire and, after a few days decided to give it a try, in the pits in Yorkshire. I wrote and asked my sister if I could lodge with them until I got a house, if, I did manage to get a job. They agreed and, went down and got a job at the pit where Alf worked. I´ll always remember the training officers words to me after the interview, he said," in broad Yorkshire" "well lad thars made a good choice coming here" there´s a 100yrs work left in this pit" he hadn´t anticipated Margaret Thatcher coming on the scene. "No one" at that time would have dreamt what would happen to the mining industry.

I was glad that at least I now had a job and could move forward. I went back home told Jan all about it and, the prospect of getting a house was about 3 months. I travelled down to Yorkshire at the week-end with my belongings and set off on another chapter of my life.

It was now March and the weather was still cold, I started work on nights at the pit bottom and didn´t know a soul, memories of starting my first shift at Easington colliery in the north-east came flooding back, and knowing how cold it was going to be, from past experience, wore my old army clothing to keep warm. There I was fully dressed in army clothing, like I was going on parade, I must have stood out like a blind cobblers thumb but, I wasn´t having any of that being cold, as I was when I first started work at Easington as a kid.

It wasn´t long before I made friends and surprisingly, there were a few lads who had just come out of the army the same time as me, we swapped stories about postings etc. The need for extra money was paramount and it was my luck that my nephew Thomas was an electrician and could get me overtime, working at week-ends labouring for them, I didn´t mind what the job was as long as I was earning money. It wasn´t too long before I picked up that it wasn´t what you knew or capable of at that pit but, "who" you knew. Working as much overtime as I could get, it worked out that I could get to see Jan and the bairn after I had been on nightshift, overtime providing as sometimes I could get a Sunday afternoon shift in, we needed the money so badly, now, we were going to set up home, which, wouldn´t be too long now so, there wasn´t much moaning coming from Jan as she too was getting mighty fed up of living at her mother´s by now. On one occasion I hired a car from a local garage which worked out as cheap as the train fare plus the fact it was door to door and could leave later on my return. These cars were old bangers that´s why they were so cheap to hire. On one occasion I had only drove about 8 miles from the garage up the A1 when suddenly the engine cut out I managed to coast into a lay by, where there were several cars already parked up, and got the bonnet up to investigate the problem. I didn´t notice a car had pulled up behind me and when I´d fixed the problem(a loose lead from the distributor) and was putting the bonnet down I noticed this guy was jacking the car up. I said what the f...k are you doing? He said if "you" are having the "battery" I´m having the "wheels". I told him it was a hire car, he started laughing and said sorry mate I thought it was an abandoned car. I told lots of people that story and many years later a comedian at the club, came out with the same story as a joke.

After about 4 months we had been given a house and moved in, and, £50 towards the expense of moving, like, my sister and Alf, had been paid. It was a colliery house and they were only 25yrs old, and the rent was cheap. One incident that happened after moving into our home, our Christine, was about 4, at the time and, like Jan she found it hard to mix. The kids next door who were 5 and 7yr olds were VERY big for their age and Jan said, several times she had ,had, to check them as they were constantly hitting her and running off into their house or taking Christine´s toys off her,, and breaking them, I said it´s only kids playing one minute they are falling out and the next minute they are friends again until, one day as I was having my dinner looking through the window at them playing in the garden the Stephen the eldest started to punch the bairn in the chest pushed her down kicked her and started to break her toys I tapped on the window and he ran into the house. I picked the toys up, I was furious, I banged on their door Steve the father and May the mother came out and I said to them,

I´ve just watched your lad give our Christine a good hiding and he has broken these toys, he shouted for him, and admitted he´d done it, and sent him in the house, to deal with him. I said to Steve to make sure that it doesn´t happen again, I will come in here, and get hold of you, and, "one" of us is going to be in hospital and, it´s not going to be me, and if you want to start now we can do. I´m absolutely fed of your kids picking on our Christine. He apologised and walked in, and those kids never picked on her again. We were good neighbour´s after that and, young Stephen went on to become a policeman. Another incident I´ll always remember is after moving into our new home. I took our Christine up to the local shops in her pushchair with me, did what shopping I had to do and walked home without her. I´d left her outside one of the shops. Jan went ballistic when she realised what I´d done and rightly so. It was my first telling off from Jan but, when we got back to the shops where I´d left her she was still there oblivious of what had happened thank goodness. All down to tiredness I suppose but the consequences could have been dire.

I still worked as much overtime as I could and, we soon had a home put together, and also meeting more and more people and, making new friends. After about 6 months I was asked if I wanted to do my coalface training which, caused a bit of a fuss because, other local lads had been waiting longer than me. It was sorted in the end by the Union and because my attendance record was 100% the animosity stopped and we were all friends although I could never get used to being called a foreign b.....d by them, if the word b.....d was used (an expression used by most people at this pit, not as a insult but), where I came from in the north-east, to us, that word meant you had to get your fists up.

I started on my coalface training and was glad as it was a lot more money per shift than what I was on now. There were three jobs you were trained for the coalface bringing roof supports in and pushing the steel conveyor to the face after the coal had been cut and the coal face ends ie. keeping roof supports up to date so the coal cutting machine could start a new cut of coal and a job called Ripping it entailed taking the stone above the coalface after it had been cut out and, set arch girders, to extend the airway road to the coalface. It was normally blasted down but if there was a lot of gas there it had to be taken down by an air pick and this was one of those. It was peace work i.e. the more you did the more you got paid, it was hard work and very dusty, make, no mistake, and a lot of men were not prepared to do it, even though the money was a lot more than working on the coalface because, it meant a lot of the time you were working under "unsupported" ground at times. I started on my ripping training and met the 3rd person in my life who took a shine to me."Joe" and even though he was 20yrs older than me he had the greatest influence on my life and, became a "lifetime" friend who I will "NEVER" forget as long as I live. He was like a father to me He was the charge man on the job and told me what was required of me and that the training would take 8 weeks. I went home that day more tired than I had ever been in my life, even the time I had, had rheumatic fever. After the first week we were having a food break, (when everyone should stop for 20mins to eat) called "snap time" in Yorkshire pits and "bait time in the North-East pits. Joe said to the other 3 men, you can get your hands in your pockets this Friday "we are" (not will you) we are giving this lad 10/- a man (50pence today), this lad has worked his goolies off since he came on the job and, it has made a vast difference to our check (pay per shift) and, that´s what they gave me every week after that, on top of my pay.

(And no tax to pay on it) As my training was coming to an end one of the older guys, Bernard, said he was coming off the job as it was getting too much for him he was 46yrs old and was knackered, he had been doing the same work for 26years and was going onto the coalface where it was lighter work. That left Joe, Jim and Bill, and Joe said to me, if you want his job you can have it. I jumped at it. I couldn´t believe my luck, here I was, not even finished my training and, had a job that was going to pay me as much, in one shift, as I was getting for a week. That was a perfect example of, not "what" you know but "who" you know. As a charge man you had the right to pick your own team of men and Joe had picked me, out of all the men he knew, I must have certainly impressed him. It once again it caused a fuss and bother with the lads who had finished their training and, were in, what you called a "market pool" where you would be sent to fill in for anyone who was absent that day. Hence the three stages of training. He told me a long time after, that I reminded him of him self i.e. coming out of the army, skint, desperately needing money, a good worker "but", wasn´t in the "know" then and couldn´t get a regular job. I went home that day on "cloud nine" told Jan and we were both, well, well excited at the prospect of earning that much money per week. It wasn´t long before everything we had on HP was paid off and, were replacing the furniture for better quality and being able pay cash for them. If we had not been buying and replacing furniture it was the "second" time in my life that I couldn´t spend my weekly wage because, I had everything I needed and, it felt "fantastic". We booked our first holiday since I had come out of the army to Yarmouth, and couldn´t believe it, I got sunstroke on the last day of our holiday. After spending 12 months in the Persian Gulf to get sunstroke in England seemed incredible.

During the early stages of my new job, Jan´s Dad had died and Jan´s mother Winnie had to get out of the pit house they had lived in for years as was the NCB ruling in those days and her coal allowance as a widow was greatly reduced. We had bought ourselves a car by this time, and, had Jan´s mother and, two youngest sisters down to stay with us on several occasions that is to say, when I went for them in the car at no cost to them for the journey or, their stay and the return journey, I didn´t mind in the least it was my in-laws and they were not well off. Every Xmas and New year that came around was spent at Jan´s mother´s and one Xmas in particular I remember was when everyone had gone to bed Jan and I were helping her mother Winnie wrap the presents up she said I´m giving you this for your Xmas box George, it was a bottle of aftershave, you have been good to us these last couple of years and deserve it. Normally it was a box of three hankie´s. The next morning there was such a loud shouting and bawling going off I got out of bed to see what was going off, it was Jan´s sister saying "you are not" giving my husband that as a Xmas present and Winnie had to swap my aftershave for the hankie´s to keep the peace with her. Such was Jan´s family. On another occasion Jan and I had booked a 6 berth Caravan down in Devon for 2 weeks Jan suggested we ask if her youngest sister could come with us. As she had never, had a holiday, and, we could use her for babysitting, in no time at all Jan´s mother and another sister had jumped on the band wagon. It won´t cost anymore Jan said, all those beds are not being used anyway. I drove up to Durham the night before we were going on holiday and brought them down and set off in the early hours in the next morning to Devon. The arrangements were that Winnie and the other sister paid for their own food and we kept the youngest one, as she would be babysitting for us. After only 2 Days we went to the camp super market and noticed Winnie and the two sister´s stood outside, what´s wrong with them I said, Jan went out and asked them and after a while came back and said, they´ve no money. Bernard one of her brothers had borrowed their holiday money and was sending it on to them and it should have arrived today but it hasn´t, and it never did, so I had to keep them all, and, going out drinking for the rest of the 2 weeks. You will get what we owe you when we get home Winnie said, when we did get home Bernard had, had, to pay some urgent debts off and had no money left. I was never repaid.

On another occasion one Xmas when we were going up I had changed my car for a Mercedes and Jan´s mother asked her could we possibly bring some coal up as they had none at all. Talk about "taking coals to Newcastle it sounded like a joke. Why can´t your 2 brother´s who work at pit give your mother some coal I asked, it´s so cold up there they need it for themselves she said. I filled the large boot of the Mercedes with large clean paper bags of coal, the car looked like an aeroplane ready for take off as we drove up to Durham. It was bitter cold when we arrived and the first thing Winnie asked us, have you brought some coal, two of Jan´s brother´s they were 15 and 16yr olds, were in the front room with blankets wrapped around them, huddled round a tiny fire, I said come on you two let´s get this coal out of the boot of my car before the springs break. They both got up and to my amazement said we are going out in a couple of minutes and don´t want to get dirty. I was shocked I went into the kitchen and told Winnie she said don´t worry George I will give you a hand, she was 60 at the time I said no you won´t and said to Jan you and our Christine get back in the car we are going home, "or" stay here, I said and I´m "not" kidding. Why? she said, I told her and, got back in the car, she could see I was "livid" as we drove off, I said, to her that´s gratitude for you, I bring all this coal 105miles from Yorkshire risking the springs on my car and they won´t help me to unload it, they can freeze for all I care. About a mile down the road I found a roundabout in darkness and unloaded the coal. Thank God there were no police about. Neither she nor Christine spoke a word to me all the way home. That was the last time as a family we went to Jan´s mother´s for Xmas or New Year.

It was about 1967-8 that our Alice had been in touch with our Lizzie and told her aunt Rose had made a visit to her house in Horden she had given her, her address in Nottingham in case any one wanted to keep in touch and also mentioned uncle Bill had died I know this might sound awful to some people but I was elated. I couldn´t feel any other way after the way he had treat both Jane and I when we went to live with them. One week-end I decided to pay her a visit and took Jan and our Christine as they hadn´t met anyone from my mother´s side of the family and also the opportunity to show off our daughter. She was quite surprised to see me and gave us a warm welcome. She never brought the subject up about me being in the homes and neither did I how I wished that I had I´m sure I would have gained a lot more knowledge of my childhood but I just didn´t have heart to question her as she really looked very old and frail. She invited us to stay the night and to go to their social club with her and Dave who I remembered as a child as uncle Bill´s mate. That evening as aunt Rose was getting ready I had noticed during the day that her hair was to say the least looking rough she was putting her make up on when suddenly she whipped a wig off showing that she was as bald as a billiard ball and said this is what that b.....d Billy Carter did to me. I was absolutely gob smacked it was then that I mentioned how frightened I´d been of him as a child and that I would never have visited her had I not known he was already dead because of my hatred of him. She said you only had a short spell of it I had to endure years of it until my bairns grew up. How deeply sorry I felt for her. She never mentioned any of her family except that her second eldest daughter had, had a child out of wedlock and that she had disowned her and brought the child up herself from being a baby in arms. There was no mention of her or Ma´s sisters either but at that stage in my life I had no intention of researching my family history and as I say deeply, regret not asking any questions about the family. She did give me a photo of Ma the first I´d seen in my life and one of Grandma and years later another of Ma was given me from Jane the only two in existence. I did write to her for a while but the contact dried up and it was years later I was to learn that she had died.

As time went on I found that both Joe and Jim had both served in the Para´s and Jim went on to the S.A.S. he was powerfully built, and, the strongest man I have ever met in my life. It was extremely hard work but, the pay was good, there was many a time getting showered my arms would lock because of the shovel work I´d done i.e. 6 ½ hours shifting about 30 ton of stone onto a steel conveyer this, was the norm, for any job on ripping and the only reason you did it was your "lust" for earning money, which, I now well and truly had and, has never left me. Of course like every good thing in life, it must come to an end and it did. The unit (coalface) had gone to the boundary of the colliery. It was a sorry day for all as; this was the last, contract ripping at the pit. We would all be working on the next unit on N.P.L.A. National Power Loading Agreement. On a fixed rate of pay which meant that instead of a four man team on ripping there would be a six man team and, in the eyes of the Union, make the job lighter and so; be able to work at the job longer. No one who had made this deal took into account that it worked out that "everyone" is paid the same as the most "idle" man there. We did start on the new unit and our four man team became six, the two new men were taking a lot of time off work hoping to be taken off the job so, we were getting staffed up with men from the market pool nearly every day. The job was made lighter "but" the pay was less than half and it was hurting like hell. So one day Jim said there´s a private firm Cementation Mining, (sub contractors) who are setting on at a pit about 5 miles up the road doing the same as what we doing now and three times as much money that we are getting here. I´ll give that a try I said, Joe said no straight away saying he was getting too old at 46 to start travelling around to different pits, but get yourselves off the two of you he said, your only young once. Jim was 7yrs older than me but, we were of the same frame of mind, a "lust" for earning good money. It didn´t matter how hard the work was, as long as it paid well. We went to the site told the foreman our work experience and said he would set us on now BUT there was a "snag" so the firm were not accused of poaching N.C.B. men, you had to have been out of work or working for someone else for six weeks before they could set us on. That was a body blow, as neither of us had expected that. This meant 8 weeks before we actually started work with Cementation working two week´s notice, just in case things went wrong and had to come back, and six week´s at another job. We got ourselves a job Alf went to the steelworks at Scunthorpe I didn´t want the travelling and shift work. I hated nightshift I´ve always said that, if God had intended us to be awake at night, why did he give us eyelids? I never missed any work but when I was on nights in the afternoon I would start with every ache you could get why? I don´t know but, once I got to work I was ok. And of course once you are down the pit it doesn´t matter what shift you are on its still the same pitch black dark. I got a job as relief milkman at the local Coop it meant, starting early but, getting up early was not, and never has been, any problem. The pay was crap I´d been earning more a shift than what this job was paying a week. Good job it was only for 6 weeks. The relief round I was given was in the village where I lived that´s great I thought and, on my first day at the dairy, I was conned twice, like every new starter. I was told how many crates of milk, orange juice etc. to load up and noticed that my float had far more on it than the others. I found out later the round was so much bigger than the rest that no one would take it because, as soon as you finished and unloaded, counted the milk checks, you could go home which meant it was a good couple of hours later than the rest of the rounds. I was waiting for the foreman to get the round book off him when a woman shouted could I please help her load up as she wasn´t feeling too good so I started to load up as she went off somewhere, I´d almost finished loading up for her when the foreman appeared saw, what I was doing and said, "don´t fall for that one again mate, there´s nothing wrong with her, she´s a lazy b.....d and tries it on with anyone who falls for it. As the saying goes, once bitten twice shy and it didn´t happen again. I had a sweat on before I even started that day. It was February dark with snow on the ground and glad, I´d put two pair of socks on with my "wellies" but, my hand´s were dropping off with the cold and I couldn´t grip the bottles with gloves on. Thank God this was only for 6 weeks. About half an hour after I set off I had to go into the side gate of one house and in the pitch black dark, this fairly large dog came out at me barking its head off it, scared the living daylights out of me, I didn´t leave them any milk I can tell you. At another house where I had to go in the side gate a cat jumped off a wall onto my head screaching and hissing, if I hadn´t had a woolly hat on which it pulled off before running off I might have needed the doctor. These "frights" were more than I wanted for the money they were paying me. I was getting disheartened by the minute. I was only two hours into the job and had, had the living day lights frightened out me, roll on day light, so I have a chance of seeing these animals coming for me. I´d finished the round and probably taken the longest on record to do it, I had to pass the houses where the dog and cat had jumped out at me this woman where the dog lived came running up and said "HEY" you haven´t left me any milk she said, I went on to tell what her dog had done, she was sorry, she said, my husband had gone to work and left him in the garden, it won´t happen again she said and besides he wouldn´t bite you he´s a big softie (they all say that) ok I said. In the next street, was where the cat had attacked me, a woman stopped me to tell me I hadn´t left her any milk and when I explained about the cat she accused me of hitting or kicking it for it to attack me. I told the foreman about the incidents, he said you did right lad, tell them if it happens again they won´t be left any milk in future. The next day that "bloody" dog was there again and the same thing happened only this time the crate of milk slipped out my hand with six full bottles in it and, I shot out of the gate, there such a din with the bottles breaking and the dog barking even louder, I waited a few minutes for the woman to come out but she didn´t so, I continued and, when I had to pass the house going back to the dairy I called to pick up the crate but there was no answer so I reported it to the foreman and said he would see to it. He got the crate back that afternoon, charged her for the milk and, then told her there would be no more milk deliveries. I can guess what sort of telling off she gave her husband. I was now on day three at my new job and already in someone´s black book. The rest of the six weeks went by without any more animal incidents.

There were two more incidents that I can remember though, and the first happened one Saturday morning, when I collecting monies for milk I´d delivered that week and went to a house where the woman was standing at the front door in a see- through negligee it was open and I could see was wearing stockings "WOW" I thought my "lucky" day this, fits in with some of the milkman tales we have all heard about. I didn´t notice at first because my eyes were looking elsewhere but as I got closer I noticed the face, it was a guy dressed as a woman, I was shocked it was the first time I´d ever seen a transvestite or, a cross dresser in my life. He wasn´t embarrassed at all, he said in an ordinary man´s voice, how much do I owe you, paid and walked in the house. I couldn´t wait to tell the lads in the club. The other incident happened one day when I was calling for money at another house this old guy said come in out of the cold lad he went on to say that he brewed his own beer and wines and, would I like to try some. Being as it was at the end of my round I did. Firstly he gave me a small glass of beer which tasted ok, then another then another till I´d had about two pints in all. I said to him I would love to stop but, I´ve got get back to the Dairy, well I set off for the dairy and almost immediately I felt like I´d had about 7 or 8 pints I got back to the Dairy and was glad I hadn´t been stopped by the police and that was another invaluable lesson about drinking and driving which has lasted me to this day "DON´T DRINK AND DRIVE".

I left the dairies and Jim and I started work for Cemmo as everyone called it. We started on development work, making new roadways and coal faces. It was the first time I´d been on this type of work, a job which I didn´t know at the time, I would do for the rest of my life in pit work. The money was as good as they said it would be, and at times even more. It´s a strange thing working in the pits when the conditions are good you earn good money and when the conditions are bad you earn less money, common sense would make you think it to be the other way round but, I never found that in all the 29 years I worked down the pits (5 in all) At one pit Jim and I worked at, there was a short spell where we were earning almost twice as much a shift as a man working on the pit top for N.C.B was earning in a week. Yes, we were working hard, "Dammed" hard but, the guy on the pit top was only being paid a pittance that´s how pit work went then. NOT GOOD. We had almost 4 years at private contracting at different pits until one day Jim and I had a massive fall out with the site engineer who was short changing us so we left. Jim went further north with another firm (once again I didn´t want the travelling) and I went back to my original pit and, the three of us always met up for a drink on Sunday mornings whenever we could.

It was during this time that Sarah the third eldest of our Alice´s children the one who I´d had to take with me as a teen-ager came to see me and Jan. She was heartbroken and asked me if I could help her to get away from home. She went on to tell me the sad story about her mother having stolen her savings. She was courting and saving up with her boyfriend and her mother had found her bank book which she had hidden. The reason why it was hidden was obvious; any monies found in your pockets some or all would be taken by our Alice and any knowledge of it would be denied as always. She only found out about the money being stolen from her account when she went to report the bank book lost, and found out that withdrawals had been made from it. As she had never made a withdrawal the police were called in Alice was summoned to the police station and after several hours admitted it. Saying it was done to give Alf some drinking money, Sarah, against the police advice didn´t press charges. It was a great mistake on Sarah´s part as another incident years later concerning her and her husband could have had grave consequences and yet again Alice managed to get away with it.

I explained to her that that was sadly the norm for her mother. Thomas and Lucy had both had it done to them in turn and that as a teen-ager I had had the same done to me and told her about the watch her parents had stolen from me as a child Lucy had all her savings which were in cash stolen out of the house just before her wedding day imagine that. Something did come good out of it for her though. As our John had been invited to the wedding he took her to the church in his Rolls Royce and let her have his cottage in Whitby for her honeymoon. Shortly after they stayed with Jan and I until they got a house of their own. I went on to tell Sarah that she could stay with Jan and I for as long as she wished. I took her home to pick up her belongings and when I asked our Alice why she had done it was told to mind my own business and good riddance to her. I said before leaving how can you steal from your own child only to be told; you don´t know half of what I´ve got to put up with. Sarah stayed with me until finally she went to live at her boyfriend´s house and got married from there. On the New Years Eve of that year Jan and I went out for the night out with our Alice and Alf, Thomas and his wife. We took our Christine up so she would have some young company and also it would be a long night of drinking as was the norm for New Years Eve. Alf had been off work for some time so to help him pay for the nights drinking I gave him £10 A big mistake on my part because at the end of the night it ended up a disaster. All went well during the evenings drinking and during the small hours the subject got round to me having Sarah stay with me. You know the reason why don´t you I asked Alf. His reply was, why should she have money when I haven't got any was one of the comments he made. I just shook my head in wonderment and thought of the £10 I'd given him to help pay for his night out. There hadn't been a moment's hesitation in taking it I told him she did right asking me for a place to stay and would have been upset had she not asked me first after what her own mother had done. Then things got a bit heated when I mentioned about him taking me at five years old to be put in a children's home, never coming to see me and then taking me out of the homes when they found out from our Lizzie and Eddie that you could get paid for me. The answer I got was go up stairs get your bairn out of bed and GET out. My last words to him as we left the house was; the truth hurts doesn't it? It was about three in the morning and we had a good two miles to walk home but; it was something that I'd wanted to say to him for years. Looking back at it all I should have mentioned the watch that was stolen from me and wondered if the reason why he took it was like Sarah having money and him not but I never got around to it While walking in the cold I thought to myself what an idiot I was for giving him that £10 then to be thrown out in the early hours of the morning with a young bairn. It was about two years before we spoke again and I made certain it was he who spoke to me first.

I started working with Joe again and working with him was a dream as I had never worked with anyone like him before, or since, everything went like clockwork for us, we knew what each other was thinking and doing at all times it was like telepathy, of all the people I worked with I never had that sort of experience. On one of our drinking sessions the subject came around to decorating in the house he said I don't do any of that. I was surprised only for the fact that until I came to Yorkshire I'd never heard of men doing home decorating, it was always done by women in the north-east. He said when he was first married and got their first house Hilda his wife said we´ll get stuck in together, and get the house decorated, I told her I don´t want anyone around me when I´m working, you get yourself out for the day and I´ll get it done. I still laugh to this day with what he said next. Sure enough Hilda went off for the day and when she came home and had a look at the decorating she screamed at me and said what the effing hell have you done. I´ve done my best he said, your best she screamed, look at it, there was more paint on the windows than was on the frames four lengths of wallpaper had been put on upside down in one of the corners of the room The ceiling you could see every brush mark and paint, there´s more paint on the floor than on the skirting boards. He said I never got asked to do the decorating since that day. The same happened with doing the dishes I never did the dishes unless I broke some so never got asked to do that job either. Then there was the lawn and boarders of the front garden. Hilda asked me to put some weed killer on the lawn and borders as the weeds were coming through fast and furious so I got some weed killer off a my mate who worked on the railways that they used on railway sidings BUT he forgot to tell me that nothing would grow for 10yrs, and guess what I don´t have to do any gardening either. The only job Hilda would let me do after that was to fill the coal buckets up. I don´t know to this day if any of this was all true or, he was kidding me on but, I still laugh about it to this day.

After some time I did notice that his pace had slowed down and was now taking time off work, it was a few years later that it became clear as to why.

Joe and I were now working on repair work in the road ways i.e. Replacing bent arch girders so the conveyor belts could run straight, it was the same money per shift as working on the coalface or ripping, and once again Joe´s being in the "know", got us lots of overtime. Jan and I bought our selves a brand new car the first and only, new car, I ever bought, a "Ford Capri" the reason it was to be the only new car I ever bought was the trouble I had with it i.e. On the second day of owning it I went to our garage to take it out and it had a puncture. Not Ford´s fault. On the 3rd week I noticed rust in the one of the headlights. Not Ford´s fault, I took it back under warranty. On the 5th week I found rust on the front and rear bumper´s once again, exchanged under warranty. After about 2 months realised breaking over 60m.m.p.h the steering wheel was hard to control bent disk´s and Steering damper once again replaced under warranty. When it was returned a buzzing noise was in the dashboard when travelling over 60 M.P.H. after several visits it was never ever found. After 3 months while polishing it, I found grit in the primer coming through the paint work it was re sprayed under warranty. After 4 months decided to have it rust proofed for £200 with a 10 year guarantee and when fitting a stereo unit, found there was no rust proofing in the side box sections Not Ford´s fault. The garage I bought it from, called it a "Monday Morning" car AND I do believe them, it all took all the pleasure away of owning a new car. Little did I know at the time of all this that, in nine months I would have to sell it.

On one of the visits to Jan´s family, I took Jan and the bairn to Medomsley to show them the homes, where I had been in, I was so interested and excited that they were still there that I failed to see the sign at the top of the drive that it was now a Detention Centre for young offenders and wasn´t until one of the guards was tapping on my car window with his trungeon asking me, what we were doing, that I realised what it was. Didn´t you see the big sign at the top of the drive one of them said, sorry I said and went on to tell them that I was showing my wife and child where I lived when this was a children´s home in the forty´s. He said don´t get out of the car and you must leave in 5 minutes, I couldn´t explain 7 years in five minutes so we left. It was several years later that I took Lucy to see it, the Detention Centre had closed, and was now some security depot and they allowed Lucy and I to walk around it, that brought a lot of sad and some good memories back I´ll tell you, I was amazed that in the village a lot of it was still intact, the sweet shop where I used to spend my pocket money If Jane didn´t catch me first, the church and chapel I went to every Sunday. The garage on the corner of the crossroad where we had pinched the tyres from, and the picture house in Consett were still there, but, as like most villages the picture house, was now a bingo hall.

It was in 1973 Jan dropped her second bombshell. Our Christine had been at school for some time now and Jan had got herself a job which fitted in nicely with her school times. Her boss, Bob, was a nice enough guy to get on with and on the odd occasion went for a drink with him. I never noticed anything suspicious until we had parted as to Jan´s pay "always" being the same even, when she had a day off or, went into work late. There were several times when, my shift work provided her the opportunity to go into work after, the shop had closed and help him out with his book work for extra money (she was good at figure´s) but, I wasn´t looking or felt that there was anything suspicious she was earning some extra pocket money for herself. It´s a true saying, the one who is being deceived is "always the last to know because, you are not looking for it, and yet it´s staring you in the face.

After a while I started to go out with him on a Friday night. One particular Friday my mate, Keith, from work was with me and Bob suggested a trip over to a "stagnight" show over at Castleton rugby club, in two weeks time, we agreed to meet at the pub, Keith was going to drive. We met at the pub two weeks later, and after waiting a good while decided, Bob was not going to turn up so, we set off only to find that it had been on the week previous. We decided then for Keith to take his car home and, would have a drink in his local club. After a few beers, I decided I would have an early night and went home. It was about 10-45 pm when I arrived home not, the usual 11-30pm. What happened next was, "one" of the saddest days of my life and became the 1st body blow that I would never get over. I couldn´t get in the back door as it was locked which was unusual I then went to the front door, tried that, it too was locked which, was usual, knocked, got no answer then went back to the back door .Jan opened it wearing a negligee which I hadn´t seen before. I said what´s going off why are both the doors locked? Why are you home early she said, I answered, why are you looking in a panic, it was you, she said going to both doors which threw me in a panic. I went into the sitting room and could see the front door was slightly open and also noticed that there were cigarette stubs in the ashtray. Jan didn´t smoke and, when I saw which brand they were "Peter Stuyvesant" I knew Bob A...... had been in my house, there was no mistake about it, she could not lie her way out of it, whether they had sex, which looked likely being the way she was dressed. That b..... rd had been in my house. I went ballistic. I quickly worked it out that, as she was letting me in the back door, she was letting him out of the front door. I was bawling and shouting at the top of my voice asking why? Why? How could you do it? I wanted to hit her so hard; I would put her in hospital at least. If our Christine hadn´t come down stairs then, I´m sure I would have, I was raging. All her attention went, on settling her down and, taking her back to bed. She came down, said she was so sorry it had happened and, that it was the first and only time that Bob had been to our house and that he had come looking for you. You´ve got it all wrong, it´s not what you think. "PLEASE, PLEASE" nothing went off believe me. I couldn´t believe a word she was saying. Knowing that it had been planned by her and Bob to send Keith and I on a wild goose chase over to Castleford to get us out of the way was getting to me. (The B......ds) I was in shock, I couldn´t talk or say anything by this time. My mind was full of, how Christine and I were going to cope because, one thing´s for certain "SHE" is going. She went on pleading and begging for forgiveness for letting Bob into the house until day light. I made the mistake of telling her that I was going to the shop to sort him out. By the time I got to the shop, she had phoned him that I was on my way to see him, he had left, no one knew where, I told the staff what had gone off the night before and when I get my hands on him "he" is going to get the hiding of his life. It was sometime later; one of the staff told me that, when he left the shop that morning, he had gone to live with his mother in Elland. He had dropped Jan like, a hot potato which, I was glad about but, it just shows what a spineless b....rd he was. I never went to work that day I couldn´t, it was the first I´d missed since going back to work with Joe. I went to his house to explain to him what had happened, he was devastated, he said if there was "anything" he could I was only to ask. The following day I went back to work and everyone could see there was something wrong, I wasn´t my usual perky self but, I couldn't tell anyone there was only Joe and I who knew and he wouldn´t tell a soul. It took 3 weeks to work out what was to happen next. Our Christine wouldn´t hear of her mother going to live somewhere else and, just us two living together. I had decided "foolishly" I would tell her the truth when, she got older what had gone off, and that her mum and I could no live together anymore. Thinking foolishly, that as much, as I hated

Jan now, I didn´t, want to paint her "black" to our Christine at such a young age. It was a decision I would regret for the rest of my life as this story unfolds.

As family life had stopped now and, our marriage could never be repaired, there were 3 unhappy people living in the house, and the atmosphere could be cut with a spoon. I decided (foolishly again) that I would leave and that way Christine would have a good home and not have her schooling disrupted and still have the few friends she had made around her. I had looked around for accommodation and settled on buying a caravan. I packed my things and left telling the bairn that I wouldn´t be forgetting her and that I would be seeing lots of her and that things would still be the same only, I wouldn´t be living at home. How else can you explain to a 9 yr old child, it was heartbreaking (how I hated that woman) because of the bairn Jan, was living in a home, second to none after what she had done to us was eating away at me, the crying, our Christine did, in the early stages of me walking out and me desperately, wanting to tell her the truth about me and her mum splitting up, was killing me. I moved into my caravan on a site which was a couple of miles from where my home was. It was September and the weather was good there wasn't a garage I could rent, and the thought of leaving a new car outside to the elements in winter I decided to sell my dream car even though I´d had all the problems with it. I sold it to a dealer and only lost £350 on it and that was including the £200 rust proofing. I went to the auctions and bought another car as there were no buses to get to work on day shift. When Jan found out I´d sold it, she wanted half the money as, we had bought it when were together I refused and "that" was, when all the dirty tricks began, and to think she had caused the breakdown of our marriage I couldn´t believe the stunts she pulled. She had packed in work (the shame of it I suppose) and was now on benefits. I didn´t care what her plight was my bairn would always be alright. I was taken to court by the Social Security to pay her maintenance, I went to see a solicitor and after a while he said to me that as she was denying the adultery and, there were no witnesses and no Bob to be found there wasn´t a good case, In the end after explaining my side of the story I had to pay her £2 a week, can you believe it, she had committed the adultery, and I had to give her money and, she was living cost free because of our Christine "Is there a God". I had to pay £10 a week to our Christine that was ok because at the time I was giving her £20 anyway besides pocket money. I asked the solicitor about a divorce and he advised me to wait until we had been separated 3yrs when I could apply on the grounds of separation at some cost to me or, wait 5 yrs and the cost would be only a few quid which, I did. Jan was found, not only to be a liar and a cheat, and, what hurt me most was, that she was the mother of my child "she", was definitely "not" the girl I had married. I hadn´t spoken to Jan since the day I left, only, if it concerned our Christine, I always told our Christine when, I would be calling for her. Two days before that first Xmas we had parted I asked Jan if she was staying at home for Xmas and she said yes, so I said I would bring our Christine´s Xmas presents up on Xmas eve. I arrived to find the house in darkness thinking all kinds of things, had, she not paid the electric bill, had the lights fused "never" in a million years thinking what she "had" done, after a few minutes of knocking, the neighbour, next door came out and said, it no good knocking George, she went up to her mother´s yesterday. I was livid to think she could do this to our daughter not being able to open her Da´s Xmas presents on Xmas Day. (But there was much, much more to come over the years) I decided not to go racing off to Durham as I knew I would get arrested for what I had in mind for her. It wasn´t until the bairn had to come back in January for school that I could give her, her presents. Jan said it was unexpected; her brother had come down for her. I never asked the bairn to confirm that story I certainly wasn´t going down that road with her i.e. asking questions about her mum and I never ever did. The same thing happened for the next 3 years even after getting her assurance she would be at home.

During the first winter in the caravan I got up one morning, and couldn´t see through the dressing table mirror, I thought to myself, I didn´t have that much to drink last night, did I? I touched the mirror and realised it was covered in ice; I sold the caravan as quickly as I could and moved into a flat in town. I had three flats in town with the same landlord each one better than the previous until I ended up with the whole of the upstairs of a house to myself except that I was to share the bathroom with a girl student who had the bedsit below me.

Wouldn´t you think a young girl would be clean and tidy about having a place of her own, nothing could have been further from the truth. Not once in the first six months or so that I first lived there did she ever clean the bath out or hoover the hallway and stairs that we shared. I didn't mind doing the hoovering I just thought maybe she didn´t have one and I always found the time to do it once a week. It was the filthy state the bathroom was always left in. She had lots of male and female friends, fellow students I suppose, visiting her at times and I suppose that they were using the bath as it was always filthy and being as I didn´t use the bath it´s self because I was working seven days a week and had a shower at work she should at least clean the bath out. The toilet was always left filthy and on three occasions I had to tell her without being abusive about it to remove used sanitary towels that had been left on the small shelf in the bathroom, there was always pee on the floor and toilet seat whenever they had been visiting her. One night when she had a load of friends in her flat they were having a noisy party with people up and down stairs to the bathroom and the loud music blaring out, when it got to midnight I went down stairs and asked to speak to the girl and asked her civilly could she PLEASE keep the noise down as I had to get up for work at 5 o´clock and all I could hear in my bedroom was the loud THUMP THUMP of the music coming up through the floorboards only, to be told F..k off I live here. I was shocked at that and wasn´t expecting that response from her I could only think that she hadn´t taken too kindly to me asking her to remove use sanitary towels from the bathroom in the past. I stood it for another ½ hour got dressed and stood at the top of the stairs and told the next young lad who was on his way up the stairs what he thought he was doing, I´m going to the bathroom he said, oh no you're not I said, I live here and your friend downstairs who has never cleaned it since she came to live here but is entitled to use it, and the next person to try and use it will be going down the stairs backwards take that message to your friend and let me tell you this is not a threat it´s a promise. He went down stairs the music stopped for about 5 minutes and then turned louder if that were possible but no one attempted to us the bathroom again. I sat there on the stairs until it was time to go to work and just before I went out of the door I sorted out a Mario Lanzer record put it on my stereogram on full volume with the arm off so it would it would play continuously the noise from down stairs drowned it out as I went through the front door and left for work. When I arrived home from work the landlord Rob was outside waiting to see me along with the young girl. The first words he said was I´ve been in your flat to turn you record player off George and let me tell you this, this can´t happen again. I said if you give me time to explain why it happened and went on to tell him the whole sorry story about her never cleaning since she came to live there, the sanitary towels the pee on the floor and toilet seat every time I used the bathroom the noisy party´s almost every week and loud music until early hours of the morning which she refused to turn down after asking politely and after last night I´d just had enough. I know it wasn´t right what I did early hours this morning and two wrongs don´t make it right but when you are continually rebuffed in sensible requests how can you put it right. He asked her if was true what I´d said, and to my surprise she agreed to everything I´d said saying that she lived here and that she would do as she liked and no one was going to tell her what to do. When Rob pointed out to her that we had to be reasonable and not be a nuisance to other tenants she said I live here and I´ll do as I like, not anymore Rob said I´ve heard enough and you are leaving right now I don´t like your attitude and don´t want you as a tenant of mine any longer so get your things together and leave right now. I don´t know why but I said to her I´m sorry It´s had to come to this BUT you have brought it all on yourself with your attitude and walked in to get my meal ready. As I walked in I looked at the stereogram and thought by the time Rob had turned it off I bet you could have fried chips on it, but at least it did the trick and there was never any mention of the incident from Rob again thank goodness.

There was one incident that happened while I was living in that house I will never forget as long as I live. It happened in 1976 just before I moved up to the village where I worked. I had bought myself a small colour TV in town and when I was on afternoon shift there was a late film on at times I could watch, so I would take the TV into the bedroom and watch it in bed. The following morning on one of these occasions I was carrying it out of the bedroom into the living room and just as I was about to set it down on its table I tripped over the hearth rug and not wanting to drop it I suddenly got a horrific pain across the small of my back OUCH that hurt I thought. By the time I was due to set off for work it was killing me not knowing at the time I´d trapped my sciatic nerve I got half way to work and had to return home because of the pain. There was no way I could have gone to work in so much pain. Besides being a danger to anyone who was working with me there was always the danger of injuring myself even more. I decided to visit my Dr. that evening I went to his surgery only to find that he was on holiday and a locum was standing in for him. What a shock I got when I did get in to see him. There was this Dr who was either Pakistani or Indian sat in his chair with legs up on his desk smoking a cigarette which I found very strange. Ah he said, take a seat and what can I do for you? I´d rather stand I said I then went on to tell him the pain I was in and how I´d done it. What he said next was a classic that I´ll never forget. He said do you know, that if I had got enough money I could prove there is nothing wrong with you. I said hold on Dr I´m not making it up. He went on to say; now look here in 1962 you had 6 weeks off with a bad back and 6 week every year since. I said Dr I have never suffered with a bad back in my life and besides that I was in the army from 1960 until 1966. MR GREEN he said, you weren´t in the army. I said I beg your pardon I was and my name is not Green and this is where the classic came in. His immediate reply was "ARE YOU SURE" of course I´m SURE I know my own name for God´s sake. His feet were off the desk in a shot and out of the surgery shouting and bawling at the receptionist. After about 5 minutes he came back looking very sheepish, and I´ve never in my whole life seen anyone as embarrassed and back peddle as much as him that evening. I´m terribly sorry he said, will you tell me again why your back hurts and where. I told him, and he said you have a trapped Sciatic nerve I´ll prescribe the strongest pain killers I can and I suggest you go home and rest it and take at least 2 weeks off work. No thanks I said I can´t afford to be off work, in that case he said take my card and ring me at any time. I often wonder if and when Mr Green paid him a visit how he went on if he wanted a sick note.

I suffered with that trapped nerve for 9 months and anyone who has suffered with one will know a night´s sleep is out of the question besides the pain. I was okay at work while I was heated up and sweating it was when I cooled down after my shift that the agonising pain would start again. One day at the end of my shift a guy from Pontefract who I got to know said you always seem to be limping about at the end of the shift is there anything wrong. Yes I said I´ve got a trapped nerve and these pain killers the doc has given me are doing no good. I´ll put that right he said I used to do a bit of wrestling when I was younger and used to give physiotherapy when I got too old for the ring. I believed him as well, he was a giant of a man a good foot taller than me one of those guys your glad he´s your friend and not your enemy. I wish you could Gordon, I will, if you do as I say, go on then I said wondering what he was going to do. Right he said stand in front of me with your heels together and feet apart raise your arms with your palms on your chest and fall back to me. I thought to myself what the hell are up to Gordon and up to that point I just thought he was going to make me look a fool. I then thought he was going to punch me in the back or something I said to him at that point for God´s sake don´t punch me Gordon the state I´m in at the moment you´ll kill me. Just fall back to me you will be okay I promise. I did, that´s when he put his arms under mine and lifted me off the floor and shook me like a rag doll. Every tooth in my head ached at the same time for just that few seconds. I shouted to him what the hell have you done while holding my jaws while the pain subsided. He explained that he had minutely opened my spinal column to let the trapped nerve out. He said if it hasn´t done the trick today I´ll do it again tomorrow for you until it comes right. I went home that day and for the first time in nine months I had a sleep at night. The pain in my leg had gone and I couldn´t wait to see Gordon and thank him for what he had done and got rid of my pain. I never saw Gordon at work next day in fact it was years later when I met up with him again and thanked him "AND" got him thoroughly drunk for his putting thousands of pounds in my pocket through not having to stay off work. However crude all that sounds it's all true and even to this day I have never had trouble with it since. Sadly four years after meeting up with him to thank him he died of a massive heart attack. Another great guy I will always have fond memories of.

Whenever I picked up Christine I would go to the local park or the pictures or shopping or take her to see the family. As well keeping her in touch with my family she would have someone her own age to talk to ie. our Jackie and Sophie providing I was on the right shift, I "NEVER" ever took her to a pub, unlike, a lot of ex husbands would do. We would have a meal in my flat before taking her home. One of her summer holidays I´d arranged to take my two weeks holiday when she was off school, and said to Jan that I would like to have the bairn stay with me for 2 weeks while I was off work on my holidays as we would be going on outings. I never thought I would get the answer she gave me, there´s "no" way is she staying with you in a one bedroom flat. I was gobsmacked. lost for word and raging at the same time, I took the bairn to the car, drove round the block, came back, walked in and said to her, you "filthy" minded B.....d she Is going to have my bed and, I´m sleeping on the settee, and slapped her across the face and walked out. I was expecting to be arrested, when I took the bairn back home but, nothing came of it. These were the obstacles that were put in my way by Jan. We started to take Jackie and Sophie on outings with us which, also gave her the company of girls almost her own age, they were and still are to this day the most well behaved kids I´ve ever met and well pleased to say they are my nieces, we had lots of fun and laughs on those outings with Christine and I, they enjoyed them so much so, they still talk about them outings which was 33yrs ago, whenever they come to see me.

After a while, a job came up, pipe laying in Alaska, for 2 yrs and coming back to the UK with 2 grand tax free. I went for the interview, got the job and was to pick the flight tickets up in two days time. I went home and gave it some more thought and (again foolishly) decided not to, as I would miss our Christine growing up. Another time shortly after that, I was offered a job on mining development in Montana, and that was to live there, and, once again I got the job, I had only pick up the tickets and changed my mind for the same reason. It will become apparent later "why"; I was foolish in not taking the jobs. As I said earlier I had changed my flats 3 times, each time for a better one, and had just got the third one decorated and furnished out nicely, when I was offered a flat in the village where worked and, thought Christine could now come and see me on the bus and make her feel grown up. We had some good times while I was living there; she was also growing up to be a proper lady. One Saturday when she came she was a bit sheepish, I asked if she was alright and she said yes, and when it was time for her to go home she asked me if I would take her home, which, was strange, as she had been going home on the bus herself and, was quite comfortable with that. I walked her to the top of the street kissed her goodbye and said I would see her next week, and that we would be going to Halifax to see the family. I watched as she walked down the street turning round and waving I just knew there was something wrong, perhaps, she´ll tell me next week I thought, as I walked home. On the Tuesday, when I came home from work, there was a letter for me with a lump inside it. It was then I found out why she had been sheepish and asked me to take her home. She "had" wanted to tell me something. The letter was from Jan, some keys were wrapped up in toilet paper, and a note, saying Christine and I have moved back to Durham where I have got a council house of my own, here are the keys to your house stick it up your arse and, "don´t" blame the bairn for not telling you, I told her not to. Once again I was devastated my bairn had been taken from me, and was now living a hundred and odd miles away. What the hell have I done to deserve this comes flooding back. I was feeling as low as I´d been the night she had committed adultery with that b.....d Bob. I didn´t know what I wanted to do, my mind was in a turmoil. Should I go now, and sort things out with Jan, and get her out of my life for good by telling Christine, she has the option of coming to see me whenever she likes, and that it´s her mother´s doing, that she now lives so far away. That week-end I did go up to Durham to Jan´s mother's, only to find she had also moved to a new address and her neighbours didn´t know the address, and I didn´t know Jan´s so, I came home. looking back, "someone" must, been looking over me, for it, to have worked out that way did, as I would "surely" have given her a smack , and most likely have been arrested and, ended up with a criminal record. She was manipulating my daughter and I didn´t like it one bit and seemed I was powerless to do anything about it.

I travelled back home in a daze thinking "WHY" are these things happening to me "WHY", I´ve done nothing wrong. I never thought that that I would feel lower than I did at that moment in time but, I would as this story unfolds, will there "ever" be an end to it? The following day I went down to the house that I had been paying rent on and my coal allowance for our Christine´s sake for almost 3 years, expecting the worst, and it was, the beautiful lawns, boarders, and hedges were all a mess they hadn´t been touched for months and months, the Cedar wood drive gates were broken, it was all a mess. I went in the house, only to find that all our beautiful furniture and fittings had been taken, every carpet, even the gas fire in the sitting room had been taken out and left with open pipes, the gas supply being turned off at the meter, every light fitting, leaving the bare wires hanging out of the ceiling, even, the fancy covers for the light switches had been taken. I went up stairs and it was the same as down stairs, everything had been taken. I could have cried it would take a small fortune to bring it back to what it was. I moved back in the house, Joe came to give me a hand to move, he took one look at the gardens and said George, you need a goat in here and, in no time at all it will have it cleared up. I took his advice and bought one and he was right, in a couple of months the garden was clear and I could now start and get it back to normal. I only wished at the time I could have got it to walk on the top of the hedges. I was telling the lads at work and in no time at all it was being used to sort allotments and gardens out which was good for me as I was having to buy food for it eat. It was in 1976 when we finally got divorced and, bought the house 6 months later so Jan could not make a claim on it. Shortly after, because Jan had put herself out of work and was on benefits, I was taken to court again, and they increased her maintenance from £2 to £10.

I carried on paying our Christine´s maintenance but stopped paying Jan´s altogether I was determined she was not going to be paid £10 a week for breaking our marriage up and all the upset for the bairn and I. One night about 8 weeks after I´d stopped paying Jan´s money. I was on afternoon shift and had just sat down to eat my dinner when a knock came to the door, it was a policeman I asked what he wanted, he said I´ve come about the maintenance arrears you owe which is £80 do you have it he asked, yes I said, are you going to pay it he said "no I´m not" I said and went on to explain why. If you won´t pay it then I´ve got to arrest you which he did. I was taken to the local police station and after 2 hours was seen by an Inspector and told I would have a suspended prison sentence until I paid the arrears and if I hadn´t paid the arrears by 8 weeks I would be arrested and taken to jail. I told the Inspector I was livid to think, that this could happen to me. Here I was a law abiding citizen been to work and arrested for owing £80 to a woman who had wrecked mine and my daughters lives and the answer I got was you "WILL" change the tone of your voice or I´ll have you put in the cells now. That calmed me down but I was raging inside and went home full of hatred for Jan and wondered how on earth I could have married her. I paid the arrears off and two weeks later I´m back in court this time up in Co. Durham.

Christine´s money hadn´t been increased as I was giving double voluntary anyway, plus pocket money and anything else she required, which Jan denied that I was. So I asked them to bring Christine to the court to prove it. The last thing I wanted to do was to get our Christine caught up in all this bickering and fighting but, I was so mad at Jan making me out to be an uncaring father. I was glad when they said they believed me. I asked them where, they thought, I could find that increase in money for her, they said you are doing a lot of overtime, and can afford it, you can have it varied every 6 months, you have only to apply. I said of course I´m working overtime she has taken all the furniture, which I don´t mind for my daughter´s sake, so she can have a full home but, I have to replace that home for myself. It was "her" who committed adultery and broke our marriage up. After all my protests I said I wouldn´t pay it as she had caused the marriage break down and that I´m having serious thoughts about finishing work and going on the dole to which the J.P. in which case you will be arrested and put in jail for putting yourself out of work. Once again I was raging inside, when will I ever get this woman out of life when will it all end? I left the court and went to see the bairn now that I had her address. It was a strained atmosphere and she asked me would I please leave before her mum came home, which hurt like hell. It was some later before she got in touch with me and said she was sorry for the way things had worked out and, hoped I was keeping well. It was the "first" of many times over the years to come that I said, it was your "mother" I divorced "NOT" you. It was from that point on that, I had to beg and plead over the years, for her to come and see me but, all I got was excuses after excuses and was years before she did come and visit me.

It was around that time and looking back when an incident happened, that I really should have taken the hint about Christine´s behaviour towards me. It was a Tuesday morning 11am, I was living in town and was on afternoon shift and was late for work and running for a bus in the bus station and bumped into a woman and nearly knocked her over, when I went to apologise it was, of all people Jan, with our Christine. I was shocked to say the least it had only been at the week-end that I had been asking her to come down and see me and her excuse was that she had other things to do. I asked her how long she had been down here, she stuttered and stammered yesterday she said blushing, and when were you coming to see me I asked, we are going home on tomorrow dad I won´t have time. I stood staring at her, raging inside, thanks a lot I said I turned around and got on my bus. It must have been about 2 weeks later when I got in touch with her and felt then that had I not got in touch with her I really don´t know when she would have contacted me. Why they were there was through an emergency with her mum's friend who was in hospital. The writing was on the wall what was in store for me in the future but I couldn´t see it.

I went to a solicitor after the increase in maintenance. Once again I got some invaluable advice which was "get the biggest mortgage you can afford" he said because, that is an investment and maintenance money is dead money and the chances are at sometime or other your ex will remarry. That was without doubt one of the best pieces of advices I was ever given. Shortly after that in 1977 I was elected on to the club committee and the same year I bought a brand new bungalow in the village where I worked. There were a lot of snide comments about that, like, by god you must be making some money on that committee to buy a brand new bungalow, but nothing but praise from all the friends I now had. Joe helped me to move once again, he was like a father to me, the help and advice he gave me and the doors he opened for me over the years, was unbelievable, he will always remain in my heart "THE" best friend I ever had in my life. Shortly after moving into the bungalow he built me a brick wall around the property and a huge conservatory on the back it, bricklaying was his trade before he went into the army and also when he first came out of the army, before starting at the pit to earn more money. When I asked how much I owed him he went ballistic " your my friend aren´t you", you would do the same for me wouldn´t' you and of course, I would have, it was a beautiful piece of work it made my bungalow stand out like a blind cobblers thumb.

By 1982 Christine´s maintenance had stopped and she was now receiving unemployment benefit so I stopped the pocket money saying that unemployment benefit should be ample pocket money for her but if she needed my help at any time she knew where I lived and after going to college for two years it shouldn´t be too long before she got herself a job. Jan´s maintenance was still on at £10 a week I foolishly took the advice of a lot of people, who were paying maintenance, and did not have the order varied to a lower sum, because, inevitably they put it up. It was around that time that interest rates shot through the roof, and I was struggling. It was a good job I was getting the overtime at work otherwise I would have had to sell it. It was some time in 1983 when Joe and I were at work, he was called out of the pit for the 2nd time in a matter of weeks, his wife Hilda had, had her 2nd heart attack and, it didn´t look too good. He had been having quite a few spells of work, and due, to the circumstances now that was the, last time he worked at pit, he decided to stay at home to look after her, they had both worked all their lives and money was not a problem. I bought an Omega watch for his retirement with note thanking him for all his advice, choosing me to be his work mate out of all the people he knew and the doors he had opened for me, to get where I am now. I took it to his house dropped it off I just said this is for you mate and made an excuse to leave, as I just knew, I was going to get a telling off. About an hour later he came down to the bungalow and did just that, he thanked me, and said there was absolutely no need for me to do it. I was later told by Hilda that he had a cry about it as; no one had ever done anything, like that for him in his life.

I missed Joe not being at work but all the doors he had opened for me were now well and truly open. I had become well known through working with him and also serving on the local club committee and along with my unblemished attendance record and, my quality of work I was now a charge man myself, and could pick and choose who I wanted to work with me. All this had come about from my first meeting Joe when I did my ripping training 16 years ago, I was very lucky, in the fact that I had met him when I did, and lucky that I never had a serious injury all the time I worked at the pit and, grateful, that I had been recognised for my hard work. I do feel that someone has been watching over me.

I had been given a new development job for a new unit. It wasn't too far from the pit bottom, it was winter and the main airway was perishing cold. I had, had toothache for a day or two and like everyone else, you say to yourself oh it will go off but mine wouldn't, it was getting worse and, for the first time in my life, I came out of the pit early, to go to the dentist. It had been about three years since I had been to the dentist and had two teeth out together and had, had extraction pain and bleeding for a couple of weeks. So I wasn't looking forward to this visit one little bit. I asked the dentist if he could take my tooth out that morning without an appointment as I was in that much pain. He said he would if there was a cancelation. After a short while he called me in. I asked for the needle in the hand or gas, he said no, because he needed a nurse in attendance which he didn't have at such short notice, so I had the needle in the gum, sent back into the waiting room for it to take effect. He shouted me back in after a while, and asked if my gums felt numb, I said yes and that's when it all started. He got the grips around my tooth and leaned over my face and said " don't let your head come forward I've never smelled a dog's backside "but" it can't have smelled worse than his breath "PHEW" but at that moment having that tooth pulled was more important. He started to pull and the pain was "excruciating" I told him in a mumbled voice there's something "wrong" He said you told me it was numb didn't you, well it isn't I said, he gave me another injection and sent me into the waiting room again. A short while after he sent for me again, asking is it numb now? Yes I said as best I could, he started to pull it again and once again the pain was "excruciating" but he kept on pulling. "DON'T" let your head come forward he was shouting by now but, the pain was so intense I got hold of his hand to stop him, "Let go of my hand" he was shouting, I then shouted at him and said "there's something wrong" the anaesthetic isn't working in the best way I could considering I'd had a double dose of it. He stopped and gave me yet another injection and sent me back to the waiting room again. By this time I was soaking in sweat like I'd had a hard shift at pit. All the patient's had gone and I'm sat there alone for a while, when a young girl came in she was called in immediately, after a few minutes she was leaving, and the dentist said to her "will you tell that big softie to come in here. I thought to myself "yes" wait until I've got this tooth out and I'll show you who's a big softie. Everything OK now he said I could only nod and he started again to pull the tooth and the same thing was happening again. This time he stopped put the light on his head and started to look in my mouth. "OOPS" he said, I'm sorry about this but you have a large abscess under your tooth and had I known I would not have started pulling it in the first place "SORRY" but I must pull it now as it is half out, your tooth is really deep rooted, you will just have to hang on, grip the chair arms and hold on tight and I'll be as quick as I can. Now I knew what was wrong it didn't seem too bad but the pain was still there even though I had now had three injections of anaesthetic. Must be getting soft in my old age I thought. After what seemed an age he finally got it out I was drenched in sweat, the assistant gave me a mouthwash I rinsed my mouth out and said to her, in my best mumbled voice, let me have a look at my tooth, the dentist by this time was standing by the window, arms folded and said "WHY" I said, I want to see if there is a pair of balls on the end of it. The assistant nearly fell on the floor laughing but he never even smirked. Probably another one who had been told as a child, you can get VD from laughing. What a miserable faced smelly breathed dentist he was, probably playing hell with himself for having spent all that time with one patient. He gave me a prescription for the abscess and I left knowing that as soon as I could talk properly I would warn everyone I knew about him.

The reason, I had put up for the committee all those years ago was, to try and get entertainment back in the club, as they had stopped it because, artists, were charging so much but, the club seemed to lack any atmosphere after that. I will always remember the first day I was elected onto the committee, and once again it had been through Joe's help, getting all his long time friends to vote for me and of course the friends I had made that got me on the committee. I had just come out of the committee room feeling good by the fact that in 11 years since I arrived here as a complete stranger, I had, what a lot of local lads, had never achieved, i.e. Having been elected onto this clubs committee you normally had to wait until someone died before that happened. When this young lad who didn´t work at pit, walked by, and made the comment "another idle b....rd" to keep, meaning, as was the norm, once, you got on the committee, after a short while they hardly ever went work, or went on long term sickness benefit. I was both shocked and livid, shocked that a member would talk to an official of the club that way (new or otherwise) and livid that he was calling "me" not only idle, but a b....rd I was just about to run after him when I was stopped by another committee man who said, don´t worry George his tap is stopped now, which meant, he can´t get served at the bar until, he appears in front of the committee, we will send him a letter out after next Sunday´s meeting which, will mean he will be out of the club for a fortnight at least, and then his punishment on top. Not, a good start I thought, what else is in store for me? That night he did come into the club, he came over to me and said I´ve come to apologise for my comments this afternoon, I was "way" out of order, will you accept my apologies, listen to me, I said, you don´t know me because, if you did, you would know, I haven´t an idle bone in my body and don´t you "ever" call me a b....rd ever again, or I will give you the hiding of your life and, if you think I can´t, come outside now. George he said, I am truly sorry I was out of order and will you please accept my apologies. On this occasion I "will" we shook hands and, he went to see the President of the club and told him he had seen me and, I´d accepted his apologies, and could he now be allowed to get served at the bar. During the next 30 years he was one of the most courteous members to me. I actually went on to create a record in the club, I was the "only" committee man in that club to serve 30 years continuously, and hold a full time job at the same time, for which, I was complimented for, on many, many occasions during the time I spent on the committee. I had some great times with outings, and brewery trips. Although I couldn´t go to a lot of them because, of my work, which was far more important to me, but the one´s I did go on I have a lot of happy memories of. On one we went on we stayed at a hotel in Scarborough and me, being a joker bought, some trick sweets and offered the waitresses them, they didn´t let on, and when we had dinner that night the first course was pea soup my favourite (which I had mentioned to the waitress at lunch time) and, had been given a jug to myself, when I tasted it, it was full of salt, she and the rest of the staff burst out laughing and said that´s your own back mate, we all had a good laugh over it. On another trip out we went for a meal, compliments of the brewery this time, the secretary and I shared a table and as both of us liked red wine and no one else did we were thoroughly drunk by the time we got home that night, and, as he didn´t live far from me, I escorted him home only, for him to fall down at his front door, and couldn´t get up, his wife came out and started to give me a telling off for bringing him home in that state so, I said to her, you can only lead a horse to water you can´t make it drink it, "shut up" she said sharply and give me hand, we got him into the house, onto the settee, and I went home before she started on me, thanking God I didn´t have to wake up to his wife. I was on a rest ay from work the following day and thank God for that also. The next time I saw his wife she was all apologies and I said I hope you were gentle with Ernie when he woke up she said I have just started to talk to him today. That was a week later, thank God also I wasn´t married to her. Ooh poor Ernie

I had had only two visits from our Christine in eight years, by the time the miner´s strike came about, and not one Christmas, New Year or birthday either mine or hers had she spent with me since the day Jan and I had parted, no matter how I begged or pleaded with her. It was always me that had to make the journey up there to see her. She had started work in a hospital at 18 after she had finished college, and the first job she had been given was with geriatrics and, as she is only 4ft 9 inches tall she quickly, hurt her back lifting them in and out of bed, she had to finish work through it and, has never worked since. It was and, had been for some time been hurting me, the fact that she was now an adult and she had only made the effort twice to come and see me since 1976. Jan had a phone installed about 1980 so I was now keeping contact by phone and no longer by letters, I have kept every one she has ever wrote to me including, all the birthday, father´s day and Xmas cards she has ever sent me to this day.

 The miner´s strike started in March 1984 until March 1985 we were put in a situation by our union, where you either became a scab, or be skint, for as long as the strike lasted, I chose the latter. There were some lads from our pit who did scab, and poor Jim had the humiliation of being, the Uncle, of the first scab at our pit. When he heard about it, he went straight to the pit, phoned down the pit and got him to come out. It was too late though he had scabbed and the village never forgave him for it he was treat like a leper as were "all" the others were, and eventually left the village. All of those who scabbed at our pit were soon transferred to other collieries after the strike. Poor Jim he was such a proud man he never got over that. The sheer size of Jim avoided the subject being brought up in front of him by any lads in the club or by anyone when we returned to work after the strike. That´s, what Margaret Thatcher and her government did to mining families. They should have closed the uneconomic mines down in a more civilised way. The lies they told on national TV that there was "no" pit closure list and the use of service men dressed as police was something that each and every one of them should be ashamed of. One of my unanswered questions is this, are politicians born natural liars or, are they trained? I suppose we will never get an answer to that one. And one of the unfortunate things about politics is, the good ones, get tarred with the same brush, as the bad ones.

Some of those scenes shown on national television were not of miners striking to save their jobs, they were someone else. No one in their right mind, can convince me, that a fellow miner would stand at the back of a picket line and hurl stones at the police at the front of the picket line, and have their fellow miners have the police try to beat their brains out with a trungeon. Those hurling stones were planted there by????? to take the public sympathy away from the miners. Has the public seen what the cost was, of trying to defeat Arthur Scargill? And "that's" what it was all about. He was the only man telling the truth on those TV shows throughout the strike. I "can't" forgive him though, for keeping us out on strike for 12 months, he put us in the untenable position as I said earlier, of being a scab for the rest of your life or, skint until it was over, it doesn't bear thinking about. However we survived living history, not an experience, I or, any other miner, would like to live through again. The wrecking of scabs homes during the strike was "not" what I condoned in any way. I remember when I first started at the pit, here in Yorkshire, when I came out of the army, and as I said my first job was working at the pit bottom. One of the privileges you got for working in that cold environment was, to get on the last cage going down, and the first cage coming up, at the end of the shift. After a few weeks I noticed an old guy, who never spoke to anyone, and that he would always be down the pit before any of the pit bottom staff, and never come out with us on the first cage out. I asked someone why one day, and was told that he didn't have that privilege as he was a "scab" in the 1926 strike. I was shocked to say the least, this was 1966 "but" it showed me, how strong their contempt was, as regards "scabs" at that colliery alone. Forty years had gone by and they "still" treat him as a leper. There was still a lot of guy's his age still working down the pit in those days that kept the man's foolish action all those years ago continuing.

Because I was single I had a full 12 months without wages and had to live on savings. There was no strike pay, the Union had made a deal with the Electricity Board and Gas Board that if striking miners paid £1 a week to them they wouldn´t cut our supply off. That is what I was given from a "donation" fund. That is what I and every other miner on strike was given, £1 a week each for gas and electric and we could go to the welfare and have a cooked dinner every day, and once a week was given 5 tins of various things from foreign country donations. I certainly don´t want to throw kindness in any ones face for the donations. I still think it was kind of them whoever they were, but, this is what I and all of us who stuck it out through the strike had been reduced to, I didn´t pay my mortgage for best part of the strike and it took almost, a couple of years after the strike, to get myself back on my feet properly. Joe was the only one who offered me any financial help, he was always asking me if I was ok for money all the way through the strike I never took Joe´s offer but knew he would be there for me if I did. There were 15 and myself on the committee and out of all of those there was only 3 that offered to buy me a pint, and 1 gave me a packet of lamb chops and another would give me joints of meat that were unclaimed raffle prizes. The steward of the club offered me lots of drinks but, I was always able to pay my round when we had a drink, but the offer was very much appreciated at the time.

I got letters from the Building Society every month asking, if there were any changes in my circumstances. I was "foolish" "VERY" foolish I never replied to them until one day I replied saying that I hadn´t answered previous letters because I had been staying with friends as I had no income and had to at least eat. This of course was not entirely true, I had been to visit friends and stayed a couple of days now and again, and foolishly thought the Building Society knew by the news that we were still on strike. The return letter I got shook me and frightened the living daylights out of me. It said you have broken your contract with us as an "owner/occupier" and had left the property unattended, would you please vacate the premises and forward the keys to this office immediately. I was crapping myself, they are going to repossess my bungalow, I couldn´t afford a solicitor so, went to the Citizens Advice Bureau and thankfully, they sorted it out for me, by me, I had to write them a letter of apology, for not replying to "all" their correspondence and that I would in the future. Thankfully they accepted my apologies and told me that they "could" repossess the property at any time, because of arrears. That was a rude awakening for me and a lesson learned. It took me as I said 2yrs after the strike ended to get back on my feet properly, thanks to our Union, and the Conservative Governments battle with Arthur Scargill. That to me and a lot of other miners who endured the strike thought it was mostly about!

Nine weeks into the strike I got a letter from the Courts saying that I was now £90 in arrears with Jan´s maintenance of £10 per week. So I applied to the courts to have it stopped until after the strike and I was back to work whenever it may be. I had to have an interview with the Clerk of the court to have the order varied. There were two of them in the room an old guy and a younger one. The older guy said "firstly" has there been any changes in your circumstances, yes I said I´m on strike and I´ve no income at all with being single. Go to work he said, I can´t do that I said firstly I´m on strike for a reason and secondly I don´t want to be a scab for the rest of my life. If you don´t go to work they will get the arrears somehow or you will go to jail. My heart sunk and it must have shown. I said is there no end to this woman´s hold on me. I said this woman broke our marriage up through adultery, and because the guy who she did it with, is not in the country , I have to keep paying her money she took my home ,my child to another county and for the last 12 years I´ve been paying her, for breaking our marriage up. How long has this to go on? It was then, the younger one spoke, and said, has there been any changes in "her" circumstances, like what I said, well, has she got things that you haven´t he said, any material things that "you" can´t afford, yes I said, (a nod is as good a wink to me).She´s got a microwave a phone and colour TV and can afford to go on holidays. I don´t have any of these things, which, was true at the time, Right he said we´ll be in touch as regards a hearing.

It was two weeks later I got a hearing and went to court wondering what the outcome was going to be, but hoped they would put the order on hold. I looked around at the people in the waiting area and couldn´t help feel that I shouldn´t be here. The appearance of most of them was, to say the least, "low life", men dressed in clothes that I would have thrown away, unshaven, hair un combed and hadn´t seen shampoo for God knows how long. Women dressed similar, hair badly in need of shampoo, children dressed in similar fashion, running amok, being effed and blinded at by their mothers. Are they going to make an example of me I thought, because, I´m properly dressed and clean appearance, and should know better, than to end up here in court. I felt really uncomfortable, I looked around for Jan, to give her a piece of my mind, to tell her this is what your quick roll in the hay has led to, "you B....rd" but couldn´t see her, just as well because they would have taken a dim view of me making a scene before I went into court. But would anyone see my side of the story?

Here I was, a law abiding citizen, served my country in the forces, got married, wife commits adultery, have to pay her money until I retire, brainwashed washed my daughter that I deserted them, arrested and almost given a criminal record two years prior, and end up with the humiliation of being taken to court among all these low life. And at the same time "WHAT" are they thinking of "ME". By this time I´m looking round to see if I can see anyone there who knows me, so I can explain why I´m there. All these thoughts were racing round my head, and feeling sick to the stomach with it all. Oh God, how I hated that woman for putting me in this position today. Thankfully I didn´t have to wait long before they called my name out. I went into the court room, there was no sign of Jan and thought, Oh hell she´s not turned up they'll adjourn it, and I´ll have to go through all this again. They asked me to explain my case as to why I was in arrears. Which I did, "THEN" I´ll never forget as long as I live, the middle one of the three women J P´s said, your ex spouse has not turned up, she has sent a letter explaining why, so, we will proceed without her. That made me feel better, at least I wouldn´t have to go through all this again.

We have decided, she said, to "reduce" the maintenance order to your ex spouse to 5 pence per year, in case, the order has to be varied again in the future, and also, wipe off the arrears. I couldn´t believe what I was hearing I thought I´d slipped into some sort of day dream. After a few seconds the J P said are you ok? Would you like a drink of water? No no I said but am I hearing this right, I don´t owe any money and only have to pay her 5 pence a year from now on? Yes she said.

I don´t want to seem ungrateful but can you explain how this has came about? Yes she said your wife has been working as a nurse for the past two years and not declared it to the court, proceedings are now pending. I hope they throw the book at her I thought to myself. That´s all, you can go now, "Oh" before I go I said, would you mind if I came across and gave you all a kiss, thanks she said smiling, but no thanks. The smile on my face was hurting the back of my neck by now. That´s all, you can go now, before I go I said, can I pay my maintenance for the next 23 years, I´ll be retired then? "NO" she shouted, then smiled, and said now get yourself off home. It was a day in my life that I remember "every" word that was spoken, and can still visualise the faces of those J Ps that day. I was "one" very happy chappy. Talk about every dog has its day or, what goes round, comes round, from that day I am a firm believer in both of those sayings it's the waiting that gets you.

As I came out of the court, one or two looked at me and must have thought there was something wrong with me, the smile on my face as I say was hurting the back of my neck it was so wide. I was walking on air and couldn´t wait to get to the club, and was I going to have a good, good drink or what! I couldn´t remember a day in my life when I'd been so happy. At last I've finally got her out of my life. BUT there was "still a twist to it later. On the way to the bus station I bumped into Jack one of the fitters from work, a great lad, with the same attitude at work as myself and also, the same sense of humour as myself. I asked him how he was coping, ok I suppose, skint, like everyone else he said, the only good thing to come out of it is, the wife has had to get a job, we both laughed. Do you manage to get out for a drink I said, no he said I haven´t had a drink for weeks now. I went on to tell him what had gone off in court and said, come with me and we´ll get P....d up today. He phoned home and we had a glorious day. When we did get back to work after the strike he insisted on returning that day out I´d given him that day. Another of the genuine people I have met in my life.

Not one of my family offered, or visited me through the whole 12 months of the strike "except", my brother Ron, who 8 or 9 months into the strike had come to pick up my father, who, had been staying at my eldest sisters for two weeks, which I was unaware of, not that I was interested. He brought him to the club we had a good amount to drink and Da was saying all night how much money he had, had to give his own daughter to stay at her house, at the end of the night James said he would give me lift home to my bungalow which neither had seen before. They both wanted the toilet before setting off back to Derby so they came in Da was still on about the money he had given my sister and I said, did "you" think about me being strike with no wages, and while we are on with that, "why" did you, up and leave Jane and I as kids and we were put in a home? Not once did you come and visit us, send a card or letter "why".

 You should be f.....g "blinded" talking to me like that he snarled, I could not believe what I was hearing. I was not going to be spoken to by him in that manner. I told our James get him out here before I crack him; the tears were streaming down my face I was so hurt by that comment alone. I wanted so much to give him the beating he deserved and it was his age that stopped me I was never more ashamed of him being my father than at that moment. He was still chuntering on when I got him by scruff of his neck and pants and frog marched him to our James van and said "DONT" ever bring him here again. He was still chuntering on when James said "One" more word out of you and, I´ll drop you off on the motorway, and off they went, I never saw my Father alive again. He died in 1988. All the family did attend his funeral why I don´t know but we did, and, as the service was being read the pastor said what a nice man he had been, Jane and I looked at each other and said at the same time "we must" be at the wrong funeral.

In February 1985 I was still on strike and Christine´s 21st birthday was here, I asked her if at least, she would come down and spend her 21st birthday with me, being as she had spent her 18th with her mother, and mother´s family, she said, "no" again, people don´t celebrate 21st birthdays now Da, it´s the 18th when you have become of age these days. So I said if I come up, would you go out for the day with me to celebrate your birthday. Your only 21 once I said, I´ll see how I feel when you come Da. This is how so many things had altered over the years, and I still think it´s through Jan´s influence. Because I wouldn´t forgive her for committing adultery just once as she put it. For Christine´s 21st birthday, I bought her an Omega watch, a bottle of Moet Chandon, I got the wife of a friend of mine, to bake and ice a birthday cake, 21 fresh red roses and a huge birthday card. There didn´t seem to be much enthusiasm and when I took her into Sunderland for a meal there was nothing on any of the menu´s after going in several places. In the end we had some sandwiches. On the way back to her home I asked again if anything was wrong that I could put right for her, she said no. Is it because I´ve come I said, no, I just don´t feel too good she said. I dropped her off and said "here" I was going to spend this on our day out, I gave her a £100, I drove back home feeling utterly dejected and let down. She has definitely grown away from me. I was also a little concerned about the fact that there was never any mention of boyfriends or going out and meeting boys and put it down to not going out much.

It was March 1985 when the strike was finally over and went back to work. We all met at the welfare grounds and with the colliery brass band playing we marched behind it through the village to the pit. It was a proud sight to see but only for the fact that we had stuck together through the hard times. The government had won the battle and no one could doubt that. We marched into the pit yard; a speech was given by the branch Secretary praising us for our efforts and could hold our heads up high unlike the "scabs" of the strike. Not one mention of the debts we had all run up. We all went into the baths/stores to be issued with new boots and clothing and to see what shift and job we would be starting on and who with. There were lads who were handing the clothing and boots out who had scabbed and some of them were being spat on by some of the lads and the name calling was horrendous until an official came and threatened them with the sack if it continued.

It was shortly after the strike amid talks about the lads who had scabbed and transferred to other pits that we found out they had been sent letters encouraging them to go back to work during the strike. I wonder to this day why I and hundreds of others with good attendance records and good at their work never received a letter. Did they know in advance that if we did scab, we would be transferred after the strike and they would be left with a second best work force? Who knows? It was a good while before the pit got back to the working relations we had before the strike, and overtime was on offer again and everyone was clamouring for it, we were as I said earlier up to our necks in debt.

On the Friday of the first week we had started back to work we all had a week´s wage to draw which British Coal had with held for the duration of the strike and everyone was buzzing, at last we would have some money in our pockets. I had my wages paid straight into my bank account and when I picked my wage slip up I could have vomited. The joy of having some wages in my pocket was short lived. Because my maintenance order was being paid prior to the strike by Compulsory Wages Order to the courts, they had taken all my wages except the minimum they allowed me which was £26 to live on until the arrears were paid up. I went straight to the wages clerk and told them that the order had been cancelled 11 weeks into the strike and should not have been deducted only to be told that they had not been informed by about it and I would have to get the courts to send confirmation to them AND then the deduction would only be stopped at the start of the next months payroll. I was livid but powerless to do anything about it. On the Monday after work I went down to the court and was lucky enough to bump into the young Clerk of the court who had got me a hearing during the strike and explained what had happened, he was surprised and asked me to wait and he would see why it had happened. He came back, apologised for the mistake that someone in the office hadn´t informed British Coal and that confirmation would definitely be sent out that day. I said British Coal won´t cancel the order until the last day of the month so how do I get my money back off my ex wife if it´s been forwarded to her. Don´t worry he said she will be informed to return it here to the courts. I was pleased it had been sorted out BUT it would take until the first day of next month until before my wages would be back to normal once more. Jan did return the money to the courts and the court sent me a cheque for it. She must have thought all her birthdays had come at once when she received monies from the court after the strike. I don´t think for one second she would have returned the money had the court not requested it.

Life trundled on for a few more years and in 1988 things were looking grim as to the future of the pit. All sorts of rumours were flying round and anyone who wanted a transfer to another pit was almost guaranteed bearing in mind it would be out of the area and mostly and probably having to work with lads who had let you down in the strike ie. scabs. One Saturday afternoon I was in the club having a game of dominoes as usual, when a lad who I knew from work came to me and said, can I have a word with you George, yes I said, I couldn´t believe what he came out with next. He said, I know you were talking to me not long ago about you wanting to sell your bungalow because your mortgage was so high well, the wife is wanting a bungalow and where yours is situated would be just fine for her so, If I offered you over the market value would you be prepared to sell it me and not gazump me. When he told me the offer which was well over the market value I said. give me a split second to think about that. Right I said do you want me to move out this afternoon or can you wait until I get somewhere to live? Seriously would you do that he said. Yes of course I will and sold it there and then. I couldn´t believe it, I knew where I could get a property for cash in the village albeit a bit run down but I would have enough money to refurbish it and at the end of the day NO mortgage. Why he offered as much as he did I don´t know I wasn´t going to question him at the time in fact it was me that was worried in case he gazumped me. A chance like this comes once in a life time and grabbed it with both hands. I did buy the property in the village, refurbished it, and the feeling of no mortgage, was like the world had been taken off my shoulders and have never looked back from that point.

It had been almost a year since I´d sold the bungalow when I met the "love" of my life, Sue, and how we met was unbelievable. I had been talking to a mate of mine Bob and he was telling me of a night he´d had out with Brian who was also a mate of ours and said that they had been over to a village about 6 miles away and they had, had a fantastic night out and meeting lots of old work mates one in particular Gordon the ex wrestler who had sorted my trapped sciatic nerve out for me all those years ago. He asked them how I was going on etc. and Bob said would I be interested in going over there the next time they went, he gave me Brian´s phone number who lived in the next village to me, so I rang him the following day to arrange to have a night out with him as I hadn´t seen him for quite a while. When I rang, a woman answered and I said is Brian there, there´s no Brian lives here she said, oops, I must have rang the wrong number, apologised and put the phone down. I tried again a few minutes later, and the same woman answered I must have been having a senior moment I´d rang the same number again I apologised again, and put the phone down. I can only think that I´d wrote the wrong number down when I´d got it from Bob. Two or three days went by and decided to phone again and I´m guessing the number by now, and blow me the same woman answered again I apologised again and went on to tell her that I was trying to arrange to see my mate for a night out in the village club where he lives, he lives across the road from it I said, I live around the corner from it she said, during the conversation I mentioned I was single and she said that she too was single, and that she and her friend go in there on a Saturday night for the last drink, and then she comes to stay at my place for the week-end so, I asked her name and to describe herself and her friend and that I would buy her a drink for the inconvenience I´d caused her, don´t be silly she said it´s been nice talking to you, like wise I said. It was a few weeks later that I got round to having a drink with Brian in his club and had forgotten all about the woman I´d been talking to on the phone, and if it hadn´t been for the fact, that it was my round on last orders I would never have met Sue. I went to the bar and saw these two women stood beside the bar and it all came tumbling back, I said, is your name

Sue, yes she said, I said let me buy you and your friend drink for the inconvenient phone calls I made you. We started talking and went on to make a date and we have been together ever since. That was 19 yrs ago we sold our properties and moved in together after 14yrs and have never had an argument or a cross word in all that time. There is one, and only one regret I have about our relationship, and that is, I wished I had met her coming out of the school gates, she´s beautiful, well off financially and a kind and loving nature, what more could any man want? I never thought I would ever be as happy as I am now.

In January 1990 Sue persuaded me to have a holiday. I hadn´t been out of the country since I left the army in 1966, whenever a holiday was mentioned I would say I´ve seen enough sand and sea to last me 2 life times anyway I surprised even myself and booked a holiday to Cyprus in January. Off we went to this new 4 star hotel, we were 2 of only 68 guests in the hotel. Every amenity was in there, heated indoor swimming pool, gymnasium. The weather was a little cool early morning and late at night. Most of the local bars were closed for the winter season but we managed to find a couple open near to the Hotel. One in particular who the owner hired us his car at a lot cheaper rate than the Hotel was offering us. We had a few trips out around the Island but, couldn´t get into Famagusta where I had visited on my way home from the Middle-east. We had to look at it through the fencing as the island had been divided up since then and needed a visa to enter. Both of us thought it was like looking back in time. Everywhere was in dire need of a good cleaning, the dust on the street looked to be inches thick, compared to the last time I saw it, and it was like a ghost town. One night we had a night in a bar close to the hotel Sue was drinking white wine I was drinking beer when she said try this George it´s really good. I tried it and found it excellent and started to drink it all night. It was my first drinking session on wine and of course was drinking it like pints of beer. After the 8th bottle the bar owner asked where we were staying and asked if we needed a taxi. I looked at him in surprise and said no as the hotel was very near, anyway after another couple of bottles we left, it was the next day that I felt like I had been kicked by a mule. We spent the day in the indoor pool nursing my head. Lesson learned "don´t drink wine like pints of beer". On the 4th day we were gathered in the main lounge and told not to leave the Hotel as the Gulf war had started and that we were to be flown out A S A P on the next available flight to UK. We were angry as we had specifically asked the Travel agent if we would encounter any problems by going to Cyprus before we booked and told everything would be OK. I did manage to get the car back to the bar owner but fuming at having the holiday cut short.

I had always said to Christine as she was growing up, and old to understand, do "not" to dash into getting married, do whatever you want to do, see whatever you want to see and then do it all again to be sure and, if you want live together without being married that´s ok by me. She was 27 when she started courting Paul, and, to my surprise brought him down to see me "hallelujah" a visit at last, he seemed a very nice lad and, came from Newcastle where they talk properly. She asked if they could sleep together, as they did when they stayed at his home. Jan wouldn´t allow them to sleep together when he stayed at her house. What a short memory she had or, was it because she didn´t like him?

I was really pleased that she was now seeing a guy because, at the age of 27 and no mention of guys I was beginning to think she was batting for the other side and keeping quiet about it. They said they were getting engaged in three weeks time. I asked them if

I could put a spread on for them here or take them out for a meal up there if they wanted, they said no, so, I gave them my car as an engagement present and said they would now, be able to come and see me as often as they like. I phoned up the week they were getting engaged and she said that they and a couple of friends were going to a night club and not having a buffet not even her mum was going, meaning she didn´t want me there, oh well, my first indication I was, I´m an old fuddy duddy and they don´t want me at the night club with them. It turned out that I was conned. About a month later I went up to see her and noticed that there was a photo of her and Paul at a party in Jan´s house, when I mentioned this she said her mum put it on the day after, now she was starting to lie to me, and worse was to come, "much" worse. They decided to get married 6 months after they got engaged and still they hadn´t used the car to come and see me. When I asked why Paul was too busy at work and also doing a delivery job at night she said. I went up to see about the wedding arrangements and see if she wanted a horse and carriage or a Rolls Royce for the wedding, only to be told by Jan I´m paying for the wedding I´ve brought her up in my home like you are sitting in my home, not anymore I´m not I shouted, and you did all that without any financial support from me? I said, I jumped up and walked out of the door Christine never came to see me to the door. The next time I spoke to our Christine was when, she said she was sending "my", invitation down and, that there was only "me" being invited to the wedding and reception, as the hall was too small to accommodate my family but, they were welcome to come to the wedding but not the reception, but can come to the club at night. I went absolutely berserk, are you telling me that my only daughter is getting married and five of my relatives can´t come to the wedding? It´s my mum who´s booked the hall and, it's the only one she could get, and beside they have "never" been in touch with me for years, have "you" been in touch with them I said. She put the phone down on me. I phoned straight back, look I said book a hotel I´ll pay for it and, refund your mum. By this time she was crying and said to me you are spoiling my wedding plans Da and put the phone down on me again. I phoned the next day to see if there had been a change of plans so my family could attend the wedding proper, when she answered I got the worst answer I could possibly get, she said, you are "not" going to spoil my wedding day because I don´t want you to give me away now, I´m getting my Uncle Bernard to give me away, "please" don´t come to the wedding, and put the phone down on me again. It was the 2nd body blow that I have never gotten over. I sat there and cried I couldn´t remember the last time I cried, in a phone call she broke my heart which was "never to be mended. This is Jan´s doing, she has brainwashed our daughter. How do you cope with a kick in the teeth like that? I love my daughter but, I have "never" come to terms with that sad day, my "only" daughter and child who is 28 years old, refusing to let her father walk her down the aisle. It should have been the proudest moment in my life. Jan should have put aside our indifferences for that day. It was our only child´s wedding day and she spoilt it for everyone except herself, "BUT" she´s got to live with that and so has Christine. I must be a glutton for punishment by keep going back for more and sadly, there was more to come.

Up to that point I didn´t even know the name of the church she was being married in, so, I found the number and address from the directory enquiries of Jan´s brother and went up to see him, his wife answered the door. I don´t know why but I was surprised when she asked me in and offered me a cup of tea but I was. I explained why I´d come up to see her and Len and that all I wanted was for me to sit in the church and watch my little girl get married. She then told me Len had died a couple of years earlier. I told her I was sorry to hear that and said Christine had never mentioned it to me. She said that she didn´t know the name of the church Christine was getting married in because she hadn´t been invited. I told her that Christine had told me she had asked her uncle Bernard to give her away as I had asked why my family of 5 had not been invited to the wedding and asking for them to be included was spoiling her wedding day plans if I insisted they be invited. She then told me that Bernard had been a Scab at their local pit which I´ve got to say hit me like a ton of bricks. He never leaves his home as he is constantly sneered and shouted at because of what he did during the strike. The only friends he would have would be the men he scabbed with. It´s a sad state of affairs but he should have thought long and hard before he did what he did. I was absolutely gob smacked and stood there with tears streaming down my cheeks to think of all the people she could have chosen to walk her down the aisle instead of her own father she had chosen him. I apologised for my behaviour. I understand George she said it´s not good for you, how on earth could she have done that to you? We chatted a while longer and as I was about to leave I asked if she knew why Jan and I had divorced and went on to tell her. She said, well, I believe you George but, she´s told all the family it was because you were violent to them which I found strange as you have always kept in touch with our Christine and it was not the impression our Julie got when she had a holiday down at your place with our Christine one time. I left and searched around the churches in the village but couldn´t find it that´s because it was in the next village which, I found out later. That it had been in the next village where she had been married would almost certainly have fitted in because she had chosen her Uncle Bernard. It does make me think that it had all been planned that way from the start as Jan would not have wanted me to attend the wedding and planned it so.

I had taken a pre dated cheque for a £1000 and a letter with me to give to Christine for her wedding present (I must have been mad but, yet I still loved her) asking her to give me an explanation as to why she chose someone else to walk her down the aisle and, if she didn't get in touch I would stop the cheque. Eventually I went to Jan's house and pushed it through the letter box and went home, feeling numb, and angry that I couldn't find the church and see her walk down the aisle. I decided to wait for Christine's reply, but never got one, I did stop the cheque when I didn't get an explanation and it's a good job I didn't hold my breath as it was 15 months later when I received a letter and photo of our Rebecca my first grandchild 18 days old, and with her new address the letter said "did "I" want to keep in contact, no mention of the wedding or that she had been pregnant. I can only think it was the embarrassment of the wedding fiasco that she hadn't let me know. I cried, and looking at the photo and wondered why she had chose to treat me like she had over the years, after a while when I pulled myself together I phoned Sue and told her what Christine had sent and travelled up to see them. I didn't know what reception I was going to get when I got there. She was shocked and embarrassed on seeing me as, I hadn't said I was coming up. I'd made my mind up while driving up, that I would tell her at last about why her mum and I got divorced and, to understand that it was not her I'd divorced but her mother but, when I held my granddaughter, I hugged and kissed her and thought it was not the right time to talk about the divorce, another time will do. I thought as I was holding the bairn, I hope to God she doesn't have any of the upset in her life like I have had with her mother and grandmother. My hoping would be in vain though, as this sad, sad story unfolds. I said to Christine you must let me know when the christening is I don´t want to miss that, and yet another kick in the teeth, Oh she said, we have already had her christened, I was bitterly disappointed and showed it. Oh well I said, you can bring her down in the car I gave you, for her 1st birthday and I´ll put a spread on, I´ll invite the family and we can show her off. She looked bemused but, never said anything On leaving I gave Christine £100 to put in a bank for the bairn and said let me know what bank, you never know how much she will end up with. Meaning I would add to it every year for use in the future. I was feeling on cloud nine driving home and hoping we were "now" going to get along fine, and although, I will never forgive her about the wedding, I won´t mention it. We phoned each other over the months and everything seemed to be fine. As it got close to Rebecca´s first birthday, I asked Christine if she would bring the bairn down and I would put a spread on for it, only to be told her mum had already made arrangements for it. It was yet another kick in the teeth for me. How can your mum have made the arrangements for the bairns birthday when I asked you to bring her down when the bairn was only 18 weeks old. There was no reply only a look of guilt. So I said ok, you can bring her down for her 2nd birthday. Time went on and I´d been up on a few visits and month or two before our Rebecca´s 2nd birthday I asked her about bringing the bairn down for her birthday I said I have had the bairns birthday cake made by the same person that made your 21st birthday cake and that I´d let the family know what date it was to be and they are "all" coming and looking forward to seeing my first grandchild. I wasn´t expecting yet, "another" kick in the teeth but, got one. She must have been waiting and rehearsing the reply because, without, a seconds hesitation she said, we can´t come down Da, we have sold the car to buy a van, so Paul can do his delivery´s at night and I can´t travel with the bairn in that. Oh I said well don´t worry I will come up and bring you all down, after a moment´s hesitation she said It´s a long way to travel with the bairn I don´t know if it will be ok. I said look Christine you travelled all the way from Germany at that age and you were all right ask your mother, and another thing Christine (I was back to begging again, and was determined, I was going to get this nipped in the bud "right now") If you decide you are not bringing the bairn down for her 2nd birthday Christine, we are "FINISHED" for good, I´m absolutely fed up with being treat this way by you, make your mind up, let me know one way or another. My head is in a whirl and I´m starting to think at this stage has Jan told her something that I don´t know about, and this is why I´m being treated so off handed. She phoned the next day to tell me what time to go and pick them up. The party and, get together, went well and, took them home a couple of days later, and surprisingly, she said she would like to come again soon, she did but, only because I went up for them.

  It was almost a year later my grandson, Stuart was born and, I was invited to the christening, on that occasion, things were looking up I went up there for his 1st birthday "BUT", the cake I had made for him the woman had spelt his name Stewart, instead of Stuart we had a good laugh about it after I took it out of the box. It was a few years later that, on one of my many trips up there, that I complained that she ought to be making a bit more effort to come and see me now and again instead of me having to do all the travelling when she said "well" Da if you hadn´t walked out on me and my mum then you wouldn´t have had to do any travelling. I thought "yes" now is the time to reveal all. I then told her the sad sorry story. There was no immediate comment from her so I said look at me Christine and said if you don´t believe me go and get your mother now and ask her to deny anything I´ve said in front of me. And yet another kick in the teeth came, she jumped up and said "my mother" wouldn´t have done that, get out of my house and don´t come back. That certainly was not what I was expecting from her. I left, with the parting words, "ask your mother "Christine" and don´t "ever" forget this "you" will need me before I need you.

On the way back home I was both, sad, and relieved, sad, that, it had turned out like it had today but, relieved that I had finally told Christine about the divorce but wished now I had done it years ago. We never spoke again for almost two years; I still sent her and the bairns, both birthdays, Xmas cards and monies to them and never received any cards from her or the bairns. One day out of the blue she rang me and said, she said Paul and I are getting divorced, he had found another woman and was living with her at his mother´s, and said would I go up and go to court with her as her mum was working and couldn´t get time off work and there might be some trouble, once again my head was telling me one thing and my heart was telling me another. It was an absolute cheek after being told not to come back to her house ever again, I just couldn´t abandon her, she was frightened and needed my help and support so I went up and we got back on talking terms again but, still no apologies to me about anything that had gone off in the past. After that I would phone up to ask how, she and the bairns were and did visit her and the bairns quite often. It had always been the case though that whenever I visited, Christine would never greet me, with a hug and a kiss on arriving it, was like visiting a stranger somehow, it was always me who did it, and on leaving I had to ask for a kiss goodbye it was as if I were a stranger. Another reason for me to think does she and Jan know something I didn´t, and weren´t telling me. and when the kids had come along it was the same, they would run a mile when I asked for a kiss goodbye and on many occasions had to leave without one, it hurt like hell to think I had travelled all that way and they couldn´t or wouldn´t give me a kiss goodbye. Like lots of kids, they were only interested in you, on arrival to see what you have brought them. I would always take them out for a few hours to the local park or along the beach, if the weather was ok and always find time to visit my family with them. I had always given the bairns from being 1 yr old £100 for birthdays and Xmas as I did for Christine until the kids came along and then dropped hers down to £20 it hurt that they couldn´t or wouldn´t write on the Birthday or Xmas cards that I received from them, it was always Christine who signed them. These little things now hurt more than the big things that go wrong (strange isn´t it) things trundled on like that for a long while and it was always, about 2 weeks before she would be going on holiday with her mother that she would mention it knowing full well I would send her the money to pay for her and the kids holiday and still, she would never come to see me, or have a holiday with me there was always an excuse of some sort so in the end I stopped asking, I just sent them money, as and when they needed it. It was so disheartening but what do you do when you love your kids? ,

It was late 1992, Joe was diagnosed with cancer of the gullet, and I immediately thought to myself "why him" why not anyone of the really bad people we all know. Hilda had been diagnosed with throat cancer many years prior and her treatment had been successful. I can only think that he had taken that into consideration before he went ahead and paid privately, £2500 for an operation, because while we working together, we once talked about either of us contracting cancer, and as Joe´s Dad had died from it and my one brothers and one of my sisters had died from it, and, also friends who both of us knew, and both of said we would take the quickest way out by taking tablets and getting drunk. Both of us said at one time or another that, when the time comes, that I need someone to wipe my backside, give me the needle put me to sleep, "please" and, let me die with dignity. Joe was a "very" proud man a "very" smart dresser and called a spade a spade and "never afraid to speak his mind I never asked him at the hospital why, he chose to pay for the operation, I had far too much respect for him. After the operation he was told it was part of the healing process that he find difficulty in swallowing, he became weaker and weaker until it became too much of an effort for him to go upstairs to bed and had to sleep on the settee. Over the next two weeks I visited him every day and one day I went and Hilda said to me, George, Joe has stopped his family (two daughters) coming to see him and was sorry but he no longer wants you to come either and this why George. He was asleep on the settee, drugged up and she pulled the covers from him and, there he was, skin and bone, with a nappy on. He can only eat melted ice cream and that´s a struggle, he doesn´t want anyone including "you" to see him in this state, this how the proud man he once was and, now reduced to this. I broke down and sobbed, we went into the kitchen, she said to me you love him don´t you, I said yes through my sobs, he, treat me like the father I should have had, she said and he loves you too like a son and you are the best friend he´s ever had. That made it even worse for me, we hugged a while, I said, if there was "any" help that you need you have only to ask. I walked home that day the saddest person on Gods earth. It was to become the 3rd of five great body blows, that, I was to have in my life, up to the present day. There was "nothing" I could do for Joe he was dying, it was a feeling of utter frustration and anger and my helplessness in the situation. I still went everyday and tapped on the window to ask Hilda did she need any help, I respected Joe´s wishes to the end and never went into the house until after he died which sadly he did two weeks later. It was as I have already said one of the three saddest days of my life. I went to the chapel of rest to see him, he was laid there like a yellow wax work dummy the cancer had spread to his liver before he died I broke down and sobbed again. I couldn´t remember a time in my life that I felt as low as this but, at least he was free of pain now.

It was about two weeks after the funeral that his youngest daughter Neen as Joe always called her, "the apple" of his eye, (she could do no wrong) came to my house and, brought the Omega watch that I´d bought for his retirement from pit, she said, mum said, it was Dad´s wish that if anything happened to him "you" were to have it back, I just filled up and, thought why? He has a grandson, I felt very honoured that he felt that way about me, she said and what´s strange George it´s stopped at the exact time of his death 1124 am. and, it can´t be wound up, also mum wants to see you. I went to see Hilda and she asked if I wanted Joe´s two leather coats a jacket and topcoat, I said yes and, still have them in my wardrobe today it´s a little piece of Joe that I´ll have until the day I die. I had the watch repaired and cost very nearly as much as I paid for it all those years ago but, I didn´t mind in the least as I now had something that belonged him which I treasure dearly and which I have left to his grandson in my will.

It was 3 years later that Sue and I went to Corfu with Terry a good mate of mine and his wife Sally, and the most disastrous holiday I have ever had. We booked the last week in July and the 1ST week in August the 2 hottest for the Islands (SHOULD HAVE

KNOWN BETTER) I bought some expensive total sun block cream on the plane when flying out. Within an hour we were on the beach I´d lathered myself with the total sun block and somehow missed covering my shins and feet "Oh my" what a mistake! After 2 or 3 hours of swimming about in the sea we decided to go and get changed and have a meal in the restaurant which was next door to the apartment. All was well until I got in the shower and could feel the pain in both my shins and feet. Within a very short time they were as red as a carrot and stinging like Hell. I had got 3rd degree burns on them. Next day my legs and feet had swollen to twice their size and spent the rest of the holiday under a palm tree at the back of the apartment applying natural yogurt on them on the advice of the local doctor who came to see me. No sooner had I applied the yogurt and it seemed to bake it like pastry that´s how hot my legs were. I couldn´t sleep at night with pain so would spend time standing in front of the open fridge door and putting hankies in the freezer to wipe my legs with them. Every morning I was out walking along the beach in the cool air to try and get ease from the pain. It took a couple of more years before we went on holiday again and still to this day I always wear long trousers as the sun just seems to scorch my legs even with sun cream on them . There has been no hair grown on my legs since that time, and I´ll bet many women wished they had the same but without the pain to achieve it.

Our friend Jim had lost his wife ten years earlier and had remarried, and, 14yrs later he was diagnosed with cancer, he was a powerful built man, an absolute power house at work and when he was admitted to a hospital some ten miles away, I took his wife Doreen, every day I finished work and wheeled him around the hospital grounds, so he could get out in fresh air which he dearly loved. He was later transferred to our local hospital when they diagnosed that it had gone into his bones and hadn´t got long to live. I still went every day after work and it worked out that Doreen could go home for a couple of hours. The evening before he died he was hallucinating, and was talking to two people one at the foot of his bed and one at the window to his left and the conversation was as plain as day, to the one at the foot of the bed he was saying "no" I´m not going anywhere I´m staying here and then after a few seconds all his attention was to someone he was talking to at the window with a look of surprise on his face at first, ok he said but wait until Doreen comes back. Who he was talking to I don´t know but, I´ve been told that just before you die someone you know and love comes to you to take you to your maker. Doreen came back that evening, I just couldn´t, tell her, as she had, had enough upset as it was without me going in to details like that. He died later that evening. Who knows what goes on when your time is up no one has ever come back to tell us have they? But we all have our own personal thoughts and keep them to ourselves and that´s how it should be.

My view, even, today is, why? "Anyone" who is terminally ill should be kept alive in a sleeping state. Going through the indignity of having to have, as I say, their backsides wiped, they wouldn´t have wanted that in real life would they? Let them die with dignity and without pain and suffering. Does the good book say "suffer not" little children but come unto me? Well that is what my dearest and best friend was reduced to, while drugged up, to ease the pain he, had to have nappy on, as he no longer had control of his bowls.

It was a short while after the disastrous holiday, after Joe had died and after the wedding of our Christine, Sue and I went to visit my sisters at Halifax and, they told me they had all been to see a medium called Bridget an Irish girl, and that she was brilliant and, would I like to go and see her. I had never been to a medium before but, had always "toyed" with the idea, hoping I could get in touch with Ma so, I said yes. They booked us in for the following week and went to see her.

The only time I had anything to do with anything like this was when I was living in a flat in bed sit land. The girlfriend of a friend I had made in the local pub asked if I would like to have my tarot cards read, my mate immediately said "don´t have anything to do with them George they´re "evil" go on I said I´m not afraid, I shuffled the cards and gave them back to her and she started to deal them out when all of sudden she picked them all up and said I can´t go any further "WHY" I said, she said, it´s because it´s not right, I said come on do it again, I shuffled and cut the cards a lot more times and gave her the cards back and she did the same started to deal them out and then picked them up again, I can´t do it she said, I told you mate, he said, they are evil keep away from them. By this time I´d had a good drink down me and said "come on" you won´t frighten me and shuffled cut the cards loads of times again and just as she was about to start to deal I took them from her and shuffled and cut the cards again saying don´t stop this time, she deal the cards without stopping this time and told me the Angel of death card is in the wrong place she said it shouldn´t be there and it has for the three hands that I have dealt, so I said come on then, what does my cards say then. What she said next I will never forget as long as I live. She said there´s a younger dark haired woman who is going to cause lots, of problems in your life "AND" you are going to die a violent death. That sobered me up instantly. George I told you didn´t I. Whether the tarot readings were true or false I sure as hell have not had another reading.

I had no idea what was going to happen when I went see Bridget but had made my mind up, that I wouldn´t give any information away, but to give yes or no answers to questions. The moment I walked in the room and before, she introduced herself, she said OOOOH, I have never had anyone visit me who is "so down". The reading was quite good she seemed to know quite a lot of things about me i.e. having gout, having just, lost someone, very dear to me recently and amazingly said that I had his gold watch, which was true, and that I should wear it so he can look over me, I filled up then and we had to stop for a short while. She even went on to say to say that I was divorced and wouldn´t re marry, and that I had, had a major fall out with my "only" child a "daughter" and should go and make things up with her. (I took that advice only to get more heartache and grief) One thing she said to me that I found pleasing because at the time I was on my Driving Instructors course at the time, she said you are going to be associated with driving the pubic around I naturally thought I would pass the Instructors course and set up my own School never imagining I would eventually become a taxi driver. Another thing she said to me was and I didn´t understand it at the time, she said you haven´t many true friends in your life but have lots and lots of acquaintances, who, some will let you down when you when you need their help most. And as this story unfolds a truer word has never been spoken to me. There has got to be something in it. For me it´s impossible for someone you have "never" met could know these things about you. But she never said there were any messages or info about my Ma. One of the things I have always said "if" there is a place on the other side as it´s called will Ma recognise me as I was only 4yrs old when she died, I hope so. Anyway,

I came away from Bridget´s feeling a lot better, and, with a recording of the reading to listen to whenever I wanted to.

Another major event in my life came in when I was as, British Coal, worded it, "Surplus" to requirements (redundant) it was not what I wanted in particular as I was in a good paid job and felt that at 47yrs old, I still had a good few years of hard work left in me. After about 2 months of lounging about, wondering whether to go back to private contract mining, which meant travelling, a mate of mine Alan, who did all his drinking in a club down the road to me, who had also been made redundant from another pit, and like myself came from the north-east where people talk properly, his only fault was he couldn´t talk without swearing, he came to see me in the club one night and said, I have the chance of buying a large window cleaning round that would keep two in full time work it´s that big, would you be interested in buying it with me? He gave me all the details, where it was and, how much it would cost to buy etc. after some thought I said yes.

It wasn´t what I had in mind as being my next job but, it was a job and earning money, we went and had a look at the size of the round and bought it. We started on the Monday morning and the first thing I learned that day was, Alan couldn´t or wouldn´t, go up the ladders, no matter though, I wasn´t afraid of heights or, so I thought, until that first morning. The very first house we went to was one that the upstairs windows were huge and the only way I could get to clean them was to stand on the top rung of the ladder I was scared stiff, I had nowhere to hang on to and was well pleased when I had finished, the thought of falling off those ladders and perhaps injuring myself for life, was the first time in my life including, any job I´d done down the pit that I´d been scared, and, it must have shown. Are you alright, Alan asked as I got off the ladders yes I´m ok I said, have you any toilet paper? It was our first day on the job and I was moaning about it. Stop it! I said to myself. I was determined not to let it get the better of me and glad, as it turned out, because the woman paid double because of the danger in having her windows cleaned. As the weeks went by, it was taking us less time to finish an area and after a few weeks we were starting at 10am and were finished for the day at 2pm, and worked 5pm-7pm on Friday´s collecting any monies owed. I tried several times to get Alan to clean the upstairs windows even, lying, telling him about seeing women undressing etc. but I couldn´t get him up those ladders. He had the gift of the gab had Alan, and used it to get cups of tea and even a sarnie at times which was good especially on cold mornings. We were earning a living at it but "nothing" compared to the wages we had earned at pit, we had both been on the same type of work but at different pits when we were made redundant. At least we were not spending our redundancy money, sadly a lot of the lads were. A great many were not even looking for work. I have always been this frame of mind, go and earn your money now, as there might come a day, "God forbid" you "can´t" go to work, and then wishing you had, when you had the chance. After about 6 months I was talking to a mate from pit and, he told me he had done a Driving Instructors course, and that you could fit it in with any job you were doing. I got all the details from him and decided to look into it. As we were finished on the window cleaning round at 2pm most days, I found, a driving school that, would take me on, and did the course. I failed the 1st one and sat a 2nd course and passed. Alan was good to me in the fact that he bought my half of the business from me and we parted ways amicably. We remained good friends until sadly he died of cancer some 5 years later. He died with the same sort of cancer as Jim, it had gone into his bones.

Both of us had a great sense of humour and could see the funny side of things and one really funny incident comes to mind. It was the day of his funeral and it was just like something you would see on a TV comedy show. We arrived at the church gates before the hearse arrived, no one had noticed the church was locked up until the hearse did arrive and someone went to open the gates "these gates are locked" someone shouted, the funeral director tried them and sent someone to the vicar´s house which was about five minutes walk away. Alan´s widow was sobbing by now saying "how" could this happen today, of all days. The vicar arrived saying the funeral was booked in for the following day and after comparing notes with the funeral director apologised to Alan´s widow who by now couldn´t be consoled. The vicar then opened the church gates and people were now making remarks like, I bet he´s overslept, he shouldn´t be doing the job, if he´s getting his days mixed up like today. Knowing Alan´s sense of humour he would be saying I always wanted to be late for my funeral "not" a f.....g day early. I was hoping no one seen me smiling at those thoughts, it was later, at the reception that lots of others had, had the same thoughts, knowing his sense of humour. Four of Alan´s closest friends went to the hearse to carry his coffin into church, after getting the coffin on their shoulders and walked two steps one of the lads at the back tripped and the coffin was almost on the floor OOOH gasped everyone who saw it, but it was quickly put right, "I bet that woke him" up someone said later at the reception. It was the kind of comment Alan himself would have made, he was a great joker and is sadly missed by a lot of people and friends like myself.

After about 4 yrs giving driving lessons the money wasn´t coming in as much as I wanted, there were far too many schools at it. So I decided to have a go at taxi-ing. There was a bus company advertising Hackney cabs for hire to drivers with lots of Hospital and School contracts so, I decided to give it a go and started work for them, at first things went well, it was longer hours but, I was earning decent money again. One experience I remember was shortly after I´d started was, I had taken a fare to Manchester airport at 4am and on my return was ranked up at the railway station it was 11am at the time and I was the 3rd cab waiting for a fare the 1st picked up and two minutes later he came back and the passenger got into the 2nd cab after a brief chat with her he brought her to my cab and said George she wants to go to Aylesbury some 250 miles away and I can´t take her because, I´m going fishing this afternoon, can you, yes I said, she got in, she was a young Indian girl about 20 something well dressed in English clothes, spoke perfect English, and I said, I will have to get a route guide from the base operator which will only take a few minutes. She then told me that only had £70 but don´t worry you will get the rest of the fare when we get there. I thought to myself at least that would cover the fuel and she looks trustworthy. I got the route guide and set off, try as I may I couldn´t get into making conversation and gave up in the end. After about 30miles or so said could she lie down on the seat, I said yes and that´s how she remained for the rest of the journey, she never spoke another word. We arrived in Aylesbury, I woke her up and said where do you want to be, I would never have guessed what was coming next, she said I don´t know I´ve forgotten the address you are kidding me I said, I was thinking I´m only getting my fuel money out of this, has she done me? She said it´s a long time since I was here, looking ahead and feeling really annoyed I spotted a police station, I said lets go to the police station and find out where you want to be, you do know their name don´t you? Oh yes she said, as we drove to the police station I´m thinking at least they will get the rest of my fare. About ½ an hour went by and I went inside to find her and a policeman came to me and said you want be 2 villages away, easy to find he said, gave me the address, it was a doctors surgery. I was not as apprehensive now. We arrived at the surgery only to find the doctor had gone home, don´t worry the receptionist said it´s easy to find, go around to the railway which is just around the corner and take the first turning on your right just after station. I followed her instructions and after travelling about mile down the road I couldn´t see a right turn just after the station so decided to turn round and go back to the surgery, as we approached the station the girl said "that´s it, that´s it" I can remember now it´s up a field. I looked and it was a cart track leading to some tree´s yes this is it she said, we drove up to tree´s and in the clearing was this beautiful massive Tudor house. She jumped out of the cab and ran into the house. Thank God I thought, we´ve arrived at last. I was knackered it was about 5pm and I´d been up since 3am.I needed to find a phone and tell Sue where I was, and when I´d be home and to find a place to park up and get my head down for a couple of hours before I set off back. After a few minutes this guy and the girl came out and he started to give me a telling off asking, why? have you brought this girl all the way from Yorkshire in a taxi. I said before we go any further, change the tone of your voice please. I´m a taxi driver and she booked me that´s why. Oh and by the way she told me you would give me the rest of my fare which is £80 plus £10 for the waiting time at the police station and your surgery it´s £90 in all, he went into the house to get the fare and then a Mercedes Gull- wing sports car comes belting in pebbles flying all over a woman got out, "get in that house" she screamed, the guy

came out again and introduced himself as Dr. A.......
and said he was sorry for shouting at me earlier but
was annoyed with the girl coming all this way in a taxi
, I realise it wasn´t your fault he said. He went on to
tell me that she had sat her doctors exams at Leeds
university, had failed them and was too frightened to
face her parents and had run away down to here, and
it had been 20 years since she had been here. Time
was getting on now and I decided against getting
my head down. It was 11pm when I arrived home;
driving with all the windows open all the way I was
absolutely knackered it took a couple of days to pull
myself round after that one. On another occasion
which was funny I was sent to the Infirmary to pick
a patient up, to take to another hospital and when
I asked the base operator have you a name, he said
fraid not, they know the colour of the cab and will
come out to it. You do get some funny names of
people to pick up and I thought I would have a bit of
fun with the operator, after a few minutes I radioed
in and said, I´ve looked everywhere and no one is
answering to the name Fraidnot , you stupid Pillock,
he shouted, but that´s the name you gave me, I said,
"silence", and then I shouted get a sense of humour
you Pillock.

I left the bus company and bought a new Hackney cab
with a guy that I thought I knew. It was a "SERIOUS
"error of judgement I made that day that would
cost me dearly and the 4th body blow. His name was
Will Do-ewe. No, seriously if that were his name he
couldn´t have been more aptly named. I really wasn´t
prepared for what was going to happen over the next
few weeks. He was without doubt the biggest con
man I have ever had the misfortune to be involved
with. The arrangements of running the cab was, we
would share the takings, keep our own tips, and after
all the outgoing costs that would be our wages. He
preferred to work at night, and I would work it during

the day, that was ideal for me as I never liked working nights anyway, he said he could earn by working Thur. Fri. Sat and Sun nights as much as I could working 6 days on the day shift. I didn´t mind though, having to put the extra hours in, to match his takings. The 1st mistake of our partnership was, I stupidly thought, he was as honest as me. We were in his house making the arrangements of buying the cab etc. and I went back the following day with half the monies required and as I left I said to him and his wife "Well" you will never get a more honest and hard working partner than me and I will never forget what his wife said, she gave a little laugh and said "he´s the same" a statement that will haunt me for the rest of. Little did I know that in a few short weeks the pair of B...... ds were going to rip me off "big "time. I was working my 2 weeks notice with the bus company and he said he would sort everything out as regards the cab, and for some reason or other (it never entered my head) I never went with him to sign for the HP agreement on the cab. It was the 2nd stupid mistake I made of our partnership. Things were going ok at first, he was working was working his 4 nights and I was working my 6 days and then found out that on Sunday mornings there was always a good contract job would come up from British rail and being the nature I am to earn more money, started to work on Sunday mornings until 11am. This would also put extra money in the fund we had set up for Insurance, and road tax etc. The 3rd and biggest mistake I made was, I never checked the meter or mileage as I handed the cab over to him at night. I "thought" he was as honest as me. As the weeks progressed, his takings were going down and, then he wasn´t working on a Thursday night. "Thats" when I "should" have realised something was terribly wrong by the time we were into our 14TH week of partnership it was the annual works holiday week in town and there would be lots of fares "and" tips to be to earned that week. On the Sunday prior to it he said I´m having the cab next week you take the week off. I was flabbergasted at his cheek, I don´t think so I said. You decided you wanted to work nights and by the way you only work 3 nights now and I´m working 7 mornings. He was not pleased, he said "right" from now on we don´t share wages, that´s ok by me I said, I´ll use the cab from 6am and bring it back to you at 6pm, just leave the cab topped up to the gunnels with fuel when you have finished with it so we know where we are with the fuel. What we had been doing prior was to put the same amount of fuel in per week from our takings and keep the receipt for proof as well as for the accountant. I took the cab back to the garage and filled it to the gunnels and left it with him. He was furious and stormed into his house. The next morning was the beginning of the end of our partnership. I went straight to the garage and filled it up to where I´d filled it up to the day prior and could put £5 worth of fuel in it. When I returned that night I showed him the receipt which had the time and the garage where I´ve bought it from and you can see "you" haven´t filled it up as I have left it. His face was like thunder he had been found out he was cheating. He stormed off without saying a word. The next day I checked the fuel and this time it needed over £7 in to fill it to the gunnels, so the next day I didn´t fill up at all and told him why, I had used only £12 of fuel that day (calculated by the mileage) and being as I have had to put a fiver in the day before and £7 in to top it up yesterday I haven´t put any in tonight. His face was like thunder again. The cheating B.....d had been found out "and" how much else, had he been cheating me with, over, the few short weeks while we had been sharing takings? The next morning he was waiting for me He invited me into his house and I was really taken aback with what he said next .George he said I can´t go on like this anymore, stop trying to cheat me and play the game with the fuel I said thinking that´s why he had sent for me. No he said I´m taking the cab on, on my own and I´ll pay you £700 for your share in it. I don´t think so I said, I want half of what money I put in and that was £1800 alone, to get it on the road, But what about the wear and tear of the cab he said, I said, give me a minute to work this out, I said. I worked it out with all the credit work we were owed and said I´ll give "YOU" £3000 and I´ll take the cab. No he said and don´t take the cab today as I will report you for taking it without my permission, don´t forget you haven´t signed for it with me. It then dawned on me that I hadn´t. I was dumbstruck, I walked away from him and took the cab and went home, waited, for a couple of hours and phoned the police to ask if it had been reported stolen, it hadn´t. What´s his game I thought, I then phoned the Finance company up explained what he had said to me and then found out it "was" true. How could I have been so stupid? I thought and thought about driving the cab and writing it off, and then thought of the consequences, I would be found out, and then have a criminal record, it wasn´t worth it so, I took the cab back to him, and said, I´ll see you in court for my money. I sought legal advice to get my money back and in the meantime found out a lot about him. When his takings had been going down when we were sharing them it was because he had been selling the credit work voucher payment for the job for a lesser price than it was worth and keeping it. I went see a solicitor and after a couple of exchanged letters I got one from his saying that I had been threatening him and it must stop, it said, which was a lie as I hadn´t spoken to him since the day I took the cab back. It was the oldest trick in the book "If" he was to get a good hiding, I was going to be the prime suspect, the yellow backed B....rd had done me again. The solicitor after many weeks of trying to get him to return my money suggested I take it to the small claims court and that´s when the 4th mistake happened I never sent my documents in

213

as evidence and when we went to court thinking that because he would be able to read my evidence he would have had some cock bull story ready to worm his way out of it (bad legal advice) although the Judge was sympathetic with me and said because you haven't done that and as you didn´t sign the HP for the cab, he will keep the cab, and all the debt, and you will forego the money he owes you. I was livid, and it showed, the judge said in most of the cases that he knew of, the cab was repossessed as the kind of person he was, he wouldn´t be able to keep the payments up. A short while after the court case I made an appeal and when I got to court I was told that I was 3 days over the limit in making the appeal. Through bad legal advice I lost it again. The "B....rd" had done me again. I was as sick as a parrot with chapped lips. "The B.....rd" was all I could think but, he wasn´t worth getting a criminal record for.

 As I was on the committee there are certain rules that apply to a members conduct both, in, and, out, of the club and this was one of them. He had robbed a fellow member out of £2800 in total, besides solicitor's fee´s. When I asked the committee for their help in having him barred from the club as an undesirable member, they wouldn´t help me. That became the 5th body blow. I was absolutely gutted when they refused to implement that ruling saying that although they sympathised with me, that, "he" might have words with the Social Security about the amount of fee´s that they were getting while on the committee "and" receiving benefits, and that is something they could do without. There was no such fear for me, as I had never been on benefits in my life except when I was ill with Rheumatic fever. My thoughts went back to the time when I went to see Bridget and how right she´d been. I had up to that point been on the committee 25 years and thought foolishly they were my friends but now I realised they were only acquaintances after all. My enthusiasm in committee work stopped that day, and those I thought were my friends, I looked them at in an entirely different light now, from that day I would never be able to look upon them as friends again. How on earth could I have deceived myself all those years thinking they were friends when "all" they were thinking of was themselves.

There was one committee man in particular and his wife, who Sue and I we were very close to and thought were good, good friends. Shortly after we had got to know them he had to have an operation on his back to have a disk removed. I was one of two out of the 16 committee men who, went to visit him. When I was on my driving instruction course I gave his daughter my first pupil hours and hours of free driving lessons (she passed 1st time) I later went on to put his wife and him through the driving course at half price and they both passed their driving tests. When his wife was diagnosed with cancer it was me that took them for appointments, and treatment, right until the end, without, a thought of any charge to them. That´s what friends do, when your friends need help don´t you? When he made no effort to help me because, like the others he was on benefits he was scared of any Social Security enquiries he showed me his true colours that day. It´s a strange world, you would think that after "all" the kicks in the teeth I´d had over the years it would be like water off a ducks back for me "but" the trouble, is I think everyone, is, loyal, trustworthy, and honest as I am, "what an idiot I am".

I had decided after that incident that I would round off my committee service to 30yrs and retire. As much as I was fuming inside about the incident I still had a lot of friends who were members, and towards the latter end of my time on the committee another incident occurred. It was one Boxing day night the President the Vice President or any other committee member hadn´t turned up, to cover the chairman's job in the concert room, where, a disco was on, and, on a Boxing day night, was renowned for trouble and, if the truth were known, that´s, why they hadn´t turned up for their duty. So, I stood in for them, and as expected all hell broke loose so, I sent for the police, and the room was quickly cleared, I thanked the police inspector in charge, and they left. It was the following Sunday when we had our normal committee meeting and the incident was discussed. Before I could say a word on the subject the secretary said, the police had been to the club and the inspector who had been to the club on the night of the incident, took a dim view of the chairman that night (me) as in his opinion I was drunk in charge of the club. I was gob smacked I had never ever been drunk while on any duty or otherwise since being on the committee. That´s a lie I said, that´s what he told me, he said. In that case I will go and see him because he never mentioned my conduct at all in fact he said I had done a good job under the circumstances that night and bid me goodnight as he left. The following day I went to the police station and asked to see the inspector, he did see me, and when I explained, what the secretary had said about him saying I was drunk in charge of the club he said, that´s a "lie" what I said was, there should have been more than one man in charge of the club for a function like that. I asked if he would come to our committee meeting and tell them that, he said yes please invite me as I would have other things to discuss with the committee. At the following meeting I told the committee that I had, had an interview with the inspector and that he had said no such thing to the secretary, and would be prepared to come to the club if invited to confirm this. The look on the secretary´s face was like thunder he was" livid", he or the committee never thought I would carry out my threat and go and see the police inspector "but", my conduct, was being lied about and I was having none of that. The secretary shouted "I´m telling "you" that´s what he said" So "you" are calling the police inspector a "liar" I said, let´s have him in here and prove who "is" lying. The President said that´s not going to happen George the subject is "dropped" now, and, "won´t" be discussed again ok?

 I left that meeting asking myself "why"? Why had the secretary lied about me? I genuinely thought he was a friend, several of the committee came to me that day, and said, George "we" believe you, and couldn´t understand why he´d made up such a cock and bull story. It had been the "first" time he had been questioned over his honesty and been found out he was lying "otherwise" he would have invited the inspector to the meeting, and I would have been dismissed from the committee if I´d been found to be lying about it. I never got to the bottom of that incident but I never looked upon him in the same light again. Yet another kick in the teeth from people you least expect it from.

It was a week after the breakup of the partnership I went back to the Bus Company and hired a cab from them. They had a fleet of taxi´s and were in dire need of drivers, I was later to find out why drivers wouldn´t stay with them. Things went well again at first and then, about a year later I realised that all the good paid jobs over the radio were going to the company drivers so, once again I left only this time I bought a car and used it for Private hire. Everything was above board now, which meant, going home at the end of the day without the upset´ and frustration, knowing you hadn´t been cheated out of any good paying jobs. There was some classic jobs that I went to, while working there, and one of them was the time I had to pick an old lady up and take her to the doctors, for the first time, it was also the first time the firm had booked her. Off I went for her it was only a 3-50 fare, got there and, could see the old lady sitting at the window looking up the street, she couldn´t see my taxi stickers because of her small hedge so, I papped the horn, there was no response so, papped it again still no response, got out of the car and the next door neighbour who was in their garden said she´s "deaf" so I went to the window got her attention and we set off. I had only got to the bottom of her street when she frightened the living daylights out of me, "SHOUTING" we´ll have to go back I´ve forgotten to turn my fire off, I went back to her bungalow, gave her my arm as she walking badly and walked her to the door, after a few minutes she came out giving me lovely smile and shouted enough to make my hair stand on end " come on I´m going to be late" we set off and got to the bottom of her street again and shouted she at the top of her voice again " STOP" I need my purse, took her back again to pick her purse up and by this time I spent about 40 minutes with her, when we finally got to the doctors she said how much do I owe you, £3-50 I said she fumbled in her purse and gave me 3 twenty pence pieces and a 50 pence piece I said this is not enough after finally convincing her the twenty pence pieces were not pound coins I then walked her into the doctors only to find that she had got her appointment day wrong by this time I had been with her for over an hour and the fare was only £3-50 how the hell could I make a living at this rate. She now wanted to go back home, when I did get her back home and walked her to the door and asked for the return fare she shouted for the street to hear "I´VE ALREADY PAID YOU ONCE, YOU BLOODY ROB DOG" I had been with this fare for an hour and a half and been paid £3-50 I hadn´t the heart to explain to her she should pay me both ways and left, "embarrassed", hoping, no one had heard her shouting at me. I thought to myself on the way back to base that´s "someone´s" mother, she "could" have been my Ma in that state, and didn´t feel too bad about it then.

I was the only driver at that firm that wore a tie and shaved every day, Sue´s grandson would valet my car every week making my car the cleanest in the fleet, I told my fares when they made comment about it, my views were this, it costs no more to ride in a clean car than it costs to ride in dirty car and that paid dividends, as I was asked for personally many, many times.

 Two people in particular come to mind, who I thought would be well out of my league but, because of my mannerism, dress, and the cleanliness of my car I was to meet, the first one was the widow of the owner of a historic hall a Spanish lady who I drove all over the place. She was a wonderful person to talk to and how we met was, early one morning before I had set off to work in town, the base operator phoned me and said George get yourself to B......... Hall as quick as you can to the "Garden House" he gave me instructions to find it, a woman needs to get to the Railway Station in double quick time. When I arrived, she was panicking, her usual taxi hadn´t turned up, and it was imperative she caught the London train, can we do it in time she said, I´ll do my best I said, we set off and was driving as fast as the law would allow it. It must have been fate for me that day, we got to the station with a couple of minutes to spare, I got her luggage out and set off running for the platform shouting, "come on you can still make it" we did with seconds to spare. She paid me the fare including, a £10 tip "wow" was I grateful. It was a couple of days later I was sent to the station to pick her up. You must be honoured George the base operator said she´s asked for you personally to take her back to B......... Hall. When we set off she said, I´d like to thank you for the other day when you brought me to the station and ran with my luggage to the train, it was very kind of you, no one has ever done that for me before, I wouldn´t have caught that train otherwise, thank you so much. At B.......... Hall she paid me including, another £10 tip. After that day she took out a credit contract with the firm and she always asked for me and unless I was on another job I got the job. As I said she was a lovely person to talk to, and eventually we got on first name terms. "Me" on first name terms with a millionaire who would have thought it. On one occasion when I took her home from some outing, the orchard which she lived in was full of apples and asked if I could have a few, of course take as many as you like she said.

I always carried a couple of spare carrier bags in my glove compartment in case one my fares needed one in an emergency. So I filled the one of the bags and took it home to bake pies and apple crumbles, both Sue´s and my favourite's, the next day I had to pick her up to take her on some outing, I thanked her for the apples and said, I had made some nice apple pies and crumbles with them. She didn´t know what I meant by crumbles and when I explained she said they sound delicious so I said the next time I make some I´ll bring you one of each which I did. She said they were delicious and after that I took her one every time I made them. Which brings to mind one of my old sayings "what does it cost to be nice?" absolutely nothing does it? It wasn´t done for gain I get a lot of pleasure from giving.

The second person was "Tadgelle," a dear old lady who I first met when I took her to spend Xmas with her daughter and family in the West country. She was one of the few most likeable persons I've ever had the pleasure of meeting in my life. We come from entirely different back grounds, she was an ex head mistress and of course you have already read of my background. The conversations we had on those journeys down to her daughters will never be forgotten by either of us and after a few journeys we became friends for life. Tadgelle was named by her father after a race horse that had won the Derby or some other classic horse race at some time or other. She is, at this time of writing 96 years old and simply wonderful, in the fact that, she has all, her faculties about her, and puts me so at ease when talking to her, like no one I´ve ever known. Over the years we have exchanged birthday and Xmas cards, and, presents (her birthday is two days before mine) one year she was "ecstatic" when Sue crocheted a shawl and some slippers, her a shawl which she wears in bed when reading (even to today) We have invited her to tea on several occasions and she feels so comfortable that she often comments "can´t I come and live with you two It´s so lovely and peaceful" the vibes I get when I´m in your home is something I´ve never felt in any of my friends home over the years. Such nice compliments come once in a life time. She is a lovely, lovely person in every way and I hope she lives for a good many years. Although, she has said many, many times that she has lived long enough now and would like to go soon. Which shocked me at times, as she is so full of bounce when she has been in my company? I can understand it to a degree as she lives on her own and it must be very lonely for her at times.

There was another incident that I will never forget while taxi driving, it was the time there was a Poltergeist in the tyre fitting bay, in the complex where our taxi base was. It was the first building in the complex about 30 yards from the entrance. Graham, the foreman, was a decent and sensible guy, always kept a clean and tidy workshop. We the taxi firm had been buying tyres from him for more than 3 years now since we moved into the same complex so we all knew him quite well, when one day, I went to have couple of tyres fitted he said to me, George what do you make of these, and showed me a heap of coins on a shelf. What's wrong with them I said, thinking, they were his tips, I don't know where they are coming from he said, with a worried look on his face. There was a mixture of coins, 10s, 2s, and 1 penny pieces, looking at them, a rough guess, I would say about £2 in total. I don't know what you mean Graham, he said, George, they are coming out of thin air, believe me. It started about 2 weeks ago when they sent me that young lad to train; I started to notice the coins on the shelf beside the washbasin, after a couple of days I asked him why, are you putting your loose change on there? He said they're not mine I've found them on the floor, so I dismissed it as customers dropping them but, after a few days I thought myself, this hasn't happened to this amount in the 10 years that I've been here. I thought this kid is messing about until one morning, a couple of days ago, I was in here on my own, the lad was having the day off when, I heard the sound of coins hitting the floor, I looked round the floor and sure enough there was three coins on the floor, I looked outside to see if anyone was about who, could, have thrown them in, and there was no one about. This is getting "Spooky" I thought. He went on to say that it's happening quite often and the young lad is getting quite scared now and to tell the truth George so am I. No wonder he had that worried look on his face. I left him to go back to work and called in every time I returned to see if any more money had appeared. Strangely enough the coins stopped appearing for a few days and Graham was losing the worried look on his face. It was Saturday morning when I drove into the complex after doing a couple of jobs when Graham shouted George come and have a look at this, I swear I haven't touched anything, it was like this when I opened up. If I hadn't seen it for myself I wouldn't have believed it. All the tyres were out of the racks around the wall and were stacked up on the floor on top of one another in neat piles. Has anyone got a key to get in and do this Graham I said, no he said it´s at head office. He was looking frantic now and just at that the young kid came into work he looked at it and said what the hell is going off Graham his eyes bulging, that´s what I want to know he said. I left and was as puzzled as Graham. During that day I called in a few times, Graham said he had told the head office about all the incidents they sent the manager to see for himself and he suggested they send for the local vicar. He came and blessed the place, when the local newspapers got hold of it they ran an article on it and found that the building had been used as a morgue during the war. This was getting to Graham by now and it was showing too he was showing signs of stress by it all, good for business though as it attracted a lot of customers who were intrigued by it all. The young lad was scared to death about it and left that week. One Saturday afternoon when our work had dried up I went to see Graham again, I felt truly sorry for him, he was a nice guy so easy to get on with and all this had really gotten to him, he was having a slack time of it too and was sitting on some old tyres outside of the building against a wall, he told me the coins were appearing again and said things were happening at home too, he was telling me that he got up one morning and every draw in his kitchen was pulled open and that he hadn´t mentioned this to his wife as he didn´t want to scare her. I was facing Graham and his new work mate who sitting on some old tyres with their backs to a wall both had their arms folded, there was a metal advertising plate on the wall above their heads when all of a sudden some coins hit it with a fair amount of force, I immediately looked to see who had thrown them, there was no one there, if I hadn´t seen that for myself I wouldn´t have believed it. I picked the coins up, there was two

2pences and three 1 pence pieces, as I was looking at them I noticed that they were all the same date, strange I thought and took them to the pile on the shelf and found that every coin was the same date 1978. Work that one out???? Sadly Graham went on sick leave, it all became too much for him and never returned. Since Graham left, nothing ever happened, in the tyre fitting bay again. "That is", up to the time of me retiring. It was very strange indeed eh? Like seeing the UFO on the north Yorkshire moors I know what I saw!

It was a good while after that incident that, I had the second UFO sighting was when I was walking home from the club one Sunday afternoon with Dave, a long time mate of mine from work. It was once again a sunny day not a cloud in the clear blue sky. There was an Air show on at the local RAF base when a Tri plane flew overhead and I made the comment of "there´s a golden oldie Dave" when we both noticed a small grey object directly in front but higher than the plane and once again about the size of your small finger nail floating down in front of it and, both, of us almost together, said "what´s that", floating down in front of it. When suddenly it stopped and shot straight up like lightning and was out of sight in the blink of an eye. I can´t believe what I´ve just seen Dave said, what do you think it was. I went on to tell him of the time I´d seen the same thing when I was on the north Yorkshire moors years ago. Once again I know what I saw. I have never seen anything like that since. It had been some time earlier when Sue and I were in the club one Sunday evening waiting for our friends to join us and when they came in they said George "be quick" go outside and have a look at what´s floating in the sky towards the Welfare Playing fields I dashed out side had a look but it was really low cloud and couldn´t see anything. I came back in and asked what they had seen? They said If we hadn´t seen it with our own eyes we wouldn´t have believed it. It was a triangular shape and massive in size and about 5 or 6 hundred yards above the ground floating silently towards the welfare, I cursed the low cloud as it stopped me from seeing it. This was a couple who I knew wouldn´t lie about such a thing and to confirm their story when I got to work next day, two taxi drivers and the base operator the night before had seen the same thing in town at around the same time. At some time or other the same craft was seen by the residents of a whole village in Belgium. What was it who knows?

Life trundled on for a few more years and about two weeks before my 60th birthday Sue said to me, don´t make any arrangements for your 60TH as I want to take you out for a meal that day just "you" and I, so, take the day off and we´ll make a day of it. That´s unusual for Sue I thought, as we hardly ever went out for a meal, because she is so picky about food, however it is my 60TH and she wants to make a fuss of me in return for the surprise party her family and I had put on for her 60th. I took the day off, and off we went, down to the local golf club where we were to have a meal after a few beers of course. After a while I noticed she was going out of the bar quite often and said, jokingly have you got a fellow out there somewhere, well after my 6th pint she said to me "who" would you have liked to come to your birthday. I looked at and her and said, no don´t tell me Tommy , a lump came in my throat and tears streaming down my face she said yes. I had said to Sue on numerous occasions in the past I wonder how he fared in life and when I get retired I think I´ll go and try to find him, here today I am going to meet him, the tears were streaming down my cheeks by now I wanted to cry out loud so much. How have you been able to do it I said? She went on to tell me how she´d done it and that it was by a pure fluke through the wife of his nephew that she had made contact after many, many, phone calls under his name in the north-east. He now lived in Manchester and between Sue and him said he would come down to visit me for my 60th birthday. But he´s late George she said he should have been here an hour ago. What actually had happened was, Sue had not taken her mobile phone and he had asked at the golf club across the road from where we were and they told him they hadn´t heard of it. (can you believe it? across the road) after trying unsuccessfully to ring Sue´s mobile phone, and her home ,he started to feel unwell, and went back to Manchester. We had a few more beers, and went back to my home, and phoned him from there, where, he told us what had happened on the day he came to visit me. Had we met that day as Sue had planned it, without doubt, should, have been the best birthday of my life. So we made arrangements to visit it him at his home in Manchester the following week-end. I invited my sister Jane to come along to the reunion at his house, It was fantastic when we did meet up, it was like having my birthday again only this time things were going right. There was such a lot to talk about, he had 8 children and 16 grandchildren, and he now had grey curly hair. He went on to tell me that his brother John, who was in the homes with, us had died a few years earlier, and that, when he, had been taken into the homes, he had been a baby in arms, and there was also, a sister in the homes at the same time which I never knew anything about. He also said he had, had 5 heart attacks. Jane couldn´t remember his sister being in the homes, but, could remember the names of women she mentioned, who worked there, so we all had a good old chin wag. We all went down to his local and with Jane driving I was able to have drink with him. He told me he had been back to Medomsley when he got himself in trouble with the law as a young lad, and that it was now a, Detention Centre, yes I said I took my daughter and wife to show them where I had stayed, when I was in the homes, and that´s how I knew it was a Detention Centre. I also took Sue many years later to show her. We had a good day in all, we swapped addresses and he mentioned his date of birth which I wrote down as well, and said we would stay in touch when we parted that night. Unfortunately, after writing one letter, and then a birthday card and £50, and a Xmas card and £50, I never, received a reply, to any of them, so, I never made any more contact with him, and he has never made contact with me. It´s a strange world we live in eh? But at least I now know how he had fared in life after leaving the homes.

That same year after Sue had made contact with Tommy we were eligible to a council flat or bungalow, and put our names on the waiting list. This would take a few years we thought, we could even be retired by the time one comes on offer. To our surprise after 12 weeks, a flat came on offer exactly where we had chosen. We now had to sell our properties, as the plan had always been that we would move in together but not until I retired. But this flat would not be on offer again in our life time so, we took it. We had been going out together for 14 years by then but, with the flat coming up as quickly as it did I was totally unprepared for it, I thought it would be years and years before we would be living together. When Sue and I had been going out together for about 3 months, everything was hunky dory, and I said to her one night, Sue I feel sure that this is going to be the best relationship I´ve ever had and hope it will be the same for you, but, there´s one thing you should know " I am not getting married" so before we go any further down the road and you get the idea that one day we will, we had better part company now because, that is never going to happen. I don't want you to get hurt, and maybe, when we are both retired, we will live together in old age. We had both come out of stormy relationships, in my case after 5 years, in her case a divorce. She said no George it´s not what I´m looking for, and I said great, it was "just" what I wanted to hear. The subject has never, been raised again, since that night. Once we moved into the flat we started to take holidays more often. I had told her many times about when I was in the far-east in the army, and said when the time is right I will take you there. We had several holidays to the Greek islands and the Spanish Island of Gran Canaria (Puerto Rico) where the Time Share tout´s are like flies. On one occasion we were so fed up with them I asked someone how to avoid them and was given the advice of tell them you're "Icelandic" they can´t speak that language which I did, "but" forgot I´d got a Daily mirror newspaper tucked in my back pocket, nice try the tout shouted as I walked away, we both had a laugh about it but it was worth a try. I know they are trying to make a living and I for one have admiration for anyone who does; it´s just so annoying when it´s every few yards you walk.

A couple of years after moving into the flat I decided the time was right and booked a holiday to Borneo, for three weeks in a five star hotel. We were amazed at how luxurious it was. It should have been classed as an 8 or 10 star hotel; neither of us had been in a place as good as this before. There were quite a few Japanese guests in the hotel which surprised me as this Island had been invaded by them during their war in South East Asia and were noted for their atrocities. However life must go on but what the elderly locals must have thought about them inwardly God only knows. The area which we were staying at was called Kota Kinabaloo, and one morning, after breakfast, we were sitting on the balcony and looking over the harbour, I said to Sue, that looks very familiar to me, it looks so much like Jessleton harbour where we had docked when I first came to Borneo in 1961, 39 yrs ago. We asked if it was Jessleton and they said yes it was once but, the area name had been changed to Kota Kinabaloo when it ceased to be a British Crown Colony. We went and took a look at it, there were two docks now, and the new one was a ferry harbour, so I went looking for a port official and asked if I could go on the old docks and film the old harbour he said no. Then when I explained that I was an ex British soldier on a memory lane tour and that I had been here in 1961 neither one of us expected what came next. You were a British soldier here he said, I nodded, he stood up straight and said wait there "Sir" he came back a couple of minutes later in a land rover and a young lad dressed as some kind of official looking at his uniform, right Sir is there anything I can help you with. I went on to tell him why I was here and could I film the old dock for old time's sake, he was amazed that I had been here in 1961, shook our hands and bowed and then told the driver to drive us round to the old dock and wait for us to finish filming. Take as long as you like he said and we did. Sue said "wow" I know you said that these people were probably the nicest people in the world but I never expected anything like this. We took the trips the hotel was offering i.e. the old railway which the Japanese had built in the war against Japan, by local slave labour, and prisoners of war. It was not a replica but the "original" and kept in pristine condition. I had the same feeling come over me while riding on it as I had when I had walked into Belson concentration camp a few years earlier. A feeling of horror, of what those workers had endured building it, and their "lives" to the Japanese had meant "nothing" to them, so long as it got built. There was also a trip to see the Urang Utang sanctuary, up country to of all places "Kota Belud" I couldn´t believe it I was more excited than Sue now. I never thought I would ever get to see that village again as, it was up country in the jungle and here we are we´re going to visit it. It was a two hour flight, and the plane was used exactly, like you see they portray those buses in South America where they travel with goats and chickens, well there were no goats but it seemed as if everyone had a cage with chickens in loads of kids with them. How times have changed in just 39 years. These people would hardly have gone further than their village in those days. Oh and no bare breasts now either. We arrived up in Kota Belud and were taken to the Sanctuary Sue said I see what you mean about it being like a sauna, We were all dripping in sweat by now. I have got to say that most of the Urang Utangs were babies compared to the ones we had screaming at us when we were be taken down the river by the Ghurkha's 39 years ago. It must have been the case that they were mostly undisturbed in their habitat in those days and grew bigger, because they were giants compared to these in the sanctuary. We were taken to see a horse racing gala at the town of Kota Belud, nothing much had changed there and was able to show Sue the shops where we bought fresh groceries, and the bars we drank in and where I bought bad man Pierre, he wasn´t known as "you little b.....d" until we got to Hong Kong.

After we had been in Borneo for about 10 days I surprised Sue and said get a case packed we are going to Hong Kong tomorrow for 5 days and maybe, we might find Fan Mao. It would have made my holiday the best ever, but considering that he was about 35 when I left Hong Kong he would be an old man and maybe dead, I hoped not. We flew to Kowloon and straight away noticed the size of the airport it was massive, there was only talk of it being built when I left there. We stayed in a four star hotel in Kowloon and although, it was clean, and well run, it was nothing compared to one we were staying at in Borneo, and also twice as expensive. Kowloon had changed for me, it was now, something Sue and

I hadn´t seen in our lives, except in films, the sky scrapers were everywhere, and for me it had been totally transformed, I was walking around all the time with my mouth open I was amazed at the change. I could only describe to Sue what it "was" like and for her to visualise it, compared to now. What really surprised both of us was how clean the streets were. It didn´t look any less congested with people than when I was last there, "BUT" there was more litter on our lawn at home than in any street we walked in and yet, in any direction, there were thousands of people, walking the streets, day and night. What´s wrong at home? One of the things I was expecting to see but didn´t, was a presence of army personnel or police walking round with guns, but, that wasn´t the case, thank God. The day after we arrived in Kowloon we had a trip up to the New Territories as it was called then, where I was stationed, nothing had changed; the camp was the same as we left it. I was describing it all to Sue and filming it when out of this building came about 20 police shouting and bawling at us and grabbing at my cine camera and I´m saying "English" "English" thinking we were going to be arrested, when a young, woman police officer, came up and said in perfect English, what are you doing? I explained that I was here on holiday and showing my partner where I was stationed 39 years ago. She told me that it was now the camp of the Chinese army and, I must stop filming as it was an offence and could be put in prison, that made me pay full attention I´ll tell you, She said you had best be on your way before things get out of hand. Which we did, we got into the car and drove to the next village Kam Tin where I had spent many hours drinking as a lad all those years ago. I told Sue that this was one of the villages that restaurants had been raided and they had found skinned dogs hanging in their freezers. The village its self, hadn´t changed much, and I made an attempt to ask about Fan Mao but couldn´t get to talk to anyone who spoke English. Looking back I should have asked the police officer but, I was just glad for us to get away from them as Sue was looking very nervous by it all. The following day we went over to Hong Kong Island and that had changed the most, every building now seemed to be a skyscraper, which, most seemed to have a shopping mall on every floor. I was filming all this when we were threatened again with arrest. Once again there was no litter laying about and also, a sight for sore eyes NO graffiti. If it can be kept free of it there with millions of people walking about day and night, once again, what´s happening at home? Sue did a lot of clothes shopping and found that it was by far the best for choice anywhere that she had been BUT expensive. Sadly our 5 Days were soon over and we left amazed at it all, and as I say mostly for me because of the vast change. I didn´t get to meet up with Fan Mao but wish him well where ever he may be and all those fond memories I have of him will always be with me.

We got back to Borneo knackered after all the dashing about sightseeing and shopping and spent the rest of our holiday, lounging around the hotel pool. As I mentioned earlier we were waited on hand and foot, nothing seemed to be a chore to them, I, was especially pleased about this, as this is how I´d described these lovely people to Sue over the years and here she was experiencing it for herself. There was one incident Sue will never forget. It has always been our custom to tip the room maid £10 a week whenever we were satisfied with them so, because ours was on her weekly day off the day that we were leaving, Sue and I gave her (Sinita), her £30 tip, with a little bracelet, we had bought her in Hong Kong and note in a sealed envelope thanking her for her services. She took the envelope after a bit of confusion tidied the room and left. After a few minutes she came back I let her in and she went running to Sue, tears streaming, down her cheeks, hugging and kissing Sue, and talking through sobs in her own language. What "had" happened, we found out later was, she took the envelope, seen what was in it and realised she had been given a month's wages as a tip. We have never been thanked for a tip like that except once in the Greek Islands. The next day we were sitting in the lounge down stairs chatting away, having a coffee, waiting for our car, to the airport ,when all of a sudden this young girl Sinita, walked up to us in a "scarlet" red Moslem outfit she looked "immaculate" and said thank you both, for yesterday, and these, are for you, and gave us a designer carrier bag with a present for both of us, a small jewellery box for Sue and pen holder for me signed "from Sinita". "Well" it was tears from Sue this time, we certainly didn´t expect that. Sue still uses that jewellery box at home today and my pen holder is in my computer room. What a sweet girl, it's one of my great sayings; it costs "nothing" to be nice.

That really put the finishing touches to the holiday of a life time. Our long journey home was made easier by the fact that the plane from Kuala Lumpa was virtually empty and we could get laid down across three seats, and slept a good part of the journey home.

The next "bombshell" to be dropped in my life was in 2007 and I would, never in a "trillion years" thought that it could happen. I was sitting in the house watching TV and the phone rang, it was our Christine, she was clearly "very" upset, Dad she said, I need you to come up straight away, it's very important I´ll tell you when you get here. Are you ok, are the bairns ok I said, but she wouldn´t tell me why, just, to come up as quick as I could. I had been retired a couple of months, so I jumped in the car and drove up there as fast as I could, with all kinds of thoughts going on in my mind. When I arrived Jan was there and then, all was revealed.

Jan had sold her house and, given Christine £40,000 to buy her council house, for her and the kids. Something Christine had never mentioned to me, another reminder of just how far apart our lives were. About 5 months earlier and, unbeknown to Jan or the kids; she had met a guy on the internet and, was having him come to live with her. Christine had never mentioned this to me either. When she mentioned this Jan said straight away, that is "NOT" going to happen, "NO" man is moving in here, if she gets married, and later leaves her he can claims half the value of the house, "IT´S NOT GOING TO HAPPEN" she was shouting. I said to Jan and what´s it got to do with "you" what our Christine does. It was music to my ears, the fact that she could lose "£20,000" that´s what it was "really" all about. Well, you had better listen to "all" the story, she said, and went on to tell me that, Rebecca had been reading her mum´s emails "to" and "from" this guy and, were "too adult" for her at 14 yrs old, (I thought to myself I don´t think so,) and had told her grandma about them. Jan said that she had read them too, and, was shocked as they were explicit and pornographic, "so what", I said she´s 44 yrs old and besides, "no one" should be reading her emails, besides that, if she wants to start courting, it´s her business. But the kids don´t want him in the house knowing about those emails for all we know he might be a Paedophile. I knew then that Jan was manipulating the grand bairns as she had our Christine over all those years. Will you take me to visit him Christine said, (and this is where the whole sorry story began)

Where does he live I asked. She went on to tell me a story that beggar´s belief. At the moment he´s in a private hospital she said because, he had been beaten up by a gang of thug´s in Birmingham, I thought straight away well he "must" be well off if he´s in a private hospital. He was 48 yrs old and many years ago he too had been in a gang in Birmingham and had suffered such a savage beating at one time with a rival gang had ended up in a Private hospital paid for by the gang leader. When he was released from hospital he left the gang got himself straightened out and became a male nurse in a nursing home in Bournemouth, she and him met on the internet 5 months prior, apparently, she had been on the computer all day and all hours during the night and was even on it when the kids got up for school. He had gone back to Birmingham to pay a visit to the gang leader, who had been so kind to him in the past and, was spotted one night by that same rival gang from years previous and given another savage beating and once again he ended up in a private hospital, paid for once again, by the same gang leader. When she asked him "which" hospital was it, so she could visit him, he said if he told her the gang leader who was a good friend would stop paying his hospital bills.

There is something "very" strange about all this I said to her but, carry on (it got even more bizarre) She went on to tell me that when her mum had read her emails she had gotten Rebecca to put a password on the computer so she could not use it at all. So, the only way they could communicate now, was through the Dating channel on the TV which was no problem as he was in a private hospital and when he got a new mobile phone they could talk. Don´t you find all this a bit suspicious I said, no she said, dad I love him and I want to visit him and be with him. I thought to myself God only knows what cock and bull stories he had been feeding her. Will you take me, yes I said, but if you think I´m driving around Birmingham looking for private hospital you are wrong, find out the name of it and I´ll take you. She started crying, I put my arms around her and said all this sounds a big con to me Christine, and I don´t want to see you hurt in any way, ask him the name of the hospital, and I´ll take you there. In the short time I was there he phoned her and said he now had a new mobile phone and could now keep in contact by phone instead of the dating channel on the TV. She told him the trouble she was having with her mother and the kids and then he ended the call with her after which she tried for hour´s but, there was no reply so, I said would you like to come and stay with me for a few days until this is sorted out, no she said, you go home and when I find out, you can take me. In the meantime the kids had been shouting and bawling at her saying he was not coming to live here, she was shouting and bawling back, I thought to myself, what´s happened to my shy and timid little girl of a few years ago. I tried to calm things down but couldn´t. Jan took them to her, old age bungalow, which was across the road to get them to settle down. I had never seen the kids behaving like that before. I thought to myself Jan, you have caused all this upset, you selfish "Bitch" I can understand her not wanting our Christine to get hurt, but, at the onset of it all was the fact she might lose 50% of the money she had laid out for Christine and the bairns. Call me selfish but I hoped it "would" as I sat there and thought of "all" the rotten things she had done and, had got my daughter to grow away from me, and at one time even she had kicked me out of her house telling me never to come back again, an old saying came to mind "every dog has it´s day" and it looked at that time I was going to have mine soon. For some reason or other she didn´t think Christine would get herself another man and want to get married again. Eventually after about eight hours with no reply from him I went home a very saddened and puzzled man. I was so saddened that all this was happening to our Christine and the bairns and puzzled, as to why, she was she believing, what, was "the" most "bizarre" story, I´d ever heard in my life.

The next day Jan phoned me to say our Christine was contemplating suicide if everyone didn´t get off her back, and that she was now in contact with him again, and that it had given him a heart attack, and it was the consultant who he knew from his last stay there, that was texting her on his behalf. How on earth our Christine was believing any of this, I don´t know, but she was, she was besotted with him, hook, line and sinker, Jan had taken Christine to the doctors and he had, had her sent to a Psychiatric hospital to be tested on to her mental state, there was no visiting allowed while, the tests were conducted and, would let me know the next day what was happening. She rang the next day saying she was bringing her home and that there was nothing wrong with her mentally. Thank God I said but where was this all going to end. I drove back up and told our Christine that I had got my friend who was an inspector in the police force (which was true) to use the Police computers (which was a lie and, the first time I had ever lied to her) to find a "private" hospital that had a patient by the name of Mark O..... in it or had he been in a hospital in a 15 mile radius the result was, there were no private or NHS hospitals that had, had a patient in them over the last month (which was another lie) but I loved my daughter dearly and didn´t want any harm come to her, as all this was getting to me now. I love him dad and I want be with him. I couldn´t get her to see sense at all and, after a few hours talking, I went home. Then three days later Christine phoned to say that M... was now living in Middlesbrough, his mate the gang leader, had found him a house and that he wanted her to go and live with him. He was not happy about her mother´s interference, being as she had never, met him, and also the kids, not wanting him to live there. He was coming to see her at the week-end and hopefully get things sorted out. I said he has made a miraculous recovery to say he's had a heart attack don't you think Christine? Please dad she said, don't you start as well.

I asked if she would like me to be there, being as it was her first meeting with him what with all that had gone off. I thought that, I could get a look at him and, get some answers as to the hospital fiasco, before my daughter got herself involved with him. But she said no thanks I want to meet him on my own. The week-end came and Christine went to meet him at the local railway station, Jan and her sister had invited themselves along to the meeting and gave him a piece of their minds. Jan phoned me and when I heard this, I thought what the hell is she doing, she's going to drive an, even bigger wedge, between her and our Christine. The next day Jan phoned again. We hadn't spoken so much since, that night she had broken our marriage up, for a quick roll in the hay and I hated every time I had to talk to her, "but", this was all about our daughter and grand kids and was, but, I didn't like to admit it, that, her suspicions where right, and that it looked like this guy was, definitely a con man. She said, Christine had met him and, gone to the pictures and, then for a meal and, he had asked her, to marry him, and she had accepted. She was going to live with him in Middlesbrough and if the kids didn't want to come then she was leaving them with her, she said, will you come up and talk some sense into her. I did and no matter what I said, I got the same reply, I love him and want to be with him, what about the kids I said, they don't want him here and they won't go with you to his home, you have a choice I said, you stay here, and court him, without him living here or, you leave the kids and set up home with him. In a nutshell I said do you love him, after knowing him for such a short time and, have met him only once in six or seven months, than you do your kids? The answer was the biggest shock of my entire life, "yes" she said, I want to be with him more than my kids. Jan was as shocked as I was, she was crying out loud and I was sat there with tears streaming down my face saying (as they are now while I´m writing this) it was the first time Christine had seen me cry, you can´t do this I said, you can´t leave these bairns and take off with someone you have only met yesterday for the first time. What if your mum sometime in the future can´t look after them? then Paul will have to have them she said, and as soon as Mark has got the house furnished out, I am going, she said, because, I love him. I was speechless I didn´t know what else to say to try and get her to see sense. The kids were at Jan´s and she said, will you come with me and break this news to them, on the way there I said, I will help you with their upkeep "if" it does come off. I still had my doubts about it. What had happened to my "shy and timid" little girl I was thinking to myself. We spoke to the kids about it, it was heartbreaking Rebecca was 14 and Stuart was 12 they were at the age where, they were fully aware of things, which made it worse somehow. I told them of my plight as a child and had ended up in a children´s home, I assured them that, that, would not happen to them as long as I was alive. We took the kids back over to their home and I tried once again to talk sense into Christine but couldn´t. Before I left I hugged and kissed Christine and said, "Christine" if you leave these bairns "you" and I are finished "forever" do you understand me. Yes she said, crying, I asked the bairns for a goodbye kiss and as usual were reluctant, and as per usual didn´t get one before I left. I couldn´t and wouldn´t say anything to Jan because the grandchildren were there and they certainly had enough on their plates to put up with today, in my own mind I blamed her for isolating and making our daughter grow away from me and all this was happening, through, that, it was like a nightmare. I drove home feeling about as down as I had ever been before, with my head, reeling at what our Christine was going to do. I never slept that night thinking about it, and not a day goes by without I think of what she´s done, and what she´s done to those bairns.

After a few days Jan rang me up and said Christine had done it, she had met him at the station again, she and her sister once again went there to try and talk sense into her and telling him, it was a whole load of lies about the hospital and heart attack and he replied, it was "Christine" who made the stories up, "not" me. Both of us were shocked to think our Christine could make up such a cock and bull story as it was totally out of character for her and, why? I asked to speak to our Rebecca to offer my sympathy and tell her to keep in contact with me. The reply she gave me was, another, absolute shock for me, without, a moment´s hesitation, she said "Granddad" I don´t want to be disrespectful "but" my life is too busy to do that and put the phone down on me. I was gob smacked. I immediately sat down and wrote Jan a letter telling her what she had said and done and that you should have a talk with our Rebecca about it and "if" you can´t get them to make contact with me within a month you can forget about the support I have offered. I am "not" having the same thing done to me as our Christine did to me which I most certainly blame you for the attitude our Christine has had towards me over the years, take my money and, treat me like she did. I told her about the money, £100 each and every birthday and Christmas that I´d been sending to them from birth and, asking Christine at the time to tell them to keep in contact with me i.e. Write a letter, phone, text, or email me, and that they had only ever, had sent me "one" card each since they could write and that it was always our Christine who wrote the cards out. I told her that I´d asked our Christine at one time and she said she was "not" going to force them to keep in contact with me so I said I would stop sending them, anymore money because, if they, couldn´t be bothered to keep in contact with me, I couldn´t be bothered to keep sending them money. Jan never replied to my letter, nor have either of my grand children been in contact since so, I stopped sending money. It hurts me. To this day, they have never been in touch, although, I always send a birthday and Christmas card to them with phone numbers and email address attached to every card just in case they have a change of heart. They have had plenty of opportunity in the last 3 yrs to phone, text, email or write to me, before I wrote this "sad" "sad" story but they haven't. I do feel in my own mind that I have done as much as I could have, and it´s now up to them to keep in contact with me.

When I look back and think of the time I came back from the middle- east and Jan was courting someone else and then, after ONE stupid night out, we got back together, had we not done that, none of this would have come about. "BUT" fate and destiny is something we have no control over

 After the trouble with our Christine, Sue and I had our next great holiday in June 2007, when, we were invited to America, by Sue´s friend, Gloria, who she knew from her school days. I was still feeling so sad at what our Christine had done and hoped it wouldn´t spoil Sue´s holiday. Gloria and Mick had two children a son, who had died of a heart attack at 27yrs old leaving a wife and 2 children, and a daughter with 2 children who lived in Florida. It was one night when we were sitting having a drink Gloria asked if I was enjoying the holiday as I looking a bit down. I said that I´d had some awful trouble with my daughter before we came on holiday and that it was still bothering me and before I mentioned anything she went on to tell me her daughter had done exactly the same thing with her children. It was years before they came to terms with it but have never forgiven her for it. That seemed to make things easier for me and the holiday became enjoyable knowing someone else had, had the same troubles.

Both Sue and I had our reservations about going to America for quite a while, what with the availability of guns and violence on the streets on films and documentaries you see on the TV, well, it couldn´t have been further from the it, at least it wasn´t anything like that, where we stayed in Tennessee with Gloria and her husband Mick, who had previously worked at the same pit I worked at. He had gotten himself a job some years ago, as a rep for an American mining firm dealing in roof supports, and eventually settled in the US some twenty years ago. They lived in a huge 3 story wooden house at the side of a lake, with a garage the size of a commercial garage, which housed 1 car, 1 jeep 1 truck 1 golf cart, a sit on lawn mower and, a 20ft boat. He, like myself, was now retired, and lapping it up. They drove us all over the place, and the thing that surprised Sue and I most, was "tree´s" everywhere you looked, was thick with tree´s, there were more tree´s there, than the jungles of Borneo. Fortunately for Gloria and Mick there was a bar at the lakeside, not too far from their house where they lived, otherwise it was a 50 mile round trip to the nearest town and, the nearest for shopping etc. Whenever we went shopping to the local supermarket the stores were the size of aeroplane hangars and "always" packed with customers even though they were open 24/7. On one of our outings we called into a store where you bought things for hunting and fishing a monstrous size place, where there was full size boats on display and guns. There was guns of every description, Sue was asked if she would like to hold a "Dirty Harry" type pistol, it was so heavy she could hardly lift it, we all had a laugh about that, then he showed her a gun that lots of women carry around with them in their handbags for protection. The price of it was "£16" that´s, when it hit home, the "scary" availability of guns as their way of life.

I told the guy who was showing us the guns, that it was illegal to have any gun in the UK and he said what if you get a burglar in your home, I said you have to reason with them "AND" If "you" use unnecessary force to apprehend them "they" can sue you for "actual bodily harm" he looked at me in disbelief and shouted his college over, and asked me to repeat what I´d told him, "what" he said you mean a burglar can sue you for hitting him, yes I said, that´s the law of our land, they laughed and laughed and I walked away feeling stupid, and wished I hadn´t mentioned the subject. Another thing that had me confused about the type of guns for sale, was, why any hunter, would need an automatic rifle to go hunting? If the people who buy those weapons want to play soldiers, or whatever, why, don´t they join the TA or their equivalent? One night when we were having a drink at their house, Mick, showed us the guns, he, kept in the house for protection, a pump action shotgun and, a revolver. Never had to use them he said, thankfully it´s quiet around here. It was true but, still, all a bit scary for Sue and I having guns around the house.

We had quite a few trips on the lake in their boat, the lake was 2 ½ miles long and we saw some of the Mansions that were all along the shore line. Gloria and Mick´s home and grounds were large by any standard but the size of these mansions were "huge" and all made from wood was fascinating to us, built in brick here they would be worth a fortune. Another thing we found strange was the lack of mosquitoes, and thank God about that too. It was June, and temperatures were 100c plus, daily, and at night the sound of crickets, and bullfrogs reminded me of the jungle in Borneo. During our stay there they had the "American Day of Independence" a lot like our Guy Fawkes Night, with hours and hours of fireworks displays. The police were kept busy on the lake that night, as it is illegal to have alcohol on boats while sailing, but it was, a sight worth seeing. One incident that happened a few days before Independence Day, and, just like at home, before bonfire night, people are setting fireworks off, an off duty Sheriff had gone into his next door neighbours garden, shot and killed him because, he wouldn´t stop setting fireworks off. Frightening eh? Chances are that would "not" have happened here in the UK. Like all good things, they must come to an end, and our holiday in the US did that. Gloria and Mick took us to the airport, and found we would be having a 24hour delay in Atlanta, to our surprise Mick talked them into changing us to 1st class because of this, and "WOW" it was the first time ever we had flown 1ST class. Looking back at it all, who would have thought the little "lad", who, had been "abandoned" by his family and put in a children´s home all those years ago, would be flying 1st class across the Atlantic, certainly not me.

Sue and I now spend as much time in Spain as we can, now that I´m retired, where for most of the time it´s warmer and to get the warm air round our creaking bones, which I have plenty of. I never thought in a million years that you could wake up every morning with a new ache but that is how it feels. The advice I give every youngster I talk to is DON´T get old it´s CRAP. But like fate and destiny it´s out of our hands.

All in all, after all those bad times in my early life, I have had the greatest of pleasure in meeting some truly wonderful people especially, Sue the love of my life, Joe, and the great influence he had on my life, and Tajalie the sweet old lady who I met at the latter end of my working life, who incidentally had only at the age of 95 started to suffer with some arthritis in one of her knees, how lucky is that? And also the good times with friends and the hundreds of acquaintances I have met on my way through life. As for the bad people Mr Peverly who flogged me as a child and the ones I met who robbed or abused my friendship, they have got to live with what they have done. I still can´t believe the terrible way our Christine treat me over the years, only my love and maternal instinct is why I stood it for so long but it´s the fact that she has abandoned her children I can´t forgive her for. She too, will have to live with that for the rest of her life. I still shake my head in wonderment at it. God only knows where her nature comes from it´s certainly not from me, and there without doubt is food for thought. I have pondered over this story many, many times and find there is a repeat of history here in the fact that my own daughter has done the exact same unforgiving deed as my father did almost 63yrs ago when he walked away from his daughter and son. It´s sad, so sad, that any of it happened but that´s life which from my own experience can be so cruel.

I dedicate this story to Joe the one person who influenced my life the most and hope he is being looked after to the standard he deserves. God bless him.